Praise for *Hard C*

"Unwrap me and I'll/give you a mouthful of truth." Truth told through the interweaving of poems and prose, so like incantations, about the crescendos and diminuendos of each and every day of caring for an ailing loved one while painstakingly navigating through the current fractured healthcare system. And though Lanzillotto's book is part tragedy — "death is death no matter how served" — it is a full-on joy to read as each poem and prose vignette ushers us snapshot by snapshot, laugh after laugh, and song after song, through the last months of a mother's life and a daughter's devotion to her. Lanzillotto writes about spending every moment of her mother's remaining days as, "… squeezing a dry lemon over cooked fish," so that by the end she is, "holding rinds, pits, seeds." The fruit born from these stories, just like her and her mother's home in the Bronx, "stamps us indelibly." We are as she says, "marked … For life," with memories of two lives tightly knitted together. When one is unraveled, we are left with an understanding of the "intimacy of illness," and the hope that recovering from grief can be "a thousandfold" possible.
—**CELESTE GUZMÁN MENDOZA**, author of *Beneath the Halo*
co-founder of *Canto Mundo*

A mother's life caring for her daughter. A daughter's life caring for her mother. In *Hard Candy: caregiving, mourning, and stage light*, cancer survivor Annie Lanzillotto gives the performance of her life — for her life and her dying mother's. She stages a drum-beating sit-in at the hospital and refuses to leave without the medication she needs to breathe. She screams operatic on the phone demanding oxygen equipment so her mother can breathe. The bureaucratic debacle of our health care system chronicled in this memoir will take your breath away, but not Annie's. Every inhale, every exhale. For motherdaughter. For daughtermother.
—**PAOLA CORSO**, author of *The Laundress Catches Her Breath*
winner of the Tillie Olsen Award for Creative Writing

I hardly ever re-read a book, but this treasure must be read and savored again. And again. I am wowed by this wonderfully rendered journey that Lanzillotto has given us all. Anyone who has mothered a mother—or a father, or a sibling or partner—will recognize themselves in *Hard Candy*. A love song to Annie's beloved mother, Rachel, as Annie recounts their journey through her mother's final illness and the harder work of Annie's solo journey beyond. In Lanzillotto's deft hands, the bond so beautiful between these two strong Italian American women in life is rendered even more beautiful now, in this in-between time during which each of them has to navigate without the other until mother and daughter can savor peaches together again one day. With tenderness, tenacity, humor, wisdom, honesty, abundant love, and even recipes, Lanzillotto draws us in so powerfully that we quickly come to share her poignant journey, her profound loss, as if it these experiences are our own.

—**KAREN TINTORI**, author of *Unto The Daughters: The Legacy of an Honor Killing in a Sicilian-American Family*

HARD CANDY

Guernica World Editions 1

HARD CANDY

Caregiving, Mourning, and Stage Light

Annie Rachele Lanzillotto

GUERNICA
World
EDITIONS
TORONTO · BUFFALO · LANCASTER (U.K.)
2018

Michael Mirolla, editor
David Moratto, cover and interior design
Annie Rachele Lanzillotto, cover artwork
Guernica Editions Inc.
1569 Heritage Way, Oakville, (ON), Canada L6M 2Z7
2250 Military Road, Tonawanda, N.Y. 14150-6000 U.S.A.
www.guernicaeditions.com

Distributors:
University of Toronto Press Distribution,
5201 Dufferin Street, Toronto (ON), Canada M3H 5T8
Gazelle Book Services, White Cross Mills
High Town, Lancaster LA1 4XS U.K.

First edition.
Printed in Canada by Gauvin.

Legal Deposit—First Quarter
Library of Congress Catalog Card Number: 2017955488
Library and Archives Canada Cataloguing in Publication
Lanzillotto, Annie Rachele
[Poems. Selections]
Hard candy : caregiving, mourning, and stage light ; Pitch
roll yaw / Annie Lanzillotto. -- First edition.

(Guernica world editions ; 1)
Poems.
Bound tête-bêche.
ISBN 978-1-77183-305-9 (softcover)

I. Lanzillotto, Annie Rachele. Pitch roll yaw. II. Title.
III. Title: Pitch roll yaw.

PS3612.A73A6 2018   811'.6   C2017-906462-2

Perchè l'anima è in te, sei tu, ma tu
sei mia madre e il tuo amore è la mia schiavitù:
—Pier Paolo Pasolini
estratto di "Supplica a Mia Madre"

Because the soul is in you, is you, but you
are my mother and your love is my slavery:
—Pier Paolo Pasolini
excerpt of "Supplication to My Mother"

Acknowledgments

"Holy Cards" previously appeared in *Philadelphia Poets*, Volume 23, Rosemary Petracca Cappello, Editor, Philadelphia, PA 2017

"Are You Gone?" "I Know You're There," "Orange and Spice," "Lilly O Lilly," "Her Blue," "Depart Soul Depart," "Breath," "Room," "All I Can Do Is Cry," "Where Will I Go?" "O Mamma" are recorded on Annie Lanzillotto's album of mourning songs: *Never Argue With a Jackass*. Lyrics & Music, Vocals, Keyboard by Annie Lanzillotto. Pocket Trumpet by Pasquale Cangiano. Production, Music, Guitars, Bass, Recorded and Engineered by Al Hemberger at The Loft Recording Studios, Bronxville, New York, 2017. Executive Producer Ron Raider. Produced by StreetCry Inc. www.annielanzillotto.bandcamp.com

Book Thanks

For funding the production of this book: Ron Raider, Ellyne Skove. For strategic planning: Neil Goldberg. For fiscal sponsorship: CityLore. For reading pieces and giving me feedback: Rosette Capotorto, Simba Yangala, Nicole Lanzillotto, Emily Jordan Agnes Kunkel, Audrey Kindred, Sophia Capotorto, Gina DiRenzi. For literary championing: Edvige Giunta, Joanna Clapps Herman, Clare Ultimo, John Gennari, Kathleen Zamboni McCormick, Salley May, Maria Mazziotti Gillan, Rosemary Cappello, Celeste Guzmán Mendoza, Karen Tintori, Paola Corso, Urayoán Noel, Steve Zeitlin, Bob Viscusi, Rachel Blumenfeld, Elise Bernhardt, Martha Wilson.

To Michael Mirolla, the whole team at Guernica Editions, and David Moratto for making stunning books. I am grateful to be part of your line-up.

Thank you Dr. Diane Pepe-Stover for your compassion, love and care for Mom, for every time you held her hand and walked with her to measure her oxygen saturation. Thank you to all the many workers at Sloan-Kettering for ministering to Mom and I in our most vulnerable hours! A special shout-out to some unsung heroes, Adrienne Bloom and all the heroic nurses and aides of the 15th floor, and the phenomenal pharmacists. Your dedication keeps me breathing. Susan Murillo, Ching Yeung, Genevieve Laurent, Paul Longo.

My eternal thanks to all of you who help me keep on keepin' on: friends, family, neighbors, poets, memoirists, musicians, theater makers, readers, all revved souls.

About the Author

Annie Rachele Lanzillotto is the author of *L is for Lion: An Italian Bronx Butch Freedom Memoir* (SUNY Press), the book of poetry *Schistsong* (Bordighera Press), and the narrator of both audiobooks on Audible.com. She is singer/songwriter of the albums: *Blue Pill* by Annie Lanzillotto Band, *Carry My Coffee*, *Swampjuice: Yankee with a Southern Peasant Soul* by Annie Lanzillotto & Washbucket Blues, and *Never Argue With a Jackass*. She was awarded the New York Foundation for the Arts fellowships in Multi-Disciplinary Performance, and Non-fiction Literature. She's held writing residencies at Hedgebrook, Santa Fe Arts Institute, and New Jersey City University, and was awarded performance commissions and grants from the Rockefeller Foundation Multi-Arts Production Fund, *Dancing In the Streets*, Dixon Place, Franklin Furnace, and the Puffin Foundation. She holds an MFA from Sarah Lawrence College and a BA from Brown University. www.annielanzillotto.com.

Contents

PART I:
Caregiving

PART II:
Mourning

PART III
Stage Light

Introduction:

Blowing Your Mother a Kiss

ANNIE LANZILLOTTO—the award-winning and much beloved New York performance artist, author of the powerful *L is for Lion: an italian bronx butch freedom memoir* and the poetry collection *Schistsong*, an "urban song-line of New York," and songwriter and vocalist—is still in her third trimester of grief—"I want it to be as public as being pregnant"—and already she has produced *Hard Candy*, a poetry and short prose collection as capacious as the motherdaughter love it celebrates and mourns, and one which pulls the reader into the depths of Annie's world. These poems pulse with intimacy that is "impossible to calculate," with the "intimacy of illness and recovery a thousandfold impossible," and with the unremitting physicality of death and dying. Yet as readers, we are allowed so many glimpses into the mutual indwelling of mother and daughter—"we lived on Persephone's precipice"—that we come to believe we might understand that intimacy, or, at the very least, its incalculability. Stirring catalogues of living and dying punctuate the volume. Omens—frightening in their uncanny ordinariness and in their power to conjure the magical universe of old—increase our vigilance to the portents in our own lives. And then there is color, and, in the process of dying, such absences of color.

The Cathedral of the Madonna of the Nail Polish: Stained Glass and Clear Windows

When I read Annie's memoir, *L is for Lion*, I was struck with its profusion of color and likened the imagery to an intricate set of Italian stained glass windows depicting pink spaldeens, faded two-family Bronx houses, multi-colored laundry, men whose minds were red with war. In one corner, black and white cars idled outside Sloan-Kettering at a green light. A peach tree encircled the entire set of windows and there were orange peaches everywhere, along with yellow *frittate* with touches of green and burnt sienna, brown maple tables, violet batteries, red lasagna, saffron rolling pins, flour-whitened dough, black pocketbooks, and blue eyes. The blue of those eyes matched the lead holding the elaborate windows together. There was a special blue chapel devoted to Our Lady of Mount Carmel, her mother's patron Saint, off to the side — "what a blessed color is blue" — where two women, Annie and her mother Rachel, knelt, holding pinkies, praying.

In reading *Hard Candy*, I find myself back in that Italian cathedral of color which is now dedicated to the Madonna of the Nail Polish who sustained her spirit by surrounding herself with infinite color — such as purple outfits, "Hollywood Sani-White" polished sneakers, "Pink Lightning" lipstick, and "Midnight Blue" eyeliner.

Stained Glass

On this visit to the cathedral, I find there are some new windows. A large double rainbow encircles one of these sets of windows. The first and most colorful has as its primary background "Red Sky" with streaks of blonde hair dyes in every hue. Large skeins of yarn frame the window in purple, indigo, blue, green, yellow, orange, and reddish-pink. Under the yarn are bulky spools of thick embroidery thread in every color of the rainbow. In this corner are some knitted hats and sweaters — knit and pearl, knit and pearl — in blues and purples and roses and creams. Over there, nail polish is lined up in so many shades of pink. One called "Taffy Pink" is being applied by a mother to her daughter's nails. Those hands look like they just can't relax. Tiny bobbins of thread are scattered here and there throughout the window in every possible shade of green, brown, brown-purple, turquoise, blue, blue-purple, and more and more tones of pinks and purples. Beings of all colors wave with one hand and hold out bowls of hard candy with the other. Those candies are in every stained glass window if you look carefully. Yellow lemon drops. Yolk butterscotch balls. Dark brown Italian imported espresso candy. Lighter brown coconut and cacao. Orange tangerine. Red raspberry, strawberry, cherry, and berry. Striped peppermint. Rust red anise. Green spearmint and eucalyptus.

Another window is spread with metallic tones. There's a little girl with a gold angel pinned on the lapel of her coat. St. Ann is depicted with a cloak covered in gold jewelry — watches, rings, bracelets, pendants, charms, chains—prayers from supplicants. From one angle you can see small shapes that turn out to be thousands of double gold stars and double pennies. Along with the dominant tones of gold and copper, there are intermingled shades of aluminum, nickel, silver, bronze, iron, and a child's leg braces that seems to be made of a dull tin.

In that blue chapel devoted to Our Lady of Mount Carmel, where two women had knelt, a piece of the large window has been replaced and there is now only one woman. And a whole new crescent-shaped window has been installed above it. It is edged by two dozen Belgian Purple Prince tulips. Apart from those tulips, the rest of the window is filled by warm, loving blue eyes that burst through a gray sky. When the light is right, we feel "the blue eyes cloak us as the heaven, as Mother Mary's robe, as infinite blue love."

Clear Windows

Perhaps most startling is another little chapel with windows that are virtually clear or only slightly clouded or with an occasional bit of bright white. This chapel is dedicated to Annie's mother Rachel, "The Saint of Crystalline." A private donation has been made to pay someone to clean these windows inside and out on a regular basis in honor of St. Crystalline's capacity to purify because when she cleaned the environment, she also cleaned the soul: "To all our souls constant renewal she gave by her ablutions." (And not just anyone is qualified to window wash to the high standard required. It is said that "sunbeams bounced from St. Crystalline's own window glass," and no less is expected here.) Step back and consider the window glass gleam. The first two windows are known as the life windows. Much of the first window you encounter represents St. Crystalline's cleaning miracles and implements, her canvasses and percussion instruments. Look, this part depicts the vision of the air sparkling. Over there you can see the miraculous disappearance of sock stains. And here are hundreds of shining tubs, porcelain sinks, toilets, and tile walls, window ledges white in nooks, bright white curtains snapping with incoming light and more of that sparkling air. What at first appears to be a rag is, upon closer examination, a paintbrush of luster. There are scrub brushes, clotheslines, mops, ropes, and solutions of baking soda and hydrogen peroxide. The most devoted are said to be able to hear the high pitch of clean glass with a white vinegar shine whenever the wind blows in a certain direction.

The second, slightly translucent life window represents the saliva that is made when devotees of St. Crystalline suck on a peppermint hard candy—ones that are always in place on her altar in fancy candy dishes made of cut-glass, white milk glass, or wicker. A small intercession to St. Crystalline enables those hard candies to cure you from nausea, carsickness, poverty, hunger, sadness, grief, a cough, stuffed nose, dry mouth, anxiety, lonesomeness, all the bitterness. They take the life taste out of your mouth, get your juices going because St. Crystalline knows that life is less hard when sucking on a hard candy. If you look carefully at the center of this window, you can detect what appears to be a lightning bolt when the sun catches it just so. It's St. Crystalline who is no longer matter, but an electric pulse.

Now the windows over here—while perhaps looking exactly the same to an untrained eye—are the St. Crystalline chapel death windows. There are some clear glass panes representing St. Crystalline's inner shine and the air she fell through at the age of two. But then, one might say, this is where the clear becomes darker. Here we see faintly outlined IV drip bags, oxygen, needles of medicine. Over there is a perpetually steamed-up nebulizer window where clouds of Xopenex and Ipratropium bromide billow. This piece of glass close to you represents breath —so it is slightly frosted, though it fades to clear when there is no longer breath, when St. Crystalline stopped "moving air." Let your eyes move slowly so you don't miss an irregular clear pane for St. Crystalline's tears and one for her daughter's. Don't be overwhelmed by the huge area symbolizing the permanent wave that was St. Crystalline's life. She wasn't.

Intimacy that is "impossible to calculate": The Intermingling of Motherdaughter on Persephone's Precipice

In many poems, we discover a physical intermingling between Annie and Rachel that existed in life and continues past Rachel's death. When Rachel is rushed to the hospital and diagnosed with pulmonary emboli, the doctor speaks to them as if they are one person: "Well you could have dropped dead." This amalgamating of life-essences that the doctor intuits is one that Rachel and Annie feel profoundly in *Hard Candy*. Rachel can't sleep unless she knows the baby is okay, so she asks Annie about the baby: Annie momentarily becomes both baby and person reassuring mother. Annie likens their motherdaughter relationship to that of Demeter and Persephone, acknowledging that the distinction has frequently blurred over the years. They have alternated the roles of kidnapped daughter and fiercely defending mother as they "reach out for each other's hand to rescue first one then the other in a revolving dance on the edge of death." Annie even jokes about the precarious balance that exists between them: "I'm a caregiver, but I get sick all the time. When I'm sick, Mom catches it. When Mom's sick, I get it. It's a bad system over here, two immuno-compromised people helping one another." We saw Annie and Rachel become one in *L is for Lion*, particularly when Annie helped her mother heal from heart surgery. They infused each other's consciousness: "I'd look at the wound and she'd look at me. My face was the mirror of her wound. She would judge by my expression how it looked, so I had to believe it was healing." The capacity of mother and daughter to unify, to support, to help restore each other was epitomized in this moment in *Lion* where Rachel literally required Annie to become her eyes.

Daughter repeatedly finds herself holding mother, rocking her, letting mother be her baby. Annie writes of Rachel that "On a number of occasions in recent years, she's introduced me as her mother." This loss of the liminal dominates the early part of the collection—"I hold every breath, every pulse, every heart beat" and "I will sit beside you,/hug you as you let go/ into my arms" until daughter and mother are in the position of a "Reverse Pietà" where, although mother is still alive, we realize that the interchangeability of their Demeter-Persephone relationship is now no longer possible. In "As she is leaving her body," daughter feels "like something is being pulled out of me ... like I am having an abortion" as she says of her mother "she is my daughter now." Even after Rachel's death, Annie "still notice[s] everyone's veins on their hands," still "feel[s] pulses and heartbeats." And when mother "comes inside" daughter, they realign from "Reverse Pietà" to reverse abortion.

The Integration of the Epic and the Quotidian in Catalogs of Living and of Dying

The collection is punctuated by catalogs, in which at times the ordinary is elevated to the epic, and other times, the style only sustains its epic quality by being firmly grounded in the quotidian. Some of the catalogs focus on living—names, foods, gifts; others on dying—illnesses, jarring juxtapositions, and lists of what one cannot do when grieving. Each balances the extraordinary and the commonplace in slightly different ways.

In the catalogs of living, the listing of names is most immediately recognizable as being in the epic catalog form. But unlike the "begats" of the Bible where genealogies grow tedious, these lists, embedded in tangible history, surprise and fascinate. In "Her Blue," we witness the multiplication of "Lucys and Rachels," as poems of names celebrate the Italian tradition dictating that you name your children for their grand-parents. The catalogs of living are also dominated by food. Annie re-members how the women in her family created "healing home cook-ing." Annie is inhabited by these women as she comes to be inhabited by her mother: "Those old Italian ladies are inside me. They possess me." The significance of the cooking reaches epic proportion by the intricacy of preparation, heightened expectations and appetites, sheer delight in eating, the abundance, the excess of history that, after all that cata-loguing of food, can be contained in the most minute flake of Parmesan cheese, a flake that then swells to a cornucopia and becomes the *"parmi-giano* snowglobe we live in," the sustenance and essential necessity of their healing family meals. The catalogs of food and the urgency of its sustaining power continue as daughter gives actual recipes for dying mother in "How to Cook for Your Mother in the Last Year of Her Life." And then there is the catalog of hard candy. Every example in every catalog is like a hologram occupying both the epic and the everyday, both immense bounty and the infinitesimal, first one, then the other, until, like motherdaughter, the two merge and simultaneously inhabit the incalculable and the commonplace. The final catalog of the living occurs in "rain reminds me" and enumerates the paradoxical riches of "Mom's old checkbooks," a wealth made possible only because "she was a master of home economics," because she clipped coupons, because she "cut soap bars and Brillo pads in half." The thrifty woman, living "the harsh realities of single motherhood," was able to "take care of her and me to keep us warm and safe," the record kept in hundreds of cancelled checks not only for electricity and phone, but for "everything she paid for over the years/all I owe her: rent, my student loans,/electricity, gas, telephone, credit card, the dentist." Pecunious means both "wealthy" —signifying the epic and excess—and "thrifty"—the quotidian, the minimal, the ordinary—and the catalog of Rachel's checkbooks, like all the catalogs of the living, dwell in both instantaneously.

The first two types of catalogs of the dying—illnesses and jarring juxtapositions—operate somewhat differently from the catalogs of the living. Rather than explicitly contrasting the epic with the quotidian, these poems simply tally the quotidian until the list is so long that it becomes epic: motherdaughter have endured such a surfeit of death and dying events that the catalogs of the dying extend to the point of painful absurdity and, on occasion, black humor. "Love Primer" enumerates illnesses experienced by motherdaughter. The list defies any type of comparison with what might be considered "normal." "Dearest *Carissima Mamma*" imagines the conversation between motherdaughter in which they laughingly recall Rachel's discussion of her medical history with Dr. Sun. They speak in lines that consciously articulate their own excess. Even Dr. Sun knows that he has overloaded Rachel with questions — "it was a draining interrogation" — about her surplus of illnesses: "'Is there anything else?' and he laughed, because there was already too much for one life of time." The black humor that infuses this passage challenges the reader to try to match it, but only playfully, because who in their right mind would ever seek such an accumulation of near-death experiences? And to give the reader, Dr. Sun, and perhaps even herself, yet one more, wholly other stratum of mother's heroic and larger-than-life ability to continue to exist, daughter — now in the absence of mother, of mother who was finally unable to outlive death forever — imagines-recalls mother saying and daughter thinking: "'And that's not even half the story,' you told Dr. Sun, because there's no room in the chart for your story, your escape from domestic violence, your life as a war bride of a sick marine." And suddenly we are awash in the pain of motherfatherdaughter.

The second type of death catalogs holds nothing back: they offer us endless lists of jarring juxtapositions that occur in the death and dying process. These catalogs not only enumerate, but pair experiences — contrasting the expected with the real, the known with the unsaid, comparing the metaphorical with the unspeakably literal, the violently different meanings of expressions in life versus death contexts. All of these juxtapositions startle and shock the reader with how unremitting death is once it has decided that there will be no *mirabilia verificatur* today, even for motherdaughter who "laughed at suffering like dancing skeletons." So these catalogs repeatedly pull unsuspecting readers, going about their everyday lives, into the frighteningly epic terror of actual death. In "Her heartbeat," we discover that the "dense silence," caused without mother's heart pumping completely deafens daughter. The sensation of mother's death experienced by daughter — where silence screams out — is utterly unexpected and wholly different from what we have been prepared for in our quotidian prayers.

In "Jesus' Lips," we are required to confront how "everything shifts" when "death becomes the goal." Here we must accept that mother's "terrified" look, represented first as fear of more needles or chest pound-ing has become a fear of death, of mother's death, of motherdaughter death: "the cognizance the panic the whimpering the fear and trembling." We're forced to translate the nurse's euphemistic "She's not moving air" to the realization that mother can no longer breathe. Daughter heard the death rattle. The poem pushes us to ask, "Did mother?" And finally we are driven to read and to admit that mother is a "corpse," mother is dead. Motherdaughter cannot feel. Daughtermother feels too much. Nothing is held back and we must watch, participate even, as what we want to believe — that motherdaughter can continue to defy death — is juxtaposed with what is.

Annie holds nothing back in her descriptions of death's physicality — likening her mother's "fragile ribcage" in "Beauty Marks" to a "little accordion." This simile seems at first to make an odd, simplistic, even perhaps trivial comparison. Then daughter says that she'll need to buy an accordion after mother's death "to continue to feel breath/inside my two hands." Here the contrast of mother's lungs with a little accordion compels the reader, at this moment of daughter's touching mother's slow physic-al decay, to face how negligible is daughter's belief that the feel of moth-er can actually be replaced, and how loss will be experienced not only in the heart and mind, but in a much more literal and startling way, in daughter's very hands.

As daughter injects mother subcutaneously with the blood thinner, Lovenox, in *"Sim Sang"* / "We are Blood," explaining graphically that she shoots her mother's side with eighty milligrams in eight milliliter syrin-ges, she ironically contrasts how the expression "blood is thicker than water" previously always made thick blood seem like an advantage. Until the first embolism. A similar ironic reversal of meaning occurs in "Rose Petals Fall": all her life, mother's "having a big heart" has been a strength, a gift, a necessity to her family until daughter discovers that from a med-ical, literal, and purely physical standpoint, a bigger heart is a failing heart.

The third and final type of the catalogs of the dead — what one can-not do while grieving — itemizes, nearly endlessly, the average and or-dinary activities in which daughter cannot engage because of the grief she is experiencing at her mother's death. It is the list's length and the move from the expected to the unexpected that jolts the reader. In "I can't listen to Sinatra," daughter's grief is so overpowering that she can-not take care of a dog let alone a mother. Not to be expected, a reader will think, after so much caregiving. Then daughter's paralysis spreads to the much more mundane — she can't grocery shop, watch TV, listen to the radio—simple, everyday activities that we often engage in to avoid doing something more demanding.

In a final stage of inaction, we discover that, at least temporarily, daughter cannot be herself anymore. The emptiness, separation from mother, becomes too much, and she can cope with her mother now existing only inside her by imagining that she, daughter, has the power to re-externalize mother, to bring her, Lazarus-like, back into the world, into the present. This fantasy of daughter or daughtermother becoming mother or motherdaughter manifests itself in a different set of restrictions. "I eat how she eats": we know how mother has been eating—we have the recipes, recipes of safety and restraint where Ginger Ale and hard candies are always on the menu. "I save electricity like she does/I save money like she does": daughter is so constrained in this catalog of paralysis that when she fantasizes she becomes her mother, she can only be the mother who holds back. "I think like she does": what part of her mother is she thinking like? Which mother? The one who cooked like crazy? Who healed her daughter? Defended her children against her husband? The mother who laughed at Dr. Sun's infinite questions about her illnesses? The mother who could no longer clean? Who said: "Don't bother" when asked about resuscitation? Is she the mother who could not remember the words: "Spider Orange Rainbow," words that daughter can never forget? It is impossible to know, but the line evokes a catalog of endless permutations for the reader.

Omens and Signs in the Magical Universe

The collection gestures to unknown forces at work in our lives, forces retained from old beliefs in the magical universe, perhaps superstitions but nevertheless ways by which we look for meanings, for more meanings than might be there because sometimes (always?), in our fullness or our loss, there is not enough. Omens are part of the magical universe. The most obvious and extended omen is the dead pigeon that appears outside mother and daughter's door in "DNR—550 days left." The pigeon is a carrier of disease, therefore dangerous for two women with compromised immune systems to come in contact with. But more than that, it seems to daughter a frightening harbinger of death: "a dead pigeon belly-up on our doorstep. That was an omen. It was clear. My Mother could die that night." Rachel's power to discover the pigeon, even apparently through a closed front door, her willingness to move it with the edge of a rolled-up *Daily News*, suggests her capacity to face death. But does it really? Maybe she just wants to get rid of the germy bird.

The gorgeous rose in "The Cut Rose" functions less obviously but more frighteningly as an omen because unlike the dead bird, it is so lovely to look at. But we are warned not to let its apparent elegance deceive us—"Beautiful and luscious/as ever, but don't let it fool you/it is falling apart/ … drawing/what it can in its slow/letting go." The rose, daughter insists, has been cut from its life source and, regardless of how it looks, is dying or even already dead. Daughter makes it clear—rose stands for mother. And daughter will not be fooled. But throughout the collection, we witness infinite moments that remind us that vast spaces exist between being fooled and not being fooled, spaces of love and laughter and lightness of being where, just for moment, just in that moment, there is connection, life, holding on, there is not letting go. Sometimes, we still do let the rose deceive us.

In "Apple Table Penny," mother is unable to draw the clock the doctor of geriatrics challenges her to make; she can't get the hands right, at the meaningless "ten after eleven" demanded. Does daughter overstate the insignificance of the exercise? Or is she really telling us what we all know about the relationship between the inability to draw time and the inability to draw breath? But do we actually want to make that connection? "Such a stupid test."

Sometimes the omens are joyous, and then we become grateful that the universe is or can be infused with so much extra meaning. Readers of "Exit Cues," like daughter, yearn for the early peaches, given by what we want to be Grandma Peachtree, to mother and daughter. We yearn for those peaches to be a sign, welcoming mother on her journey back to Grandma. Welcoming daughter to her own journey.

That dead pigeon, rose, undrawn clock, early peaches and other omens feel like they are harbingers, that the world still speaks to us in some ancient, perhaps Catholic, perhaps more deeply pagan way. But they demonstrate not so much their power as our own, our capacity to make meaning even in the face of meaninglessness.

Moments of Recovery and Social Class Distinctions

So much of Annie's work is underpinned by a sense of social class—the need for Rachel's careful spending, the "never splurging, never wasting." But in "Sloan-Kettering Downton Abbey," the healthcare they both receive knows no social class barriers, and this is joyously and humorously celebrated. Motherdaughter and daughtermother, for the first time in their life, are hospitalized simultaneously at Sloan-Kettering. Annie, contagious, is in "isolation," a condition about which she wittily remarks: "I love the privacy. I love there's no smells from other people or other's beeps ... I love the 'room of one's own.'" Annie's appropriation of the literary terminology only increases the enormity of the distinction between these Bronx Italian women and the Bloomsbury upper class where the phrase originated. For both groups it leads to creativity, but for Annie there is always such a lust for life.

Even more than the private room, is the peace and contentment Annie experiences because she and Rachel are both being completely cared for: "It is the first time in my life that I know all our needs are met. We are safe, cherished, watched over, in two beds! Which has never happened." Never mind those Bloomsbury £500s where a woman is alone in "a room of one's own." Here, in Manhattan, one of the best benefits of a "room of one's own" is not being alone: "We need this on a more regular basis ... A place where we are not all alone making every decision about our care."

Resurfacing in Blue

Annie began her slow process of resurfacing and recovery the night of her mother's death—July 13, 2016. In "Her Blue," Annie's eulogy song to Rachel on her new album, "Never Argue With a Jackass," Annie recounts looking for her mother the evening of her death in what she expected to be a blue sky but was, in fact, a thickly overcast one: it was a "gray sheet of paper." A confused and overwhelmed Annie asked Rachel where she was. As Annie turned onto the Williamsburg Bridge, her mother turned up, as we have come to expect her to. The clouds opened to reveal Rachel's bright blue eyes: "there in the overcast sky, were two cut outs of eyes, her eyes, with the brightest blue light shining through, pouring through —and a cloud shaped into a smile." And, in this very first step of resurfacing, Annie returned to her role as daughter—as baby, the one who is being rocked to sleep, the one being sung to, the one who could turn to Rachel and her magic eyes once again for protection:

> I looked up at her bright jewel eyes smiling down on me, down on all of us, down on me, as she did ever since I was her baby,

smiling down, singing, rocking me to sleep, comforting. Her face in the sky was as big as when I was a baby, and I felt the magic sparkle from her eyes that I have all my life looking up at her.

By day 58, Annie is "beginning to accept the absence," and in two of my favorite lines from the collection on the paradox of what she's accepting —"the endless hours/or the fact that hours will end"—we appreciate the craft and its crafty ways whereby grief, when allowed to be meta-morphosed into poetry, lures and slowly coaxes the artist back to life.

Blowing Your Mother a Kiss

Annie and I first met close to twenty-five years ago at a conference when Rachel was recovering from a triple A dissection, and Annie thought she was going to lose her then. Annie asked me how to say "Goodbye" to her mother, and I thought of my own Italian mother—chronically ill, but also so vibrant. On momentous occasions of parting—from my first day of kindergarten to my first European flight, to my first marriage —my mother would say "Goodbye" to me in exactly the same way: she'd blow me a kiss. So I rather confidently suggested to Annie that she should "blow her mother a kiss." I'm honored that Annie carries that memory —and practice—with her to this day. She tells me that every morning she blows a kiss to Rachel's photo, and to the blue clouded sky—and every morning, she feels how light and air-filled and easy this gesture is. Annie says this helps her to have joy in eternity and to let go! Blowing a kiss always symbolized an act of a little letting go of me by my mother. It was only after her death, when it was my turn to let go, that I realized exactly how hard that light gesture could be to perform. Reading the poems in this collection brings that back to me—as it will to many, many readers.

—*Kathleen Zamboni McCormick*
2017 Purchase, New York

Professor of Literature and Pedagogy, Purchase College
author of *Dodging Satan: My Irish/Italian,*
Sometimes Awesome but Mostly Creepy Childhood
2017 Foreword Reviews Gold Medal in Humor

Another Kind of Motherhood

EVEN AS A child too small to reach doorknobs, I had a presentiment of my mother's death. Life is a set-up. Death is the cap on the bottle. We get our hearts ripped out over and over. I understand women who wear black in mourning the rest of their lives. I became suffused with my dead. They felt all around me, inside me, communicating in an ancient eternal language. I needed to be recognized as a mourner and treated with compassion. There is company in mourning. When I go to the cemetery and stand by my mother's grave, a gravitas takes hold between us mourners, spirit respecters, rememberers, honorers, candle lighters, flower waterers, the ones left behind, paused in prayer and reflection, touching marble stones, staring up at Bronx clouds. We give each other room to grieve and kind nods. We drive slowly, to and from the grave-sites. I pass marble wings of angel after angel and I feel safe enough to soften, in the middle of the Bronx just off Tremont Avenue.

Caregiving my Mom enlarged my heart and spirit. Enlarged is the right word, even if medical. I felt the pain of the heart tissue stretching to its capacity, pumping more than it was used to. I tapped reserves of patience and kindness. It's another kind of motherhood. From the time I was twelve, my mother and I lived alone together and it always felt like 'me and her against the world.' Just months after she passed, my appreciation of her acumen for homemaking and home economics grew wildly. She succeeded in raising me alone as a single mother. Mom's sharp-witted consumer advocacy kept us alive as she dealt with the crags of healthcare systems. Her lessons of survival are indelible within me. All my life I witnessed her as she telephoned companies and lobbied store managers. Most recently she had started her own campaign to get the local supermarket to stop selling salmon from Russia. "Russia is spoiling U.S. produce," Mom told the store manager who listened intently through many frozen food aisle political sessions. All the customers in the aisle heard Mom's views repeatedly. She made sure to encourage everyone to buy fish from the U.S.A. Finally, she prevailed. The store only stocked fish from the U.S. Mom initiated a similar campaign about garlic from China.

A month before she died, a month to the day, to the hour, Mom edited the last word in one of my poems and inaugurated the deepest period of mourning in my life. It was June 13th, 2016. I wrote the poem, "Palm Trees in Caution Tape," about the massacre in Orlando, Florida at the gay nightclub *Pulse* on Latin night. I handed Mom the crisp white sheet of paper—the new poem, to read while she sat in her easy chair. She always gave me the straightest answers. She sat quietly, thoughtfully reading it through a couple of times, then said to me: "How do you spell morning the other way?"

"You mean m-o-u-r-n-i-n-g?

"Yes. Spell it that way."

And that's how I ended the poem and began mourning. On my wall now, over me as I write this, are framed "kitchen notes" she handwrote to me. On a paper plate she wrote: "Dear Annie, See You Later! Love, Mom." I feel joy in her large handwriting, no doubt she already applied her Pink Lightning lipstick and was ready to go out the door with energy. I feel reassured that she is busy doing celestial work while I'm here writing.

—*Annie Rachele Lanzillotto*
July 16th, 2017—The feast day of Our Lady of Mt. Carmel
Yonkers, New York

PART I:
Caregiving

For all who mother their Mother

Last Call

"Have some wine, Ma."
"Just a drop."
"I know I know. Cin'dahn!"
"I don't think so."
"No? You don't got another ten years?"
"No."
"Five?"
"No."
"No? Three?"
"I don't think so."
"So this is it?"
A nod.
We clink glasses
drink the wine down.

Though we are careful with each step, to not trip
careful with germs, careful with eating and washing
we know life's a game
where the final buzzer will sound
at any moment
the length of the game don't matter
ain't in our control
it's how you play that counts
and death death is a friend
who'll drop in every once in a while
to say, "Hey, you know I'm close by"
the knock startles you at the door
forget goodbyes
either it's been said by then
or it don't matter
Live knowing that
Live by the bell
Live cause
this is
the last round

DNR

550 days left

I WAS IN A RUSH. I couldn't leave my mother for more than an hour or two alone any more. I was going to physical therapy, a last ditch effort to take care of myself while I cared for Mom. I settled her in her chair, propped up her feet with a pillow, poured her orange Gatorade, arranged clicker, tissues and telephone on her little table, and left. I opened the hall door and took a big step — over a dead pigeon belly-up on our door-step. That was an omen. It was clear. My mother could die that night.

Ever since the apartments went Co-Op and installed large glass panes for front doors, birds flew headlong into the glass. I didn't want to deal with a dead pigeon. I don't have a spleen and my immunity is com-promised from chemo and radiation years ago and my mother had me convinced that dead birds carry disease and all this swirled in my head as I stepped over the pigeon. I hoped my mother wouldn't see it — dead birds upset her. Somehow I know this is a *mamma* pigeon. It is the clear-est omen one could have.

I came home a couple of hours later, the pigeon was still there and Mom knew all about it. She already had called the office to have the grounds crew come remove the bird. Hours passed, no one came. Final-ly she'd pushed the dead pigeon a few inches away with a rolled-up *Daily News*. I tell her: "Let's take a ride. We can put a couple of tanks of oxy-gen in the car in case you need it." There's a new baby in the family, my sister's granddaughter. It's imperative Mom meet her. We hit the road. When we walk out the door the bird is gone. "Did someone remove it or push it into the garden?" Mom examines the garden. No bird in sight. We get out of Yonkers and head north.

On a long list of her diseases, my mother now has recurrent bladder cancer. On one recent trip to Sloan-Kettering, a nurse saw me pushing her in a wheelchair. The nurse looked at us startled. "I remember when she pushed you," she said. "Now you push her." This nurse has been at Sloan as long as I have — thirty-seven years. I've had her in different clin-ics over the decades. We've aged together. She remembers when I was eighteen with Hodgkin's disease and my Mom was my caregiver, hold-ing my coat, pushing my wheelchair. Now Mom's the patient and I'm the caregiver. Plenty of times we both sign into Urgent Care, one after the other. I'm a caregiver, but I get sick all the time. When I'm sick, Mom catches it. When Mom's sick, I get it. It's a bad system over here, two immuno-compromised people saving each other's lives.

That night at my sister's house, I went to bed early to read, only to be woken up with shouts: "The ambulance is on its way!" My mother couldn't breathe, knew something was really wrong, and told my sister, "Call 9-1-1."

A CAT scan gave an answer. "Pulmonary emboli," the E.R. doctor told us. I asked the prognosis and she clarified: "Well you could have dropped dead." She talked to us like we're the same person. They put Mom on Heparin, and she began yet another long uphill journey to stay alive.

Mom cried out: "I wish I could just up and walk outta here!"

A young doctor carrying paperwork found me in the hallway. "I asked your mother if she wanted to be resuscitated if necessary."

"What'd she say?"

"Don't bother."

After fourteen hours at Mom's side I take a break. I wish it was the old days when I could drop by aunts' and uncles' houses and at the spur of the moment, they'd fill the table with a feast anytime of the day or night. I was exhausted and needed nourishment. I remember visiting Grandma Rose on White Plains Road in the Bronx, as you entered that apartment building you smelled all the Italian women's cooking. I would lean against the wall of brass mailboxes and bask in the aromas. Fried eggplant, garlic, olive oil, steak *braciole*. I wanted to knock on all the doors and eat at all the apartments, walk up all the flights and smell all the cooking. There were pots on every stove. On my father's side, I could drop in at his sisters' houses and there was always all kinds of food. No sooner than you stepped in the door and Aunt Archangel was pulling out dishes, a whole spread like it was Thanksgiving and I was just stopping by to say hello. Then I'd cross the street to Aunt Tessie's and she'd cover the table with multiple courses. Then I'd cross the street to see my Grandma Anna. I was never done eating. I couldn't say, "I just ate." That had nothin' to do with it. These women fed you, heart and soul. I need that now. Something on the stove. Plenty on the table. Healing home cooking. Then a brief deep nap. Those old Italian ladies are inside me. They possess me when my goddaughter Melissa and her little girls Caroline Rose and Elizabeth Rachele come down for a visit, and I make thirty meatballs big like peaches. Chop meat, parsley, bread-crumbs, garlic, good oil, a coupla' beaten eggs. Mix it with my hands, roll the balls lightly in my palms. Spareribs, two dozen. Large pork ribs. I brown the ribs and throw them in the gravy. It stews for hours. I turn with Mom's tallest wooden spoon. Then chocolate pudding. I turn over the meatballs, let them cool and rest. The meatballs, the spareribs in gravy, the chocolate pudding. In Italy where we're from, in the south, the heel of the boot, some dishes take days to make. The almond bis-cotti, *gli biscotti d'mandorle*—three days. Some processes have to sit for hours, sometimes overnight. *Limoncello* takes at least three weeks. It's gotta sit. Maybe a month. *Vino* takes years in barrels. When my nieces arrive I put on a big pot of water for the spaghetti. You might think—they're kids—you could'a grabbed a pizza. But no. It's too late. My mother taught them. They expect meatballs and spaghetti to come outta Great-Grandma's kitchen where there's always something cooking. They know the difference between *fettuccini, linguini, spaghetti,* and Mom's favorite, Angel Hair. They twirl their forks with the long strands and they've been saying *parmigiano* since they're two years old, shaking the cheese shaker like a snow globe for a forceful flurry. After we eat I photograph the empty plates. The table looks like we slaughtered some-thin'. Red gravy splotches on white plates. We push back the chairs and lay on the couch. I play a video from three years ago—when we had the same exact dinner. Close-ups of my mother spooning meatballs onto all our plates and the one-year-old holding a strand of pasta up in the air over her head like a trophy and the two-year-old throwing her head back to fit a fistful of strands down into her mouth, and the *parmigiano* shak-er being passed around the table, the white flakes of cheese snowing down onto our plates. This *parmigiano* snow globe we live in—*parmi-giano* inside and out. We have the gravy inside us. The gravy has to be inside us all. And my mother walking into the kitchen, walking into the window light 'til we can't see her anymore.

To Mother Your Mother

the seams on the sidewalk set the rhythm
to the wheels all our lives
from my baby carriage
to her wheelchair
steady rhythm like turning
pages of a book

The omen of the bird comes to pass
Mom cannot breathe not one deep breath
"Call the ambulance," she ekes out
ribs bobbing

this is her still life
quarter moon slice over peach tree
over Mom on wooden bench
her white princess sneakers
bend into white arches
sliced moonlight

she's a baby now at eighty-nine
whimpers in the morning whines at night
points at something she needs and lost the word for
I jump to get it, knowing she's done this already, all of it
for me and would again if only
if only she could

The Rackets

I DROVE STEADILY, continually checking the tank valve so that we wouldn't leak any oxygen. We needed every minute. Mom survived the bilateral pulmonary emboli attack in Connecticut. Now we had to drive home to New York. The problem was, oxygen cannot be delivered across state lines. No one could authorize giving us two tanks of oxygen for the trip. Not the doctor, not the Patient Advocate, not the social worker, not the Discharge Coordinator, not the Charge Nurse, no one could get Mom more than one green tank, a two hour supply. Enter the quagmire of Medicare contracts with 'durable medical equipment' suppliers.

Sitting in a car for hours and not drinking enough water increased Mom's chance of blood clots, now she was being sent home without enough oxygen to take a pit-stop. I coached her to move her legs and ankles up and down in the car to circulate blood. I sped. I lowered the level of oxygen for a while to buy minutes. We prayed the oxygen tank didn't leak, or the nozzle washer break, or the pin housing loosen, like they routinely did. We prayed we didn't hit traffic. My plan was this: if we ran too low on oxygen, I would find the nearest Fire Department for help. Firemen are much more helpful than anyone. They deal with high alert. So many years of our lives have been on constant high alert. I always had a contingency plan my whole life.

The next six months I worked hard to get Mom a portable oxygen concentrator on wheels. This is like carrying a vacuum around every-where you go that makes oxygen out of air; now you only have to worry about running out of batteries, again every two hours. You don't have to worry about oxygen leaks or explosions. After six months of continual battle, a concentrator was delivered to our door by a durable medical equipment supplier. I examined it and realized it only "pulsed" oxygen. It was not capable of "continual" oxygen. The pulse of oxygen was dependent on the patient's rhythmic inhalation / exhalation. Mom needed continual oxygen. With heart failure, her 'air hunger' caused anxiety, panic and terror—she was not able to regiment her inhalations and ex-halations. The oxygen company said they had no such "continual flow" machines. After weeks of phone calls, my sister succeeded in identifying who at Medicare evaluates the performance of the suppliers who win the contract bids. "Medicare's Competitive Acquisition Ombudsman; the C.A.O." Now we had someone specific to call when we needed interces-sion. Mom called the C.A.O. to report the oxygen company as an inept vendor. The C.A.O. immediately called the oxygen company while Mom was on the line, and said a complaint had been filed against them. Mom said: "You should lose your contract with Medicare, the way you treat people with one foot in the grave!"

The oxygen company man replied: "A continuous flow concentrator was just delivered to our warehouse! I was *just* about to call you Mrs. Lanzillotto!" It was at our house the very next day.

"Jackasses!" Mom said.

The oxygen company workers routinely lied. What was the racket with durable medical equipment? Once we got the portable oxygen concentrator, I called for extra batteries so that when we hit New York City traffic getting to Sloan-Kettering, I could change the battery and Mom would have uninterrupted oxygen—and wouldn't die in the car! I also called for a car plug. When I say "called" I mean spending three hours a day on the phone trying to achieve these goals, navigating the obstacles and lies of the oxygen company. First they said: "You can't have both an oxygen tank and a concentrator in the house. You don't qualify."

"We have frequent power outages," I explained. "We need a tank in the house in case the power goes out."

"If the power ever goes out, call us and we'll deliver a tank."

"She'll be dead by then."

"That's the system."

Then: "You can't have extra batteries for your portable concentrator. You only get two. Then you plug in wherever you go."

"Two hours is not enough time to get to the doctor. We get stuck in Manhattan traffic."

"Don't get stuck in traffic. You only have two batteries."

Finally I learned their language—lies. Lies to survive by: "One of the batteries is not working. Please deliver another one." When the delivery guy came, I lied again: "Another delivery guy picked up the bad battery already. No I don't remember his name." And that's how I got an extra battery. I needed more and I still needed the car plug. I pulled the same routine, but when the delivery guy came, he lied first:

"I have no batteries, just the car plug." And he handed me the wire.

I screamed at him: "We needed batteries! They promised us batteries!" But Mom, sharper and calmer than me, noticed pink bubble wrap sticking out from the delivery man's armpit. In the pink bubble wrap, as she surmised, were the new batteries. He was lying to us. Why? How could he profit? Mom pulled me aside, pointed out the pink bubble wrap and hushed me with her time honored wisdom:

"Never argue with a jackass."

Phil was his name. He looked at the concentrator and tried to pull one battery out, the one I said didn't work. He couldn't get it out. The rubber handle was awkward. Phil used force, then gave up. "I am afraid to break it," he said.

I lost my cool. I telephoned the oxygen company and yelled: "Phil is afraid! Phil is afraid! Where are our batteries?"

"I gotta go look in the truck," Phil said. But he lied again. He only walked out of the apartment and into the hallway. I followed him. There they were—the pink bubble wrapped batteries tucked under his armpit—just as Mom had eagle-eyed.

I went back into the apartment, removed the batteries from the concentrator and hid them. A few minutes later, Phil walked back into the apartment with the batteries in his hand, saying: "I found these in the truck, they are for someone else but I can do *you* the favor." He lied again and again. What could be his racket? I had always tipped these delivery guys good.

"Yeah you're doing us a big favor," I said, and grabbed the batteries from him.

"Where are the old batteries?" Phil asked.

"I already gave them to you. You brought them out to your truck." And that is how we got the batteries we needed to go to the doctor, enough to swap out so Mom could breathe in peace, her last year of breaths on earth.

Bottom line. I found these batteries selling on eBay for $500 each. Therein lies the racket. Mom figured it out: Phil could sell the batteries online and report to the company that he had given them to us. He'd pocket a thousand bucks. There's always a racket. Durable medical equipment, as it turns out, is the biggest one of all.

Riverriverriverriv

on the river riverriverriverriv
                on the river riverriverriverriv
        Mom is up   the river riverriverriverriv
    Mom is on   the river riverriverriverriv
Mom is over   the river riverriverriverriv
Mom is riverriverriverriv
  Mom's hospital room overlooks the river
   riverriverriverriv is mighty riverriverriverriv breathes
            O how men wanted to cross
            O how men built braces across
          O how men sunk caissons
          O how men worked in compressed air
                O men with picks and shovels
        venous air pressure   bled out their ears
            tons of cement   in her banks
        Roebling's 80 ton wire rope   machine
spinning cables   from giant spools of steel
    1000 tons   it all started with a boy   twisting
    wire together   around his finger imagining steel rope
                    at its greatest   tensile strength
Mom's not enjoying being on the river riverriverriverriv
        She's hooked up   to oxygen   heart leads
            catheter   I.V.   BIPAP   pulse oximeter
        riverriverriverriv's good   for me   to take breaks
    look at boats   white creases   in the gray wrinkled face
    to stare into slow motion   million wing-tipped waves
where I imagine what used to be   people communing
    with the river   hand hewn log canoes
        swimming   washing ancestors   clothes
                    lifeblood   fishing   diving
    wolves splashing   bears shaking the river off their pelts
            ice 1647 Tobias and Harman ran across frozen
    riverriverriverriv to escape the   New Amsterdam Dutch
        where being gay
                was akin to being a murderer
Ahh ... the river holds all our dreams   and capital offenses
    this hospital solarium I make my Bellagio for this hour
        blessed blank   white space   paper
    holy blue ink I make   my mark   grateful for this
        Mom
            breathes
        day

Superstar Angel

7 years, 3 months, 5 days left

MOM WAKES UP FRIGHTENED with very low oxygen. I put the pulse oximeter on her index finger, give her a nebulizer with the strong cocktail: Xopenex and Ipratropium bromide—this is the expensive first world stuff—our U.S.A. privilege in thousands of dollars of tiny plastic vials. I instruct her to take three deep breaths. Burnt raisin toast, just the way she likes it, a soft circling rub of her back, a sip of cough syrup to stop the incessant hacking, a half pill of Xanax inside her bottom lip.

She moans, whimpers, yells: "How long will this go on?"

She will survive this episode, this COPD exacerbation, however her bloodwork indicates her heart enzymes are up—tiny heart attacks. Her heart is dying, failing, dying. No wonder she is terrified. What must it feel like, to try to pump yourself up while your heart is dying? All the time now, she speaks of her father, this is something new, as if she is a child again and she remembers that his love was the best comfort she ever had:

"I remember my father holding my hand, walking me out of the hospital. I felt so guilty leaving my friends behind, all my friends who couldn't walk." She stares into the past in the air, then squeezes my hand and blesses me for life. "You're my Superstar Angel. What would I do without you? God will bless you. God will bless you."

"This is my blessing Mom. This time with you." And it's true. These years of hours of caregiving are allowing me to learn and grow in patience and kindness—the pre-requisite of the task. I tap my reservoirs of care. The opposite is also true. I can be impatient. I can snap: "Lift your feet up off the floor when you walk. Please I can't stand the shuffling." I get tired of being the resuscitator, the cheerleader, the one whose message is: "There is more life worth living I promise."

I spend every moment with my mother—like squeezing a dry lemon over cooked fish. I am holding rinds, pits, seeds. Squeezing, saving, drying lemon in her blue sky kitchen. Full lemons are juicier but that's all. I beg my shrink for meds that calm me down. "I can't be impatient," I say. "I need to be a lamb, not a lion." I get on calming medications. I need to be in a rhythm that works with my Mom's. I want to learn more about Pasolini's life with his mother. I can imagine their routines, how they move around each other in the kitchen, the way he looks up her while he sits and eats *il pranzo* and she stands, wiping her hands with a dish towel. I wonder about their conversations. Artists, gay, without children, Italian, living with and attached to their mothers. He's my role model in a way, except I don't wanna die slain and crushed on a night beach, though death is death no matter how served.

Apple Table Penny

The doctor of geriatrics asks Mom to remember
this series of three words
then he asks her to draw a clock
and to draw the time ten after eleven.
She tries, but this is confusing.
She leaves his office upset.
She practices drawing the clock at home.
Such a stupid test, and demoralizing.
Any one can get confused.
We haven't drawn clocks
since kindergarten.

The next year she practices
the clock drawing before her appointment.
He asks her to remember three new words
"Spider Orange Rainbow"

Words I can never forget as
I see the effort across her brow.

Beauty Marks

Her third eye grew back!
Seventy years ago a doctor convinced her
to let him cut it off
"You're so pretty, you don't need that
in the middle of your forehead."
When she got home that day, my father told her,
"You cut off your beauty."
Now it's back, in the center of her forehead.
I tell her, "That's your third eye. Very powerful place.
Intuition. Wisdom. Vision. Power." She makes nothing of it.

I bathe her soup bone body
examine the beauty marks and moles all over her back
doctors say are not suspicious just Italian I guess.
Water pools in her clavicle. I never saw that before.
She revives in the tub, "This is Heaven,"
can barely lift her arms to curl her hair
pencil on Midnight Blue eyeliner, ask,
"What do you say to people who say—
'if you can get out to a doctor, why can't you come visit?'"
I answer, "You're a great work of art,
there's only one of you. People have to come see you!
Tell them—I'm a great work of art.
People travel all over the world to see a great work of art.
There's only one of me. You have to come see me."

Her feet swell and I prop them up with pillows
"Take another twenty" of Lasix.
Her feet take on the ribbing pattern of her socks
the ridges of her softest shoes.
These days her feet need to be free, held high,
"The feet of angels never touch ground
in Renaissance paintings,"
Audrey says, "just comb sky."
I wash Mom's feet, rub cream—hold them high as angels.
The bathroom is our ablution space. She huddles over the sink.
I hold her fragile ribcage

ribs expand and contract in my hands like a little accordion.
A bath is a lot of exercise — she steps out of the tub
heart pumping uphill — she just climbed a mountain.
I know I'll have to go get one
when she's gone, a little accordion
to continue to feel breath inside my two hands.

Sim Sang / We are Blood

our sap and blood
flow thick and sticky

I can hear our Barese ancestors yell
Cim ciang! Sim sang!
We are blood! *Cim ciang!*
in the wind between Grandma's peach tree branches
I inject Mom subcutaneously with Lovenox
eighty milligrams in eight milliliter syringes   .

Her blood stopped flat
I must thin this blood
thin the blood, thin the blood
Fludicamente du ciang

with each shot in the side of a pinch
of her belly from where I came
familiar words thicken
words I've heard all my life
"we are blood" "blood is thicker than water"
the ring of the Barese yell
cim ciang, sim sang, tu ssi ciang mi
we are blood, we are blood, you are my blood

Mom's blood stuck

refuses to flow

cinga, seis, litri du ciang—five, six liters of blood
coagulo, coagulo, coagulo—coagulates, coagulates, coagulates

stuck in veins blood
deep stops in legs and lungs

though our hearts
our hearts
thirst
still

Love Primer

WE ARE FROM THE BRONX, which stamps us indelibly. When you grow up daydreaming in asphalt rainbows in oil streaks on Bronx side streets, you're marked—you walk Bronx, talk Bronx, you think Bronx, act Bronx. For life. So, me and my mother are Bronx. Next, she's a lady and I'm a butch. That's its own thing. She teased me that I was her chauffeur, she'd say: "I'm the chauffee." She loved making up words. There's an element of the chauffeur thing that was strange, you see my father, *riposa in pace,* wrote 'chauffeur' as his occupation on their marriage license, this just after he came home from WWII, after surviving the battle of Okinawa. It's just like my father to come up with 'chauffeur' in a hefty Bronx sarcasm and wit and an Italian way of cloaking everything. He was on the front lines with the First Marine Division, an embattled private, cannon fodder, but how do you put that on a newly minted marriage license in 1947? How did any marine address the blank after 'occupation' on their post-war marriage papers? Civilian life with its stupid questions begged stupid answers. After boot camp in his first post at the sub base in New London, Connecticut, my father drove jeeps to take military higher ups where they had to go. And so, with a wink in his eye he told the Bronx City Clerk on the Grand Concourse: "Chauffeur." I imagine my mother's surprise. She was charmed by that. They laughed. In her last years of life as I drove her everywhere she'd joke: "I love being your chauffee!" It had to be a private joke to herself. She must have said the same thing to my father as they left the courthouse. I can hear her: "If you're a chauffeur—then I'm the chauffee!" Maybe it was a Grand Concourse Lanzillotto in-joke. Their first joke as a married duo.

We are Barese Italian. The Greek coast of Italy. The heel of the boot. We got a lot of Greek in us. My mother's father's side came from Greece hundreds of years ago, sailed the Aegean Sea to the Adriatic Sea and settled in *Cassano delle Murge, Provincia di Bari.* Motherdaughter love is so great in Greek thought, that the turning of winter spring summer fall is explained by Demeter's fierce love to rescue her kidnapped daughter Persephone. When Persephone is returned to her mother, the earth blooms with fruit and flowers, when she is taken away from her mother the earth sheds its leaves and falls into a barren winter. Hades hands Persephone pomegranate seeds to eat to make sure she returns. Pomegranates appear in my dreams. In one dream a hot policewoman hands me a pomegranate candle. Demeter's hunt to rescue Persephone knew no bounds. She was willing to sacrifice the whole earth to be reunited with her daughter.

A few times my mother introduced me in public as her mother. I remember once at Joanna Clapps Herman's book party for *The Anarchist Bastard*, we were saying hello to Joanna's husband Billy who was born just hours and blocks away from Mom, and they shared a Bronx repartee. Billy introduced my mother to his brother-in-law John, and my mother with all naturalness says: "This is my mother," and points to me. The truth of that moment didn't escape either of us. It was my turn to mother. Our mothering was reciprocal. We laughed with the profundity of it all.

In illness we had the opportunity to give each other mothering love; to care for one other to a life and death degree, ministering to each other's breathing, fevers, delusions, pulse rates, electrolytes, cancers, moods, insurance paperwork; we lived on Persephone's precipice, reaching out for each other's hand to rescue first one then the other in a revolving dance on the edge of death. Between the two of us we nursed each other to health and saved each other's lives through nineteen pneumoniæ, four cancers, one super bacteria, one aortic dissection, chemo, radiation, two post-op staph infections, twelve surgeries, countless viruses, aches and pains. The list doesn't come close to the thousands of hours we cooked chicken soup, shared boxes of tissues, cans of ginger ale, nebulizers, back-rubs, glasses of water, green Jell-O. Intimacy is impossible to calculate; the intimacy of illness and recovery a thousand-fold impossible. Illness is time slowed down to a still life, infused with attention to inhales and exhales, deep chest wheezes, coughs, heartbeats and pulse, temperature.

How will I mourn my mother? In the last years I carted her oxygen everywhere we went. For as long as she had the strength to walk, I put the oxygen tanks in a shopping cart so that she could stand and hold onto the cart, then when we got where we were going, we could put our coats and bags in the cart too, and make our way, one of my hands pushing the cart, the other on the small of her back for support and a precaution against falls. I pushed her and the cart. We had a good time wherever we went. Not without incident of course, oxygen tank valves opened in the car setting off loud shooting jets of flammable oxygen, panic attacks, fatigue, monitoring minutes for the amount of oxygen reserve left, frustration banging into doorjambs with wheels, prohibitions of using public bathrooms with all that equipment. I took it in stride. We'd don our yellow face masks and go grocery shopping—a giant achievement for as long as Mom had the strength. Routinely, I'd go into the staff room and grab a folding chair for her to sit in the aisles. I pulled my sternum cartilage heaving the oxygen tanks and got costochondritis which led me to often roar and growl in pain in public. It felt like I was being stabbed in the center of my chest. My roar was loud. My mother, witnessing the pain of my injury, began to say: "I'm destroying my daughter's life." I begged her to see things differently. I repeated: "Mom, I wouldn't want to be anywhere else than right here with you now."

Dark Blue

742 days left
Baltimore Riots and Nepal Earthquake, April 28, 2015

On the verge of opening this morning
two dozen Belgian Purple Prince tulips
from bulbs I planted for Mom last fall
Through months of snow and ice I prayed
she would live to see the shoots rise, bud, open
and here we are, "Another spring," as Nina Simone sang
Tulip leaves are more hardy than roses
Purple tulips open into cups for the sun
cups of purple light with yellow sunburst hearts

Sun cups   *Le tazze di sole*
Cup the sun   *Alle tazza di sole*
Sun the cup   *Al sole la tazza*
Sunny cups   *Le tazze soleggiata*

This morning Mom woke up
whimpering, "I have such a chill."
I covered her. "Pull the blinds over the window.
Keep the window open. Let the air in."
Later she felt nauseous. "Maybe it's the broccoli."
She lay on her right side.
"Rub my back. Lower. Maybe it's just gas."
Later I was in the closet grabbing laundry.
"Which are you doing?" she asked.
        "Both."
        "Hah?"
        "Both."
        "Hah?!"
        "Both!"
        "Oh both. Well you have your head in the closet.
Turn around and answer me."

The pain of age, fear of death
She opens her arms, drops all bravado

toward me she walks with outstretched arms
into my big hug, whimpering, as I hold her to my ribs,
"I just wish I could be fifteen again."

I pinch her belly skin,
jab the needle in quick and sure
tell her to sing to break her gut tension
push the plunger quickly.
Lovenox, her daily dose of blood thinner
keeps away killer clots.
I put the used needle in the royal blue cookie tin
on top of the fridge. I have hundreds of needles.

Into my bowl I spoon oatmeal, flaxseed,
peanut butter, papaya, yogurt.
I sit and turn on the news.
Stark images back to back:
a tidal wave of dark blue clad cops
muscular Baltimore boys jumping on cars
throwing rocks at the sky orange with fire,
Katmandu children wrapped in blankets not moving
the earth shaking its crust.
"One place is destroyed and fighting for their lives,"
Mom says, "and the other place they are destroying."
"Let's pray for all those who can't get their medicines today."
Nepalese breathing rubble, Baltimore asthmatics
whose Ventolin melted, exploded
when the pharmacy was torched
Oxygen, Prednisone, Xopenex, Ipratropium bromide
Dilaudid, Percocet, Oxycodone
the pain killers the pain
killers the pain
killer
the
pain. Kill.

How to Cook for Your Mother in the Last Year of Her Life

MOM CAN STILL EAT BUT she needs to be coaxed. She's napping more, talking about her father all the time, slowly entering the ether, falling asleep in the chair with her mouth agape taking bites of air. Last night she dreamt of her mother Rose. "I'm sleeping in the next room," Rose said to her matter-of-factly.

Now Mom's singing the R&B song: "Are you ready? Yes I'm ready." She keeps saying: "I'm ready. I want to get on a plane. I want to fly."

I banter back quoting Sinatra: "Pack a small bag."

Quickly she responds: "I won't pack at all." She's on her way out. I massage her fontanelle. I have felt my own soul rev up like a cyclone and try to pull out of the top of my head, wanting to get the hell outta here.

I make chicken soup. This is sustenance. No matter how rotten she feels I can get a few tablespoons of this broth elixir into her. Sauté the holy trinity: yellow onions, celery, carrots, in your pot, white enameled cast iron is the best for this. If you have whole fennel, chop some of that in! Add boiling water. Add chopped fresh parsley, bay leaf, a piece of fresh ginger. Add your favorite chicken part: a breast, a thigh, whatever you like. Add cut potato. Cover with room for a little air to escape. Let this boil for an hour. You can add oregano, and spice to taste. This is great to get the whole apartment simmering as an arena of healing. Mom likes it served with a little *pastina* mixed in, or angel hair pasta broken in half. Very soothing. A good energy boost. It builds the blood.

The next essential meal is scorched cinnamon raisin toast. Set the toaster for seven minutes. Don't leave the room. One slice of raisin bread. When it's toasted with some scorched black on top, unplug the toaster! Butter the toast and serve. Blackened toast cures upset stomach. Good any time of day. Five a.m., midnight, anytime. Great for when your mother wakes up in the middle of the night.

Next, stuffed Italian peppers, the long light green peppers. "They used to call them Italian Peppers," Mom says. "Now they call them *Cubanelos*. If you ask for Italian Peppers they don't know what you're talking about." Lightly sauté chop meat and chopped yellow onions. If you have a whole fennel, that too. Sprinkle fennel seeds. A dash of turmeric. *Basilico*. When the sauté is done, the onions translucent and the meat cooked, add chopped parsley — all you want! Close gas and cover. Add cooked brown rice. Add raisins. Mom adds raisins in everything. Add two eggs, chopped *mozzarella* and *parmigiano reggiano*. Mix with your hands. Cut a circle at the stem of the pepper to take the stem, pulp and seeds out. Hopefully, you have a hollow straightish pepper with good room inside to stuff. Stuff the mixture into the pepper. Push it in with your fingers. My Mom can fit one and a half times the mixture that I can. I don't know how she packs it in, especially with peppers with a curve. Do your best. Pack the pepper. Put it in the oven.

Zucchini always goes down easy no matter how old or frail you are—especially great for lunch. In a saucepan an inch of water, bring to a boil, add sliced zucchini rounds, a drop of olive oil, a clove of garlic. Cover. Turn off the gas after a few minutes, keep covered.

Other staples are Hot Mickeys: sweet potatoes wrapped in tin foil and baked. Jelly donuts, crumb buns, something sweet helps her mood. This is the successful way I get calories into her. A banana a day helps keep electrolytes. Ginger Ale is great for when the meds make her nauseous. Fresh roasted red peppers with fresh mozzarella fill her with *gioia di vivere*. A pot of lentils at least once a week. Add a piece of ginger to the pot of lentils. Magic.

The Saint of Crystalline

Still she will put her nightgown in the bathroom sink to soak
but she has stopped picking up after herself and after me
a plastic cup on the floor stays
a photo of her great-grandchildren under her desk stays
she has stopped moving objects, stopped cleaning dish or fork.
This is the point of no return, *alea iacta est*
windowsills are blackening. It is all up to me now
I am the one who cleans. Everyday
she says, "I just have to get myself together."
By this she means: calm down, dampen the fear
that runs like a clock.

Air sparkled. I don't know how she did it
miraculous disappearance of stains
socks flying in wind, bleached white wings
on the line, pocket holes joined
sheets' faces without a wrinkle
coins, pens, gum, retrieved from coat linings
windows bounced sunbeams, the kissing sound
of her rubbing window glass into rectangular rinks of light
tub, sinks, toilet, tile walls, maple table
chair legs all slick with shine
wrought iron milk pails, pot belly stove
a waxed top coat shine on every thing
immaculate holy glow of floors and ceilings
meatballs like clockwork every seventh day

I see time pile up, windows spotted
laundry in heaps, the teapot's stained belly
dishes, everything piling, the floor dirty in spots
the side of the fridge with gravy splatter
my brown paper lunch bag under my desk
with a month old banana.
I have to get on the ball. Figure it all out.
I wipe the table, but it doesn't shine
I need her elbow grease.
I wonder how she made every surface bright

through all of my constant creations of mess
decade after decade without ever not one day faltering?
Not one day sending laundry out, ordering a food delivery?
I don't know how she did it but I do know her ablutions
gave constant renewal
to all our souls.

My Rag Goes Everywhere

My mother got three bloody noses Saturday
took me a good twenty minutes each bleed
pinch the bridge of her nose
balance ice along the ridge
rip brown paper off a bag and fold it three times
to tuck under her top lip
calm her down!

I told her not to bend down after that
not to pick things up
I started seeing things
flecks of paper and crumbs under the table
dust clutching wooden chair leg bottoms
cobwebs adrip in ceiling corners
dirt peeking out from the top of the ceiling fan blades
grit in the cracks in the floor
coffee grinds in the rubber rim of the fridge door
smudge marks on light flip plates
slats of the humidifier hull
crevasses I
don't even know
exist
static electric dust in the air—afloat in particles
I walk into a room, spot a fleck on the floor
stoop to pick it up.
My rag goes everywhere!
My rag goes everywhere!
My rag goes everywhere
my eyes do

The Art of Cleanlihood

Spotlessness manifests in windows
washed in afternoon shade.
The whitest white enameled pots
and bathtubs arise with cream of tartar,
hydrogen peroxide, elbow grease.
Hot running water is the top supply
then a bar of brown soap, bleach, steel wool.
For soap suds voluminosity add baking soda.
Removal of rust off chrome is best achieved
with a bath of Pepsi Cola. Salt and
turpentine mixtures, droplets of ammonia,
solutions of baking soda and hydrogen peroxide,
baking soda and ammonia and warm water,
all require a practiced hand
to test temperatures and ratio equivalents.

Handshake the bow with a firm but flexible grip
hinge and swivel at the wrist, easily draw
the bow back and forth across the floor
with precision. The mop stick is a violin bow
each stroke of the floor adds to the symphony
of the well kept house. Swirl arches
with the mop-bow. Let it glide.
Practice your stroke
for maximum satisfaction and effect.

Circle the rag in a swift buffing motion.
The rag is a paintbrush of lemon oil luster
down the oak banister, around maple dowels
each chair strut and table leg, tabletop and shelf
the movement of the rag makes a shellac effect.
Shellac itself comes from a she-bug, the lac bug
whose ancient resin brings
all things to a shine for all time.

Mop, rags, scrub brush, *gli stracci*
clothesline, rope, pulley
le bucato, la corda, le puleggia
these are your artist's instruments,
bucket, gallons of agents.
Sheets, tablecloths, curtains
le lenzuola, le tovaglie, le tende
the high pitch of clean glass
to a white vinegar shine
these are your canvasses
and percussion instruments.
Step back and consider
the window glass gleam
the window ledge white in nooks
the curtain's snap of incoming light
This is your painting, your order of the day.
Here is your poem, the brightening,
the shine, the purification,
your *opera domestica*.

Sloan-Kettering Downton Abbey

MOM'S IN 519. I'M IN 721. This has never happened before. Our doctors and respiratory therapists and friends go up and down to each of us. We needed it. We were taking care of each other but in a mucous factory for weeks—putting the pillows out the windows to air out and get sterilized by the sun, cooking chicken soup. The laundry stayed piled in the hallway. The food shopping never got done. I took us in, like surrendering at the station house. The bacteria rose in my throat, a tidal wave, pushed me under, not breathing, while others waved to me from shore. Can't tell you when it started. I'd have to back-up and back-up again. I forgive myself for getting sick again though again I can point to—like my father before me—a shared food or handshake that augmented what he called "the battle with my phlegm." I woke up with a closed neck baked with mucous. I panicked. I went to a local doc who gave me a loading dose of Prednisone. Mom and I have been doing hospital / hospice care for each other for months—weeks—years—decades. We were both sick as kids. Mom was a cripple and I was a chronic asthmatic. Now we both need to be home on oxygen. My oxygen saturation numbers don't match this claim but I feel better on oxygen. In the hospital, oxygen is my lullaby.

I'm in quarantine. Isolation. Great way to get a "room of one's own." I love the privacy. I love there's no smells from other people or other's beeps. The high pitched beeping of monitors drives me nuts. I love the 'room of one's own.' I love the yellow masks and gowns. I love the hierarchy and gravitas. I love being shielded and I love being dangerous. The sign on my door reads: Droplet Precautions. My droplets, my sneeze, contaminate—droplet bullets shoot out my mouth.

There's an intimacy in illness that Mom and I share. A slowed down-ness. A tender care. A need for simple food, bright entertainment, plenty of water. To have my Mom in Sloan-Kettering at the same time as me feels special; it is the first time in my life that I know all our needs are met. We are safe, cherished, watched over, in two beds—which has never happened! It's always been one bed one couch, one of us on the couch. We are visited by people, wonderful nurses and friends to talk with, friends bring our favorite things and the food is the best in the world. Mom looks so happy having her little room; bed, table, snacks, TV, phone, tissues, oxygen, nurse call button. She needs this. And for once, I can get some rest. I am so calm here tonight knowing Mom is calm and safe and has Nurse Melissa to watch over her and someone to watch over me. I have Nurse Fallon on duty. So, me and Mom are both okay. Safe. Well fed. Oxygenated. Hydrated. Medicated. Rested. Visited. Electrolytes balanced. Remembered. Communicated with. We need this on a more regular basis — community — tribe — healing residence — a place where we are not all alone making every decision about our care. Basic needs met. Clean. And the relief of retreat, of quiet, and not having too much clutter and accumulation to deal with.

Marco is the waiter for the floor. Marco caters to me. Brings me my meals. Brings me extra muffins and tea. Asks me if I want anything extra. Sloan-Kettering is our Downton Abbey. The short ribs and roasted potatoes are the best in town. The music therapist can sing *The Sound of Music*. The arts & craft room sends us paints, sewing projects, beads, anything we want. The visiting dogs, bedside massages, good company walking around the halls, some of the cleaning staff put down their mops and pray with me and sing gospel. We have a jam session with the music therapist. I call our band "The Metastatics." My friends come and are focused. They put away their cell phones. In a way, I'm having the best time of my life. Pampered and served, and a comfortable bed, a bed at all. Being in the hospital is luxury, a whole bed for myself, and constantly clean sheets. Anything I drop on the floor, they remove and replace, oxygen cannula, cup, pillow. The "environmental specialist" comes with her mop, sings gospel, and over me, prays.

Mom is going to a special cosmetics class for cancer patients. She is thrilled. They wheel her in. She gets free samples of expensive products and a make-up bag. I go down and see her in her hospital bed, fully made up like she's going out dancing. She says she had to take off the lipstick they put on that "puffed" the lips. She got regular lipstick, the kind she likes. I rarely see her this happy, as our two-week stay in Sloan-Kettering. She's glowing.

We talk on our cell phones from room to room. On my phone, the digital voice assistant never understands my Bronx accent, so I switched it from English to Italian. Instead of saying, "Call MSKCC" for Memorial Sloan-Kettering Cancer Center, I say: *"Chiama \ Em Essa Kappa Ci Ci \,"* and not only does the phone *capishe* me now, but I bring a smile to my own face every time. And believe me, I call \ *Em Essa Kappa Ci Ci* \ more times than I want to count in life.

Mom and I go over the renowned menu, curious about what the other will order for dinner, what sides — roasted zucchini and snap peas? What dessert. Pie? Pudding? Pound cake? Ice-cream? Peaches in the can?

I coach her how to navigate the complicated TV channel system. When Downton Abbey comes on tonight we will both watch, and talk about it after. Usually we identify with the servant staff; the cooks, the servants, but not tonight, tonight both our feet will be up and our arms won't hang off the side of the couch into the air.

Gum Is Not Food

340 days out

A KNOCK AT THE DOOR. I'm used to people coming and going by now; visiting nurses, social worker, case manager, psych consult, physical therapist, oxygen tank supplier, long-term care supervisor, spring water deliverer. This one came without notice. Just appeared at the door. Dressed all in white.

"Are you the nurse?"

"Yes," she nodded sweetly, popping gum.

"C'mon in. I'm Annie. The daughter. My Mom, Rachel is in the living room. What's your name?"

"Darnell." She puts her bag on a chair, takes her jacket off. I mechanically tell her to wash her hands, that we have paper towels, liquid soap dispenser and hand sanitizer in the bathroom. My mother and I say this almost simultaneously:

"Make sure she washes her hands." Marching orders to anyone who enters the apartment. My mother listens for how long people have the bathroom water on. Enough to thoroughly wash hands? She'll comment later. Was there a paper towel in the bathroom trash? Proof she washed her hands? I have a box of yellow flu masks and gloves out on the snack table. I quickly surmise how the nurse is breathing. No sinus congestion. She asks if we have a blood pressure cuff, and I hand it to her, and she proceeds to wrap it around Mom's arm. She pumps the cuff and looks at her watch and repeats this until it is clear to my mother she has no idea what she is doing.

My mother tells her: "You are not a nurse."

"No, I'm the aide," she says slowly and sweetly, gum popping.

Darnell's hours are two to six. One night we offer her a bowl of chicken soup. It's time for my mother's dinner. We are not comfortable eating in front of someone without offering them some too. We share what we have. We know by now that Darnell has three school age children down south, and that she is here to get training so she can earn more money when she goes home. So, we're sitting at the table together, the three of us, while she chews her gum while she eats our healing chicken soup. My mother and I are stunned and nauseated. Since she's up north for training, we take it upon ourselves to teach her how to eat.

"You gotta spit your gum out," I tell her.

"I'm cheeking it."

"Hah?"

"It's on the side of my mouth, in my cheek."

"What?" She's breaking our cardinal rules of eating. My mother and I have a whole silent conversation with our eyes, but we both preach out loud to Darnell. "No," I say, "you can't eat like that."

"What's a matter wit' you?" Mom chimes in, "you can't eat chicken soup with gum in your mouth."

"Okay," she says, "if you say so Miss Rachel."

After a coupla more spoonfuls of soup, I hand her a napkin. "Spit it out."

"I swallowed it."

"You what?"

"It's food."

"Gum is not food," Mom says. "Look it up on that fancy phone of yours."

"You taught your kids to swallow their gum?" I am amazed.

"Yeah. It's food."

"Gum is not food."

"Where do you think gum goes?"

"I don't know. The stomach takes care of it."

"It's not digestible," I tell her. "It's not food. You gotta spit it out. Gum is not biodegradable."

She giggles. "We swallow gum all the time."

"You let your kids swallow gum?"

"Yes, it's food."

"Google it," Mom tells her. "Gum is not food."

I love when my mother is adamant.

"I guess it's made from trees, but there's no way you can eat it," I start reasoning. It's impossible to continue eating our soup. Darnell's shift is over and as she leaves we make her promise to look into what happens when you routinely swallow gum. When she's out the door Mom says to me:

"How do people survive? It's common sense, gum is not food."

Now we have a new story to tell. Having all these strangers in the house is useful that way; we get the perk of having a common source of aggravation to unite us and make us laugh, and the bonus of taking our mind completely off our mutual breathing problems. The gum conversation continues. I tell Mom what I remember about Primo Levi's writing about gum removal in my favorite book, *The Periodic Table*:

"You know all those black circular spots on sidewalks all over? That's gum, old pieces of discarded gum that never go away. Primo Levi was a chemist. Once he had to figure out a chemical way to remove the black spots of gum from the sidewalk. Gum is not biodegradable."

"Of course," she agrees. I look on my phone and Google: "Is gum food?" "Can you swallow gum?" "Is gum biodegradable?" And there it is; facts. Gum, as it turns out, is now made from plastics and rubber, and can cause intestinal blockages, and no, is not biodegradable. Darnell never believes us though. She comes back popping gum, and laughs if we bring up the topic.

The Cut Rose

I often think of my mother
as already dead. The cut rose
in the vase, head leaning
over the side. Beautiful and luscious
as ever, but don't let it fool you
it is falling apart.
One petal at the foot
of the pink glass angel
at the base of the vase.
Petal by petal the rose
lets you know — it lived once
for as long as it could
in its most beautiful manifestation
but now stands not before you
just leans in
the water, draws
what it can in its slow
opening
letting go

Rose Petals Fall

off the pink rouge rose.
"Give him a rose for his wife," Mom says
as Al steps toward the door to leave.
"But it's falling apart," I say as I lift one out of the vase.
"Doesn't matter," Mom insists, "it's the thought."
Al tucks the stem in his flannel chest pocket, three petals
to the floor. Later I see two more
down the outside staircase
where Al walked to his car.

Mom too is falling open
Her heart, forty percent ejection fraction
soft and giving, open valves open walls
"Her heart is so huge," the doctor told me
after the last echocardiogram.
That we always knew, I thought,
but not how the heart gets bigger
as it fails, opens
toward its last set of beats.

The seal is broken open open O
pink rouge rose petals, her skin
the softest you will ever touch
falling open
falling
the most gorgeous stem
you will ever receive

Above the Heart

Mom's feet were swollen this mornin'
I couldn't go out anywhere
missed the reading on stage in the city.
This is no 'quality of life' — her legs up
and not enough energy to smile
or take a few steps

I can barely remember how she walked
without hesitation without a walker
without being tethered by the nose
to an oxygen tank
how she walked to the bus to work
crossed large avenues in traffic

Remind me:
How was her gait and stride, head held high?
How did she hold her arms overhead with strength
enough to set her own hair with rollers?
How was the spring in her step, the bounce?

It is sundown
lilac carries in the birdsong
breeze over traffic waves, streetlight
pale light sky complexion
gray-blue, again I cry
walk the rectangular path to keep
my own blood
in motion

It's Hard Having Strangers in the House

Thirty-four minutes until the aide leaves
no one can count these hours
the oppression of being watched
like we are waiting for something to happen
death to
boil over

Mom is in her chair
as if death will seize
her in day light

Why do I think death comes
in the dark like a thief?
As if death knows
dark from light
quiet night
mice and ghosts in agreement
these apartments safeguard the silence

one scream could shatter night

April Showers

99 days out

In the thunderstorm I go out
and sit in the car.
I just gotta get out of the house.
The aide is here for a couple of hours.
The apartment feels too small for the three of us.
When one walks, the other one has to turn
with her back to the wall to let the other one by.
I go out even though I'm too tired
to go do anything.
In the thunderstorm I sit in the car
let the deluge down the car windows
clear my head. Blast some music
the way I can rarely do in the apartment these days.

This is the best aide, Clara, the one we pray we keep.
She's capable of conversation. She's older, mature.
Mom and her talk about life and laugh together.
They are both mothers who have known poverty,
working class service jobs,
the paucity of tips, hard times.
It's written all over their faces, in their vocabulary,
their nods, the way they watch the world
from the porch.
I appreciate who they are.
Still, I get the hell outta there.
Talk to raindrops.

The other day Mom dumped the leftovers
off her plate onto the floor
just tilted the plate, swiped the food
with her hand, then she snapped awake up
as if from being hypnotized,
        "Why'd I do that!?"
        "It happens," I said, and quickly swept up.

Dream Before Dying

Mom talks in her sleep to her mother.
"Yes, the oven's on. What time is Patty coming?
Will she eat chicken?" Another night,
"What time is Patty coming home?
Maybe she'll have a piece of lasagna—
I don't know if she eats that."
One night she wakes up laughing,
"I was just talking with Grandma,
she said, 'That's all the food there is?'
I told her we had chicken soup.
She said, 'That's all?'"
On December 27th she yells in her dream state,
"Is the baby okay on the bed?"
I am her baby. I reassure her, "Yes Mom, I am okay."
Another night, alarmed: "I forgot to feed the baby!"
I say, "Mom I am okay. You fed me. We had dinner."
"Okay," she says, and goes back to sleep.
I know she worries about me.
I know I have to convince her I am okay
in order for her to let go, in peace.
She needs to know I will be okay.
In one type of dream she says, "I can't find my clothes."
Over and over she reports trying to either leave the house
or to get back home, but she does not know
where she put her clothes. She is terribly frustrated.
Another series of dreams, she yells,
"Stop! That was my stop!"
I say, "Mom, you are okay."
She wakes up and says,
"I'm on the bus and it misses my stop."
I too have a version of this dream where I am on the bus
and my mother gets off a couple of stops before I do.
I look back at her as the bus pulls off. It is dusk.
Weeks before her death she is tormented by nightmares
that my father is chasing her. She sits up and we talk.
She quotes my father to me.

"We finally left your father for good, when he told me:
'You better leave, before I really hurt you.'"
May 20th she dreams, "I saw a man
in the house carrying food."
That's gotta be death, I thought.
A man in the house
carrying food.

St. Jude lost his head

I glued it on
backwards

We're all just glued
and taped together
while we feed the meter
of our soul's time here

St. Jude looks down at me with compassion
All the saints do
They don't react
just look down with pity

La Madonna del Carmine fell to the floor
smashed her ribs — her whole thoracic cavity
broke open on Mom's linoleum
the diamond pattern blue onion motif
La Madonna in a gold sewn cape

Two kinds of Holy Water
my mother crossed my forehead with
as I left for an EKG and Stress Echo
Medjugorie and *Monte Carmelo*

Squeeze a lemon on the top of my head Ma
Make me complete as bitter greens and fava beans
I'll play all your Saints numbers:

12-12 Sinatra and *Our Lady of Guadalupe*
7-16 *Our Lady of Monte Carmelo*
6-13 *San Antonio*
10-4 *San Francesco*
7-26 *Santa Anna*
12-13 *Santa Lucia*
11-1 *Tutti Santi*

Grandma Rose used to say, "Doesn't the car need oil?"
as she doused *olio d'oliva* on *cicorria e fava*

Thank God the aide's not coming tomorrow

I want a day just me and Mom
to be on our own time schedule
I gotta leave her for an hour and I regret even that
but making music is my tow rope outta here
to the hopeful place full of color and light
and my friend Al listening behind the sound proof glass
the recording studio saves me right now

I want another chance, another day
to talk with Mom, garner her street smarts,
the way she sees right through people
how she's not fooled by anyone
"I don't give a good—you know what—anymore,"
she says to Clara the aide,
after telling the guy upstairs
to stop flicking his cigarettes into the garden.
"We pick them up," she says,
"who do you think cleans up after you?"
He nodded mutely, a quick assent
to the truth-teller tethered to oxygen.

Thank God Clara can come three times a week.
The other health aides were at best, no help at all.
Sometimes we had to take care of them.
One came eight months pregnant.
"Don't strain yourself," Mom told her, "put your feet up."
Another was old and feeble, all out of breath from the bus trip.
We were afraid she might have a heart attack.
"Sit down," Mom told her, "have a cup of tea."
I put on the water to boil.

Lesbian in Quarantine

it's 2:17 in the morning, I am wide awake
in Sloan-Kettering of course, Mom is downstairs.
Now we sign-in together routinely.
Anytime one of us gets sick, so does the other.
The Urgent Care triage nurse joked:
"I get both of you tonight, or just one?" She knows.
Urgent Care was so busy. Stretchers and wheelchairs
backed up all the way into the hallway by the elevator.
The triage nurse told me she had a nightmare
patients were lined up across 67th Street waiting to see her.

I'm back in quarantine. Yellow Gown
Yellow Mask, Peacock Blue Gloves
There are stations the world deplores, to be a lesbian
in quarantine. There are stations the world adores,
not a lesbian in quarantine. Do *you* wanna be
a lesbian in quarantine? It's like AIDS hysteria plus—
behind a thick door, an allergy to poverty.
Bonjour mon coeur, I am poor.
I am a lesbian in quarantine—Droplet Precautions!
Even one drop of me is too much for you.

In Sloan-Kettering there's only a couple of destinations.
In the old days either you get sent home
or you get first class—admitted, given a bed upstairs.
Now there's a new designation:
the Observation Unit, second-class limbo.
There's no comfortable beds
and you can't order all the food,
you can't get the short ribs down here.
The nurses have to order for you from a limited menu.
It's no good. No perks. No massage. No visiting dogs.
I can't believe they keep my mother in "Obs."
I'm suffering over it. She can't get her cup of tea.
I take a walk all suited up in quarantine gear
go down the elevator and around the floors.
I find Mom's room and stand outside the open door.

Of course she is up, uncomfortable, and glad to see me.
I complain to the nurse, I want Mom "admitted"
so she can relax. Even though I'm sick
I'd do anything for her.
Move mountains. Stand hours. Nudge nurses.
Walk though I can barely breathe.

Adults

The hardest thing about being adults
is we forget we are babies.

Mom at eighty-nine needs to be held
to my heartbeat, rocked and swayed into peace.

Getting my body
around her is a challenge.

I'm too big
for all the chairs.

Lately I've been breaking chairs
the struts bend and break beneath me.

We still have the maple rocking chair
she rocked me in as a baby.

I wish I could get in that chair and hold her
over my shoulder as she did for me.

Maybe this is why we shrink as we age
so others can hold and carry us again, or try to.

Mom, I will rock you
though we don't have a rocking chair big enough.

I sit beside you, hug you as you let go into my arms,
rock, hum, sing *"Que Sera Sera"*

as you did a thousand nights

Misnomers

ANOMIA IS A CONDITION where you forget or confuse the names of things, and you can get this from small strokes. Mom had this, but she also had a sharp sense of humor about this pervasive word/noun confusion. She loved "Yogi-isms" and had her own routine of misnaming something that changed the meaning entirely. This, on top of her increasing deafness, made for frustration and more laughs. By the age of eighty-nine, it was time for her to tune the world out, and to tune in angels. In the meantime, we laughed when we could. One day she came in from the porch and said alarmingly: "Pakistani are invading the garden!" It took me a minute to figure out what she meant—pachysandra. FaceBook she called: "YouFace." On her thank you card to Dr. Diane Stover, she wrote the word 'pneuminous.' Instead of correcting her spelling as she'd asked, I thought about it, after all pneumonia, pneumatic—pneuminologist, it made sense. I said: "Ma, I think that is a word, numinous. I think I know what you are saying." Numinous indeed was most appropriate on many levels for our revered Dr. Stover. My mother had hit the nail on the head. *Numinous: indicating the presence of divinity. Suffused with divine awe. From the Latin numen, "divine will" or "nod."* Dr. Stover was sainted in our family and in Sloan-Kettering history as Chief of the Pulmonary Department. She had taken care of me since I was eighteen, and then my Mom who she loved dearly. The Numinous Pulmonologist.

Whenever Mom sat down to write cards, she'd ask me to help her come up with things to say, and to spell word after word. I will always hear her asking me: "What should I write?" "How do you spell—marriage?" I'd inquire: "What do you want to say?" I was her scribe, her word atlas. She'd turn her calendar page and make a list of what cards she needed that month. We'd go to her favorite dollar store where she could linger in the card aisle and choose pretty ones for a buck each. She loved writing cards, underlining words for emphasis, adding X's and O's. She wrote affirmations and nicknames for her grandchildren, like "Beauty Pie."

She'd get mad at herself when she misspelled a word. With Wite-Out, glitter and glue, we had fun with mistakes. The act of writing cards became a craft project. How beautifully can you glitter a heart over a spelling error?

As time got closer to her death she became forthright, writing declarative sentences; affirmations with an urgency. "Take care of yourself

#1, you hear me!?" I loved this strong patina, a woman telling it like it is, seeing the folly of our youthful ways, how we waste time and money and squander precious life itself. She saw through all of us, to our hearts and souls. When we messed up, when we took her for granted with our sharp tongues, she saw good hearts—when days of life, we wasted.

Mezzomorte

if no one is talking to one another
there's nothing to live for

I yell to rouse Mom out of her La-Z-Boy chair
her head slumps over
the right arm of her chair
where's she's been twenty hours
I make noise in the kitchen—bang life into the atmosphere.
I yell for her to help me stuff the peppers.
She says weakly, "We will make stuffed peppers together?"
She pushes herself up out of the chair's plush blue arms.

I got Pasolini's *l'angoscia* being the daughter
spiritual resuscitation is my order
I turn into a spiritual marauder
with a single word at her state of languish
when all I wanted was her ardor.

Cook, clean, slave, heal
then knock it all down with a few staccato syllables.
On the chair all day
letting the TV scale hours away
Confused. Tired. Whimpering. Panicked. Ready to not live anymore.
Always apologizing. Languishing.
Depressed over the hardships of her children, "I feel so bad."

In the kitchen she struggles
to push knife through onion.
I slam pots and pans, the oven door.
She pleads, "Annie pleeeeease."

I leave the room.
Swig ice cold vodka
bite into a tomato whole—
tear it apart with
teeth

Reverse Pietà

We're the Pietà over here
only it's daughter holding
a skin and bones mother
head all the way back
I hold
my mother
skin bones breath
Still she breathes

I wonder about the individuality of breath
as it miraculously moves her body
in waves
her chest fills and ebbs
what moment
the breath will wander off
go some other way

She says, "I am destroying my daughter's life."
"You gave me life," I say,
"you've already done all this for me.
It is my greatest privilege to help you.
This is where I want to be.
I wouldn't want to be anywhere else."
She repeats to friends and neighbors,
"I am destroying my daughter's life."

I wonder if Jesus ever said that to Mary.

Separation Anxiety

MOM AND I AREN'T getting along. Our old separation anxiety routine. We fought before I went away to college, we fought when I thought I might die to my first cancer, and now we fight as she prepares to die. My mother says the words I loathe: "I am concerned about you." The word 'concerned' feels like a sledgehammer—she thinks I am going in the wrong direction, and it bothers me more because the phrasing is filled with politeness. I'd rather she'd just say Bronx style: "What the hell's wrong wit' you!"

I call my shrink and beg her to put me back on Lexapro—which takes me from capsize to a level horizon line. It is swimming with a life jacket on; you can't really swim, but you know you won't drown.

Every day is an administrative nightmare. The list is long. Call Medicare and Medicaid and the "Medicare approved Part D Prescription Drug Plan sponsor" to see if Mom's blood thinner pill can be approved for the insurance designation "Long Term" so Mom doesn't have to switch meds and get daily belly injections. In the end, this is a dead-end; we are mandated to switch from pills to needles, giving me yet another task—to inject Mom's belly every morning—the belly I came from. More needles, more pinches, more panic for Mom everyday until the day she dies. Call Medicaid to see how to get "Long Term" coverage" without the monthly spend-down. The anxiety of not knowing if Mom is covered month to month is killing us both. You find out retroactively if you were approved for coverage for the month. You never know for sure. Call the Department of Social Services at three different phone numbers to leave messages to find out who Mom's caseworker now is, and did they receive her spend-down receipts for this month? Will her E.R. visit be covered? One number is out of service. No one answers the other numbers. I leave messages. Days later we get a call back. We ask: "Where are her pharmacy receipts?"

"Even if they are in the building," we are told, "it may be days/weeks before they make it to this office."

Call the oxygen company and argue to get clean long tubing so Mom is not tethered to one room and can reach the toilet without disconnecting her oxygen. Argue to get the plastic bottle that humidifies the oxygen because the continual blowing of air is giving Mom nosebleeds that now on blood thinners, don't stop. How many times can we go to the E.R. for non-stop bloody noses? Ask for the supervisor. Ask for the supervisor's supervisor. Get hung up on. Call back. Go through the answering service all over again. Ask for Ronald since I remembered his name. Finally Ronald tells me the industry term for the bottle: "humidifier reservoir," now that he has the correct term, he places the order. Argue with Ronald about why Mom needs a portable concentrator. Ronald says: "The home concentrator and the tanks are fine. If you want, we can send you small tanks and your mother can put two of them in her backpack." Her *backpack*?! This is a hard candy moment where I either scream or swallow my rage. Usually I do both, and later suck on one hard candy. I need the candies that last a long time. The Italian hard candy.

After I scream at Ronald, my mother says: "Give me the phone."

I remember her motto: *Never argue with a jackass!* She calmly asks Ronald: "Ronald, I have to ask you something. No, no, let me ask you. Do you think, that at ninety years old with heart failure—and I can barely walk on my own, do you think I can possibly wear a backpack carrying two oxygen tanks? No, answer me."

I am amazed at my mother's composure. She is the best consumer advocate and survival warrior I've ever known. It is phenomenal seeing her in action. Ronald informs my mother that the oxygen company from now on, summarily refuses to talk with "your daughter" and that my mother herself must make the weekly call to order the week's oxygen tanks.

There is an Omnipresent Caveat, *Acies Caueant Omnipraesens,* to all of these healthcare nightmares, and that is money. A portable oxygen concentrator, only as big as a pocketbook, costs three thousand dollars and can be bought on the internet. That would have saved two years of our suffering and problems.

I call the doctors' secretaries back and forth to coordinate their schedules so we don't have to make constant trips into the city which is unendurable for Mom. We need to stack appointments. Because of the computer system, the secretaries, now called "session assistants," cannot change your appointment until they cancel the one you have, so you risk losing your slot in the time it takes to look up the other doctors' availabilities. There are dozens of session assistants and one may book the slot you have if you release it. It takes months to get a slot. I have to make all the calls back and forth. Is Doctor A's clinic days on Tuesdays and Thursdays, is there any way he can see her on a Friday when we have to be there for Doctor B whose clinic is only Friday, and Doctor C who only does Wednesday/Friday? It's a second grade math problem with no equation, no solution, no—solve for X. Before computers my doctors had brilliant secretaries who could keep it all in their brain. They understood the needs of the patients and had the capacity to switch schedules around according to what was best for everybody. There are one or two left; when I get them on the phone I know I've hit the jackpot.

"Circumlocution," Charles Dickens called this loopy process of navigating bureaucracy. In this case, it is the patient/consumer who is blindfolded, spun around three times and directed into an endless closed-circuit loop of phone connections, message machines, middlemen. Office workers stare into screens, talk into receivers, follow troubleshooting flowcharts. The world is on call waiting. Nobody knows anything. Insurance rules and formularies keep changing, so as soon as anyone knows anything, the rules change.

Once I got pneumonia because I couldn't get a clean filter for my CPAP machine. The lady on the phone said: "You're not due for a clean filter at this time."

"But it's black with dirt," I told her, "I need a clean filter."

"You're not due for a clean filter at this time."

"Then I can't use the machine."

"If you don't use the machine and fill your hours quota, then you will be deemed 'non-compliant' and you will have to pay in full for the machine. The internal chip records hours of usage. Medicaid does not pay for non-compliant patients."

"But, I need a clean filter!"

"You are not due for a clean filter at this time."

"I want to talk with your supervisor."

"There is no one available at this time, but they will tell you the same exact thing."

Brains are as off as computers are on. Humans walk around carrying six hundred dollar brains in the palms of their hands. Brains off, computers on. Neck realignment is the business of the future. This one circular dead-end conversation almost killed me. I couldn't afford to pay for the whole machine, twenty-seven hundred dollars. I couldn't afford to be "non-compliant."

Omnipresent Caveat, *Acies Caueant Omnipraesens*

So I used the machine with a dirty filter. Gunk, dust, bacteria—was blown deep into my lungs by the forced-air CPAP machine—which is like sleeping with your nose and mouth attached to a leaf-blower. Double lower-lobe pneumonia landed me in the hospital where I contracted a MRSA colony in my lungs: Methicillin-resistant Staphylococcus aureus; a 'super bacterium.' I was put in quarantine for weeks. All for a two inch filter that cost a buck-fifty tops, postage included.

This is how the poor die.

After several weeks in quarantine, the "General Medical Team" wanted to release me from the hospital on home nebulizer treatment. The resident in charge offered me a series of paper prescriptions.

"I ain't leaving with paper," I told her, "get the prescriptions filled downstairs."

"Then you'll have to wait hours."

"Fine."

The doctor encouraged me to leave without the medication: "This way, you can leave sooner. You can fill them on the outside."

"Says who?!" I knew that a month's supply of Xopenex and Ipratropium bromide, at the time—cost three thousand dollars, and that I would not be covered by Medicare or Medicaid at any outside pharmacy. Xopenex was approved by the FDA in 2002, and Ipratropium bromide in 2004. At the time of my hospital release in 2012, the out-of-pocket cost of Xopenex was at its zenith; Xopenex was priced at up to twenty-five times more than the previous generation drug which caused tachycardia. Just five years later when a generic form of Xopenex came out, my bill would plummet to fourteen cents. I ordered hospital lunch and kept my feet up.

I called my friend David Freeman and asked him to come over with his drum. This would take all day. I staged a sit-in; refusing to leave without medication in-hand. I needed it to breathe. How could I go home without it? David showed up with his dunbek and played through the ensuing farcical six hours. I instigated a series of conversations between Patient Advocate, the General Medical Team, the social worker, the discharge coordinator, the charge nurse, and the rabbi who was the chaplain on call that day. All this while wheezing and hoarse. I sucked on lemon drops. Several of them at a time were in my quarantined room in yellow masks and gowns, blue gloves, trying to figure out how to calm me down and get me to agree to leave the hospital without the medication in hand. In the meantime, I got another nebulizer treatment with the super effective Xopenex / Ipratropium bromide cocktail. After the necessary series of phone calls they made to my neighborhood pharmacy, Medicare, Medicaid, and the private insurance company that Medicare used for Part B, one of team figured out:

"Ahh, you can't get these medications covered from an outside pharmacy because they are "life-sustaining" medications. You will only be covered if you are in a nursing home or a hospital."

As a one-liner this might, for a beat, be funny: "These medications are not covered because they are life-sustaining." Phrased plainly: "Life-sustaining medications are not covered." Period. A dizzying overlay of talk ensued about Medicare Part B and Part D and the insurance designation between if you administer a medication *to* yourself, or if a nurse administers it *to* you.

"Remember the Alamo," was all I could think of saying. Three hours into the siege, the young doctor actually said: "As a compromise, we will give you one box."

"Compromise? What compromise?" With asthma exacerbation / double pneumonia / pulmonary super-bacteria colony, I could be dead in three minutes. What was there to compromise? This felt Faustian; the devil was in the room, a devil named Transaction. It would be impossible for me to get this medication on the outside. Unless I was rich, of course.

Acies Caueant Omnipraesens.

Still, I considered the deal. "How many doses is a box?"

"I don't know," the young doctor said, and looked at her beeper. She had long brown hair, she was tall with big brown eyes. She looked like a horse. I didn't want to give her a hard time.

"All love here," I said, and wove the air with my hands between her heart, the medical student's heart, and mine, "but I refuse to leave without the meds." I looked around at each of them. "Remember the Alamo." David kept drumming.

The Patient Advocate turned out to be lawyer-like, my guess is he was a lawyer in place to protect the hospital—very unlike the beautiful Patient Advocates I remember from the '80's who actually rallied on the side of the patient when you needed an intermediary. No, this Patient Advocate five hours later, brought up a paper for me to sign, stating I understood that I would be billed by the hospital and responsible for the bill of three thousand dollars for this medication. If I signed, then I could go home—breathing medication in hand. I sucked on a lemon drop, signed, stayed alive. It's no coincidence that one of Mom's anthems was the Bee Gee's "Stayin' Alive." When we blasted it in the car, she knew all the lyrics and rocked out on the choruses.

Holy Cards

9 days left

After funerals I open
my mother's replica antique wooden box phone
and add the next Holy Card to the deck she keeps there.
Here are the ancestors, a card for each one
like their rookie baseball card, now rookie angel card.
The cards have pictures of saints and angels
and on the back, prayers. The only individual details
are the person's name and birthdate dash deathdate.
It's wild seeing who died within weeks of one another
strange groupings that never would have happened
while they lived.

Very few of my friends are represented in this deck.
My dead friends didn't have lavish funerals
with Holy Card expenses, coffins, plots, the whole nine yards.
"Put me out with the trash," Tony told me.
I make them by hand now, a Holy Card for each soul
missing in this deck. I don't wonder anymore
why my mother keeps these cards and all together
in her old antique telephone, this wooden box
hanging on the paneled living room wall
with a black pear-shape beaker
on a cord to hold up to your ear
and one to talk into, and two round brass bells
set into the wooden face of the telephone like big owl eyes.
Two round brass bells that never ring.
Her "telephone to the dead" I call it.
I flip through the deck, read the names,
examine the dates, look at the saints,
see who has the best pictures with gold trim,
wonder who's next.

My mother and I sit on the porch through sun downs.
We wait for death to swoop
down on us like a bird of prey

an owl with silent vast wings.
The telephone's brass hook and catch are bent.
At night as we relax on the couch
the door of the phone
swings open

Salt

When she has ten days left
to live I am home, her breath
I watch all morning.
I know she is low in sodium.
I put a few coarse crystals on her tongue
so she perks up, lifts her head again.

When she has five days left
she is in the hospital and I am home for a moment
to get my own medicine and a change of clothes.
There is a big crash. Something fell off
the top of the refrigerator and crashed onto the floor.
It was the salt. A big tall canister of sea salt
broke open into a heart. Coarse salt
a white heart shaped mound on Mom's kitchen floor.
A salt heart
exactly what she's dying of
$NaCl + H_2O = NaO + ClH$
a lack of salt in the bloodstream
as her cavities fill with fluid
pericardium, abdomen, ankles
her heart can no longer pump.

For decades we heard her say
as she hoisted plates of steaming food onto the table,
after everyone else was seated and she took a seat
nearest the kitchen so she could jump back up,
"There's no salt on anything. I don't have to tell you,
I don't cook with salt." And we all laughed
because we'd heard this at every meal forever.
Salt. Salt. Salt. That's all I can think about. Salt.
Mom needs salt.
When she has four days
left to live the nurse brings a shot of Lovenox,
an I.V. bag of Azithromycin, a horse pill of Potassium,
and a giant salt tablet that is very hard to swallow.
Mom insists, to the nurse:
"One thing at a time! Come back in ten minutes.
What's this a gas station? Do I look like a car?"

July is not the time to die

when medical residents just start their rotation
barely have their socks on, practice their stares

yours will be the first death certificate she signs
your last official paper will be her first

we got lucky, assigned a young forthright butch
who makes eye contact and touches Mom's arm

The day before Mom dies, she looks up and asks her:
"Am I going to get better?"

The resident continues the eye and arm contact
pauses, and says, "We'll wait and see."

Later in the day, the Chief says, "You need rest, Rachel,
you need rest." And Mom agrees, surrenders to this mission.

We were on the precipice of the decision
to up the regularity of the fentanyl and Ativan

which would keep Mom in a sleep forever
and yet stop her terrified episodes of "air hunger"

a term we cannot bear
it's an impossible decision

in her wakeful moments Mom is full of love
and witty interaction. But more and more terror

whimpering, and it is not bearable to let the day staff go.
With night, you wait and wait and can't get what you need.

The alternatives are not alternatives at all
Mom was clear months ago,

"No intubation. No chest paddles. No rib compressions
—ever"

So this
is it then.

the day before she dies

Word comes
from our cousins
Archangel "Aunt Angie" has died.
My godmother, my father's sister.
Mom still had twelve hours of breaths left,
each breath the beating of wings.

These two blue-eyed blonde Bronx beauties
Angie and Ray had shared a house
on Saint Raymond's Avenue for years,
raised their children in tandem, upstairs/downstairs.
Young and strong, babies in their arms, on their tall stoop,
who could have guessed they would share
death within hours?

In Catholicism you have a godmother in case
anything ever happens to your mother.
I will lose my mother and godmother within hours.
It is the week of the feast of Our Lady of Mount Carmel,
my mother's patron saint. This comforts me.
Our Lady will throw open the doors to receive
Archangel and Rachele
I keep my mother's scapular on her neck
rosary beads in our hands
I whisper to her, "Look for Aunt Angie."

All of my cousins are grieving.
We will share our loss together.
Later a cousin will tell me,
I can hear Aunt Angie saying,
"C'mon Ray! Let's go!"

I can see them smiling as they climb
the biggest stoop of their lives.

Kicking into the Next World

1 day out

Mom is unconscious
as she kicks in the bed
kicking kicking like a fetus
kicking to break through
kicking kicking
her whole legs kicking
hip and knees pumping
my mother is kicking kicking
to get through to the next world
even as the fentanyl slides her mind away
on a magic carpet
her feet pump, ankles working
she
steps

With hours left
I ring tuning forks around her
and whisper a final chant in prayer:

May all her suffering cease
May her mind be at peace

May all her suffering cease
May her mind be at peace

May all her suffering cease
May her mind be at peace

May all her suffering cease
May her mind be at peace

May all her suffering cease
May her mind be at peace

May all her suffering cease
May her mind be at peace

May all their suffering cease
May their minds be at peace

dignified bliss on fentanyl and Ativan

peace
world peace
breathing peace
soon

rapid heart
I hold Mom through it all.
Every breath, every pulse, every heart beat, I hold.
The nurse comes in with just hours to go
presses two fingers on Mom' pulse,
"Yes it's getting weaker," he says
like he is rooting her spirit on

Mom's pulse came into me

As she is leaving her body

I feel like something is being pulled out of me
my daughter now
I feel like I am having an abortion
My gut is a tense rope
I bleed I flood
through my underwear, through my pants
a gush of blood
this is the last time
I will bleed this way
in my life

Breath

Breath come inside me
Come inside Come inside Come inside

Breath come inside me
Come inside Come inside Come inside

Breath come inside me
Come inside Come inside Come inside

Breath come inside me
Come inside Come inside Come inside

Breath go outside me
Go outside Go outside Go outside

Breath go outside me
Go outside Go outside Go outside

Breath go outside me
Go outside Go outside Go outside

Breath go outside me
Go outside Go outside Go outside

Inside Outside
Inside Outside

Inside Outside
Inside Outside

In Out
In Out
Out

Staccato

as a dunbek

her heartbeat

came inside me at noon

her breath

came inside me at noon

no inhale
no exhale

no Tt tt t Tt tt t Tt tt t Tt tt t

I leave the oxygen mask on her anyway
oxygen never hurts
may help the cells even without a beating heart
let the cells bathe in oxygen

The head nurse comes in
places her stethoscope
on different places on Mom's chest
listens, nods
takes off the oxygen mask
turns off the loud omnipresent blow
with a flick of the tiny black toggle
up on the wall

silence is completely deafening
the room without forced oxygen hose
dense silence within Mom's chest

a gray green pallor sets in her face
as blood recedes

I always believed in the power of an hour
as the prayer says "at the hour of our death, Amen"
but death it turns out
is instant

PART II:
Mourning

*"Once you lose your mother, you'll never
get a straight answer again."*
—Amelia King
in a private conversation to me, 1993

The women circle around

in the hours after you die
in an ancient ritual
we wash we dress you
in purple cotton
how heavy your head is
it takes two of us now
to cradle your head
and a third to pour water
to wash your hair
what in life was light
in death is heavy stone
with two arms I lift your head

we blush your cheeks
the gray green pallor that came
over your face in an instant
is covered with rouge
your beauty—magnified
I pull apart roses
as cells release oxygen, carbon dioxide, nitrogen, hydrogen,
your arm skin bubbles
I cover you in pink petals
I fold your hands, secure your Mt. Carmel
scapular around your neck
rosary beads around your hands
the manicure I gave you last week
and pedicure, is perfect
You'd be happy, you're going out like a lady, a queen

You follow Jesus' death schedule:
First the I.V. "feels like a nail in my wrist"
just like Jesus just like Jesus nailed in the hands
I couldn't take away your suffering, just alleviate fear.
I kept bothering the nurses to get one to come with
the solution so the tape wouldn't pull off your skin.
Your skin was so thin and fragile and see-through.
Skin is the most important thing in the world.

What protects us from the world. Our only boundary.
Thursday night garden of Gethsemane, all of us there,
around your room, asleep apostles.
I didn't sleep I stood, talked to you all night,
held you in my arms, whispered, sang
as Gina instructed me to:
     "Keep talking to her. If it was me,
      I would want to hear my children's voices."
In the middle of the night I sat down in a chair at your bedside
Audrey stood over me and passed out with cataplexy
slumped straight down on top of me.
I called Simba and Nicole and Emily to grab her
and help her down so she wouldn't hit her head.
Now I had you down on my left and Audrey down on my right.
The nurses climbed over us all, to enter or exit the room.
Then Friday noon — your last breath
Then three p.m. — we wash and dress you
just like Jesus just like Jesus

You died in peace, without a blemish
you weren't alone for a moment
I made good on my promise:
"Not one more needle. Never a nursing home."

After you go, I cannot be touched, I cannot hold anyone's hand
I still feel your pulse beating. I feel the wheeze in my chest.
Dr. Stover comes in. "Doc, I need a Z-pak. I have a bad wheeze.
I probably need this room," I add half-joking.
The words, "It was her time"
I begin to hear inside me.
You had to go.

I tell Simba, "She wanted to go out a blonde.
That's my one regret. Mom wanted to get her hair dyed,
and we never got to it." Simba says she can comb the blonde in.
She runs out, gets blonde in a bottle, and combs it gently.
Magic. You are blonde and as gorgeous as ever
and I know you are happy.
The women hold hands all around you
sing the *Ave Maria, Luck Be a Lady, Que Sera Sera*.

I go sit in the hallway as the charge nurse
comes in to take you. I do not want to see the body bag.
I leave you with the circle of women.
I leave before I hear the sound of the zipper
I cannot bear to hear

Jesus' Lips

Day 1—I am numb as if I just got off roller skates
my whole self vibrates.
I get in the car and drive downtown.
Audrey and Simba haven't left my side.

At the basilica of Our Lady of Mt. Carmel in Brooklyn
I walk in a daze around the room of saints.
I stare at Jesus, limp in Mary's arms.
His head too, bowed to the right,
just like Mom's. I reach in my breast pocket.
There is the "A + D" ointment packet, open
that I was using on Mom's lips and cheeks
so the oxygen blowing wouldn't chap her lips and skin.
For days I've been applying ointment
with my finger as I do now
to Jesus' lips

Day 2—I cannot be touched
I cannot hold another's hand.
I need to keep the vibration of your pulse
your weakening pulse
your weakening slow breathing
You pulled through so many times before, so many crises
why not this one? It's dizzying. Confusing.
Sodium. Saline drip. Diuresis. Salt tabs.
Belly filling up with fluid. Death rattle.
Your head slumping over to the right.
Dry mouth. Loud oxygen.
In and out of cognizance the panic the whimpering
the fear and trembling, cold body hot blood
leaks out your arm so red so watery
the blood thinners the music the sparkling eyes

now I sit in your chair alone in the abyss
without your hand to hold
this is freedom this loneliness
like skidding on black ice, I brace for the hit,

I know it's coming watching you go downhill
kicking in bed on the last day
the nurse rooting you on as his fingers clasp your wrist

When death becomes the goal
everything shifts

2:16 a.m.

First trimester of grief, Day 4

in my dream
I apologize for not being able to save you from your pain
"What are you kiddin?" you say,
"You did everything for me. Even my blood you kept warm."

in my dream
you kiss and kiss my cheek, forehead,
a mother's healing kisses, comforting,
"Don't cry Dolly, you did everything for me
you kept the blood warm in my veins."

When you were cold, I circled everyone around you
to press palms to your hands and feet,
to conduct our body heat into yours.
I had my hand on your heart and over your head.
You got warm and stayed warm
your whole last night and morning
'til long after you were gone
For hours your body stayed warm
even as we washed and dressed you the last time
you still had warmth.

You died perfect
In peace
Without a blemish
Not one mark
with your lavender manicure and pedicure
the way St. Theresa is described
in death the scent of roses

in my dream
I hear you loud and clear,
"Stop doing things for me! Do for yourself!"

in my dream,
weeks later, I hear you,
"Don't do anything else for me!"

Her Blue

First trimester of grief, Day 7

Her blue shines through it all
Her blue shines through it all
Her blue shines through the whole life through
Her blue shines through it all

She came to us October 20th 1926 and departed July 13th 2016
That night I looked to the sky for her sunset
You know when I talked to my mother
about how she survived everything
how she kept sparkling—I mean her sparkler
her blue eyes were her superpower!
So when I asked her how she got through it all
and still kept sparkling her spirit
you know what she told me? You're not gonna believe this.
      "Colors!"
Colors! And that's how I knew:

Her blue shines through it all
Her blue shines through it all
O her blue shines through the whole life through
Yeah her blue shines through it all

She blew my mind
For her work she surrounded herself with colors
every shade of pink of lipsticks and nail polishes
blondes of hair dyes, in her knitting, blues and purples,
roses and creams. She wore purple from head to toe,
even her gloves—her purple
She'd never wear black
Her sneakers she polished white once a week on Fridays
She had this bottle of "Hollywood Sani-White"
underneath the kitchen sink

So on July 13th 2016 when I looked to sky for the sunset
I expected colors, long smooth brushstrokes of pinks,
her pinks, her brushstroke perfect manicures.
I expected the sky to be brushed like her manicure.
But instead it was overcast. The sky was gray
a gray sheet of paper, a gray expanse
I was stunned and confused
I looked to the overcast sky and yelled, "Ma where are ya!?"
I drove left onto the Williamsburg Bridge
looked up at the overcast sky
and over the bridge up
there in the overcast sky,
were two cut outs of eyes, her eyes
with the brightest blue light shining through,
pouring through—and a cloud shaped into a smile.
My mother's eyes were in the sky!
I looked up at her bright jewel eyes smiling down on me,
down on all of us, down on me,
as she did ever since I was her baby,
smiling down, singing, rocking me to sleep,
comforting. Her face in the sky
was as big as when I was a baby,
and I felt the magic sparkle from her eyes
that I have all my life looking up at her.
And I knew:

Her blue shines through it all
Her blue shines through it all
Her blue shines through the whole life through
Her blue shines through it all

Audrey and Simba were in the car and saw what I saw.
We were headed to my mother's patron saint
La Madonna di Monte Carmelo.
To the Basilica in Brooklyn to meet Nicole and Emily
to pray for her, at the "Feast of Mt. Carmel."
All night long, pairs of bright blue eyes shown through the gray sky
Her message was clear: "My blue shines through it all!"
That is how you get through all the travails of life.
You keep on shining.

This is her story:
Two sisters married two brothers.
They each had two daughters.
Lucy & Rachel, and Lucy & Rachel.
Italian tradition dictated you had to name your children
for their grandparents. So all these four girls were named
after their grandmothers Lucia Armienti and Rachele LeRario,
my great grandmothers.
Lucy & Rachel, and Lucy & Rachel were raised as sisters
in a six-room second-story walk-up on Teller Avenue in the Bronx.
My mother was the baby. She was obsessed by airplanes.
Whenever she heard an airplane overhead
as it approached La Guardia
she ran to the windows to watch it.
One day, July 16, 1928, she leaned too far.
She was two years old, she'd climbed up on the window ledge
to watch a plane. She fell in a seated posture
two stories, and a third story down
into the concrete sub-basement alleyway.
The neighbors all said somebody threw a doll out the window
but it was the feast day of Our Lady of Mount Carmel,
La Madonna di Monte Carmelo
and my mother survived. She'd need all kinds of surgeries
and she'd wear leg braces and be a cripple through her youth
but she survived. She would learn to walk again
and to dance. Because:

Her blue shined through it all,
Her blue shined through it all
O her blue shined through the whole life through,
Yeah her blue shined through it all!

She had a beautiful sweet father named Giuseppe.
He took her to Orchard Beach in the Bronx, as therapy.
He held her hand and buried her legs in the sand
took her into the ocean and held her up high
so the waves could beat against the backs of her knees.

The day she was able to walk out of the hospital for the last time
her father held her hand. This is what she always remembered.

She felt so bad leaving all the other crippled kids in the hospital,
all her friends. This stayed with her the rest of her life,
as did the genteelness of her father, Giuseppe with his gentle hand.
She credited her parents, immigrants off the boat
for being progressive enough to agree to the surgeries
which were radical at the time because what they did
was an experiment. They operated on her "good leg"
to slow its growth so that her legs would be even.
She was always thankful to Our Lady of Mount Carmel.
Throughout her life, she gave away as many scapulars as she could.

For years, 'til she was a teenager
the doctors showed off her legs.
She'd have to walk into rooms and strip down
in front of many many male doctors
who tried to convince other families
to agree to the series of surgeries on their crippled children.
She did this for many years.

In school, the two Lucys and the two Rachels
caused a lot of confusion.
"You never knew who the teacher was calling."
So their friends gave them nick names that stuck their whole lives.
My mother Rachele or Rachel was now called Lilly.
Her sister Lucia or Lucy was now called Patty.
So now you had a Lucy and a Lilly and a Patty and a Rachel.
No, you had a Patty and a Lilly and a Lucy and a Rachel.
All four of them made it into good old age.

Her blue shines through it all
Her blue shines through it all
Her blue shines through the whole life through
Yeah her blue shines through it all

Born Rachele, called Rachel, then Lilly
She loved music and became a great dancer
She played the radio all her life
As long as her foot was tapping, I knew all was well.

Like a miracle in 1926, the year she was born
so was the Paramount Theater at 43rd and Broadway

as if it was built just for her.
She was born one month before its opening!
As a teenager she hung out there all the time:
    "We'd spend the whole day there,
    bring a sandwich, hear the live music, the big bands,
    and they'd always have a movie.
    We'd take the train there and back, and think nothing of it.
    I heard them all and had all their autographs:
    Sinatra, Billy Eckstein, The Modernaires, Benny Goodman,
    Tommy Dorsey, everybody you could imagine.
    Sinatra was my favorite. He had charisma, pizzazz.
    I remember the first time I heard his voice.
    I was sitting on my bed, with the window open.
    Someone on the block was blasting a radio.
    The song filled the block and came into my room,
    "That Old Black Magic." That voice, I thought, that voice!"
    Ah, times were so different.
    All the time we walked over to the club house
    at Yankee Stadium where the players talked to the kids
    on their way out of the park.
    I had all their autographs too, DiMaggio, all of them."

Her blue shines through it all
Her blue shines through it all
Her blue shines through the whole life through
Yeah her blue shines through it all

She became a hairdresser.
The "in" hairstyles of her day were the "Permanent Wave"
and "Two Swirl Curls & a Pompadour."
She loved that one. She'd give everyone that style.
She'd say, "This is perfect for your head. This will frame your face."
Throughout my teenage years with her
she gave Permanent Waves to her sister Patty
and her Mother Rose, and to her neighbors, especially the elderly.
She'd go into their homes.
She'd cut the hair of her cousin Lucy.
She had a mission of beauty.
She taught me how to section a head:
    "You wash the hair and dry it
    then you block the head with small pieces of felt.

The felt has a slit in it, perfect for the size of a roller.
You clamp it and block the hair.
You section the head, like bricks. Curl by curl.
This is one section of the head.
This is another section. This is another section.
The rollers all fit. A normal size head is four sections on top
and a couple going down on the sides.
If the head's bigger, you have more sections.
If the hair needs a trim, you cut it while it's blocked.
If you see the wave's going a certain way,
you cut into the wave.
You have to look at the head to see the way
the hair naturally goes.
Then you moisten the head with Permanent Wave lotion.
You take a piece of cotton, and it has to be saturated,
each piece of hair."
Permanent Waves smelled like ammonia.
All the plugs, clamps, curlers, end papers, rods,
her gentle finger spinning technique
so you didn't stretch the curl when you pulled out the roller.
But the smell of the ammonia, I couldn't take it
so I had to run outta the house.

Her blue shines through it all
Her blue shines through it all
Her blue shines through the whole life through
Yeah her blue shines through it all

Once she described burning a woman's hair:
"I was still in school.
I worked for nothing at the time.
I made my own apprenticeship.
The shop was called Lou Bud's.
It was on Ahun-fiftieth Street off Third Avenue
above a bank. I walked into the shop
and said, 'I want to work.'
I told him I'd work for nothing. I wanted experience.
He gave me a chance. He saw I was neat, clean and efficient.
I knew what I was doing, I just needed experience.
I did a Permanent Wave, and I started kibbitzing with the girls,
we used to have a lot of fun. I forgot to shut the machine off.

The customer said, 'Miss, it's getting hotter and hotter!'
I said, 'That can't be because it's off.'
I went running to the back
I saw smoke coming up from her head
I yelled to my boss across the shop, 'Mr. Bud! Mr. Bud!'
I motioned to him to help me.
We pulled everything off, one, two, three
and put the cool dryer on.
We took the curlers off, *boop,* the hair came right off,
boop, the hair came off.
But it was all in here at the base of the neck.
I was very fortunate.
She had exceptionally thick hair
what we used to call like a horse's hair.
She never knew. She was very happy.
I learned that lesson good.
Next time I paid attention. It never happened again."

She's got a couple of stories that she loved to tell
that are emblematic of her life:
"One day I was wearing a brand new coat.
I earned the money working and saved my nickel tips
and treated myself to this new coat.
It was black wool with a velvet collar,
very stylish at the time. Before I left the house,
my father pinned on my lapel, a little gold angel.
One afternoon I was on a break from work,
I go into Bonwit Teller. It was a very good store.
I put my coat on a hook and was just trying on new clothes.
When I went to leave, I put on my coat
but it wasn't my coat! It was this ratty old coat!
Somebody had switched the coats and stolen my brand new coat!
So I went to the store security guy
and told the story but he didn't really believe me.
He thought I was trying to get a new coat from an old coat.
They asked if there were any identifying marks on the coat.
Then I remembered the little gold angel
my father had pinned on the lapel.
I told the guy—my father, this morning,
pinned a little gold angel on my lapel!
They spread the word to the security guards

throughout the store. There was a glint of something shiny
that hit one security guard in the eye
off the lapel of a coat on a woman leaving the store.
The angel on my coat!
And that's how I got my coat back."

Her blue shines through it all
Her blue shines through it all
Her blue shines through the whole life through
Yeah her blue shines through it all

Thank you Mom for teaching me to love the world
how to be kind, how to sparkle
to cook, to knit, cast-on, cast-off
to sew a button and a hem
to give haircuts, to block a head
to push back cuticles and polish a fingernail
in three strokes from the center out
to fold a fitted sheet, to polish silver
to wash the glass of windows and hurricane lamps
to get the belly of the white enamel pot to gleam
to cut coupons, to float on water
to never argue with a jackass
to roll *braciole*, meatballs, breadballs
to raise a *focacc'*, to cut a *focacc'*, to flip a *frittata*
to rinse out the day's clothes and hang them over the tub
how to sparkle how to sparkle how to sparkle
how to forgive, to forget
to be a consumer advocate
to survive, to shine through it all

Thank you for being astute, street-smart, wise
for seeing through to the heart of issues
for never being distracted by B.S.
I will continue your nightly prayers for world peace.
I will miss your commentary on the news, politics,
Yankee games and UCONN women's basketball games.
I will miss your blasting the radio in the house
as you cooked gravy on Sundays.
I will remember how when we went to Italy
all through the north you didn't speak

not in *Roma*, or *Firenze*, or *Venezia*
but when we got south, to *Bari*, to *Acquaviva delle Fonti*
and *Cassano delle Murge*
when you met your first cousins
Isabella, and *Rosa*, and *"i tre Michele"*
how you burst into the language of your mother's youth
expressions of slang from a hundred years ago,
and I'll remember how we all laughed and laughed
no one had heard those expressions for a generation!

I'll remember how you outsmarted everyone.
Once there was a leak in the bathroom ceiling,
water came down from upstairs through the bathroom light fixture,
The local handyman came to look, and tried to put her off, saying:
      "Next time there's water leaking, call me back."
      "Oh what a good idea," she said, and as he left,
she sprayed water on that line on the wall. She called him back.
"You're so right!" she said, "it's dripping again. You're brilliant!
Come you'll see!" And he came back and fixed the leak.

In her youth she was a heartbreaker.
      "Boys I didn't even know were sad around me.
      I hurt their feelings if I didn't say Hello.
      I didn't even know them!
      One boy, the landlord's son Louis
      wouldn't leave me alone.
      He begged me to go to the movies with him.
      He pestered me. I couldn't stand him.
      He practiced the violin. He was terrible.
      I can still hear it. *eeeee-errrr eeee-errrrr*
      So one day I told him, 'Louis, tell you what.
      Give the money to Benny
      and I'll go to the movies with him.'
      Benny was a kid up the block I liked better.
      And so that's what Louis did.
      Louis was so happy to do so!
      and he stopped pestering me."

In her seventies and eighties,
she drove around with her friend and neighbor Al Paoletta.
A bunch of seniors would walk into McDonald's

with used paper cups
and drink the coffee with refills for free.
Al drove. Al's car had no reverse.
Mom would open her blinds as a signal to Al and Rosalee
and they'd bring in food and all share their dinner.
They went to Nathan's for hot dogs on coupons.
Al shouted out the car window,
"'Scuse me Miss, do you mind if you leave that parking spot?
I need a spot I can drive into and out of
without going in reverse!"

Another story she loved to tell:
    "Al's friend Larry said, 'Let's go to Macy's
    to get new watchbands. I got a friend there
    who'll give us a deal.'
    So we went to Macy's.
    Larry had dementia. So when we got there, he said,
    'What are we doing here?'
    So I told him, Don't you remember Larry?
    You're buying me a diamond ring. You proposed!"

Things she told me:
"One day you'll find your niche"
"Broaden your circle of friends"
"If you don't try, you'll never know."

Her blue shines through it all
Her blue shines through it all
Her blue shines through the whole life through
Yeah her blue shines through it all

In her last voice message to me, she says:
"I'm dozing off. I just want you to know I'm going to sleep."

She always sang me to sleep with *"Que Sera Sera"*
and now I will hear that song in her voice for all time.

Some of her last words to me were
"Let's go home and make meatballs."
I will Mom, I will.

Saint Ann has a light blue cloak

First trimester of grief, Day 13

Covered in gold jewelry, prayers from supplicants, gifts
of devotion: watches, rings, bracelets, pendants, charms, chains.
White roses around her shoulders, down the sides of her cape,
she looks at us with pity, her right hand points to a scroll
that rolls from her hand to Mary's, her daughter.
Row by row the men of the Holy Name Society command us
when to exit down the church aisles,
the women of The Saint Ann Guild in white filigree dresses
light blue gold-trimmed sashes, holy medals,
summer shoes, styles of hair from every decade,
frosted and feathered to old school brunette beehive.
The big band plays, saxes, trombones, trumpets, as the saint arrives
at the open doorway, church bells fill the sky, applause and tears
sunlight popping on her gold bejeweled cape.
Saint Ann is lifted, floats down the church steps
onto Jefferson Street where she's been
in procession for a hundred and six years.

As I walk the streets of Hoboken to follow the saint,
Sinatra is everywhere, his voice, his tilted fedora,
his blue eyes in shop windows, his face printed
on a surfboard, everywhere you look.
Sinatra snaps me back to my mother instantly,
how we danced in her foyer
on her blue onion on white diamond linoleum
held hands and spun around to "That Old Black Magic."
I love the recordings from his later years
when his voice grew balls but the early versions
made Mom swoon, she's fifteen again
sitting on her bed by the window, all her life before her,
his voice comes in from the street, fills her room with
that last elongated "Love" I cannot imagine my mother's life without.

Mom's wit, charm, and kindness are unequalled.
All other people I meet pale in comparison to her.

Soon the vendors will start grilling big hot sausages
peppers, onions, *broccoli rabe, zeppoli* in vats of hot oil
shaken in brown paper bags with powdered sugar
I will have to open my mouth as wide as it can go
dive in breathlessly

Go to the old church

early. watch the man with the keys
on his belt loop light candles
on the altar pull the sanctuary lamp
down on its chain through the pulley
O red perpetual flame

I ask Mom in my sleep: "Where are you?"
She tells me: "I am inside you."
Suddenly it all makes sense.
The irony of death is that she comes inside me.
I felt her pulse and heartbeat come inside me.
She lives in me, in each of us.

The irony of death is we feel loss
when really we are made more whole, more strong.
This is exactly why Christ had to—
had to—die, to come inside each of us.
We don't need to "eat the body, drink the blood"
it is spirit that is our strength and nourishment.

I dream of a vaulted heaven

I turn into the couch pillows
I ask her: "Show me where you are. Take me with you."
We ascend fast—bright
through vertical levels of sky
Mom shows me Heaven
Up we go
Heaven is just like you'd expect
just like renaissance paintings
just like sky
we float up up
white light
Mom is going up and up and up fast
vaults of light
I ask: "I want to meet the people you saw
when you said—I have illusions."
Beings in all colors are all around waving
Mom is friendly, everyone waves
Vertical tunnel of ascension light
Heaven is a tower, a bright upward tunnel
light and colors
All is effortless, free, easy
the rising of the soul into light
Ascension is the opposite of gravity
there is no density of matter
no body to be anchored to
Colors Light
Upward fast movement
Mom loves Heaven
Light beings, colors
Mom soars, swirls
Heaven is a fast lift

Aunt Evelyn is there, smiling
a profile of her face, big, looks at me
up close, smiling, her dimple giant
deep in her cheek
She wears thin gold rimmed eyeglasses
a cigarette between her fingers

Mom has lots of friends as we ascend
through colorful bright levels
vertical vaults of sky

I took my eye

off the bird
and she is gone

Ahh ...

she just moved to a higher
branch
and song

Mangia Piangia
First trimester of grief, Day 16

I can't stop crying as I eat George's gravy, the first gravy
I've eaten since Mom's gravy, thousands of Sundays
thousands of stirrings over the hot stove to feed us.
For years on stage I tried to perform the *Commedia dell'arte lazzo*
"Pasta'Lacrime" pasta'n tears, but I could never
fulfill *Pulcinello's* act, to eat spaghetti and cry profusely.
Gravy sated me in every bite, Mom was alive, her gravy endless.
Now she is gone and cry is all I do. All pasta is *pasta'lacrime*
now every time I eat it's *mangia piangia.*

Gravy is soul spackle,
a charged life-giving sustenance
generations of blood and mother's milk, language
and a thing lost, *giustizia e libertà,*
all the immigrants' strivings to make a life, *sistemazione,*
beauty, grace, *le piazze, le fontane,*
tutte le anime che hanno mangiatt' vissuto e morto.
Gravy runs through us.
Gravy is bigger than all of us.
The pots have been passed down for generations.
We've been nourished on gravy all our lives
licked our mother's wooden spoons
ate meatballs after they were fried
and before they made it into the gravy.
George's *rigatoni* fills holes in my heart.
His meatballs are light, they have *riguth'* in them.
My mother's were bigger
with garlic, breadcrumbs, *basilico,* darkened edges.
She ran her oil hotter.
It comforts me to know my mother
was part of a grand tradition
turning meatballs, milk soaked bread
whatever
your mixture.

This is your time

You keep telling me: "This is your time."
I saw a double rainbow. This is your message:
"Double rainbows from now on."
You communicate to me in doubles.
Two songs came to me in two days.
Everything in doubles.
"Are You Gone?" and "I Know You're There."
Songs like birds, appear and surprise.
In the ocean a silence
between ebb and flow
sing deep calm rhythm
phrases, verses float
melodies and words come locked together, wed.
I sing. Double rainbows.
Double gold stars. Double pennies wherever I go
to emphasize how great I should feel.
Double free. You free me of all my sins and faults
of every time I gave you a hard time.
You are gone 37 days. My gut burns. The burning abyss.
I will sing this, what else can I do?

I bend to pick up a penny.
Metals call me. Copper. Copper calls.
Spirit communicates in metal.
Metal conducts a charge, pulse, energy.
Copper is a conductor. It is not pennies *per se*,
but copper you communicate to me through.
O! The mother who never raised her voice!
Who never overate.
Who said: "Just a drop, just give me a drop."
Who never bought herself a vacation.
Was that the price tag of my "education?"
That you could never afford a vacation?
Where is the logic in that?
If I would have known that was the true cost
I never would have went to school.
No one scrimped and saved to send you to school.
Perhaps if I never got cancer, perhaps if I could have paid
those student loans myself. Can this baseball hat hide my tears?

I walk into the big cold sports bar
look at the cheerleader hostess, and say: "Just one."
I have entered the world of saying: "Just one."

Are you gone

Are you gone—or is it me?
Are you gone—how can it be?

Without you—how can I talk
Without you—how can I walk

Without you—the world's less bright
Without you—morning is night

Without you—how can I talk
Without you—how can I walk

This deep wound—I cannot hide
A burning—abyss inside

When your eyes break open my sky
When blue eyes break open gray sky—like a child I cry

Are you gone—how can it be?
Are you gone—O is it me!

Without you—how can I
Without you—how can I

I Know You're There

I know you're there—you were always beside me
I know you're there—now you're inside me

I know you're there—in the whistling wind of trees
I know you're there—in the butterfly flapping breeze

I know you're there—in the nectar of the flower
I know you're there—in the Queen Bee walkin' with power

In the birds in the air—I know you're there
In the wave of my hair—I know you're there

In rain falling from trees—I know you're there
In leaves wind and breeze—I know you're there

In the sun bustin' through clouds—I know you're there
When I'm talkin way too loud

On the knock on the door—I know you're there
When your picture falls to the floor—I know you're there

In my dreams guiding me—I know you're there
In the skyward bend of the tree—I know you're there

Every time I'm safe when I shouldn't be—I know you're there
In close calls saving me from injury—I know you're there

When I'm awake at night—I know you're there
At eleven eleven—when I turn off the light

In the jasmine breeze—I know you're there
Shiny pennies down at my feet

I know you're there—double rainbows arcing 'cross sky
I know you're there—when strangers smile kind

I know you're there — rain gently tapping me
I know you're there — whispering singing to me

I know you're there — through clouds the sun bursts blue sky
I know you're there — out the corner of my eye

of my eye

I am beginning to accept the absence

58 days

the endless hours
or the fact that hours will end
I'm looking forward to floating up
through the heavens with you
to learn of vaults and veils
the vaulted sky
the veils between living
the difference between feet and wings
the heft of sky and air
Will anyone remember how you could sit on your legs?
How you always twisted one leg up under as you sat?
Your crooked pinky? Your last giant laugh on earth
that came with your last great bath?
Lucy gave it to you, the Nurse's Aide who I call
The General, because when you need something done
she gets it done. The General strode into your room
unsnapped your gown, gave you a scrub down
right there in the bed. We forgot the words
"Palliative Care" during that blessed bath.
You laughed and laughed and laughed.
What a relief to be treated normal
not with kid gloves and soft voices.
The General laughed and laughed
and I laughed and laughed
and The General scrubbed, rotated you,
scrubbed. Total ablution. Spiritual. Physical.
Muscular. You were reinvigorated from head to toe.
Alive. Happy. A scrub-down is so radical,
so much work, but you did it!
And the full body smile The General gave you
lasted until the very end of your waking minutes.
"Where's Lucy?" you would ask
through the last days
a big smile over your whole being.
The laughing bath
one great parting gift
a full bodied bath
of laughter

How did we get to eternity already?

I put *biscotti* and a cup of *espresso*
next to your picture on the altar I made
in your memory. Later a roasted red pepper
Pugliese olive, *mozzarella*, tomato
whatever I eat, I make an offering to you.
I hear you saying, "Just a drop of coffee."

Here I am
without you
Here I am
your eyes break through overcast skies
Here I am
heart aching

The landscape of my heart is changed.
If you travelled over my heart
you would lose your balance
on the rugged ridges

I am nauseous and dizzy
I wish there was a gyroscope
on the horizon
to orient humans
back to level

I need to be more still
to walk slowly
just take slow walks
regain
level

In the diner

I sit down in the booth and cry
"Don't think of the past," the waitress tells me, "the future!"

I have a conversation with you in my head
while I sit across the table from someone who happens to be alive

I hear you argue, answer whatever they say
so I am silent

I loved how in your last years
you told people exactly what you thought.

I say in my head: "Back off Ma—get outta my way."
I gotta learn now to have my own conversations

Your voice is loud and emphatic whenever somebody says:
"If you need anything, we're here. Don't be afraid to call."

You say from the other side:
"Yeah, we're here so you're there and I'm here."

Me:
silence.

I am having more of a conversation with your ghost
your voice inside me, than with whoever sits across from me

You always asked diner waitresses to "put on a fresh pot"
so that's exactly what I do now—it feels so self-preserving

We've gotten the bottom of the pot
the dregs, enough in life

The least we could demand is a fresh cup
of coffee—for godssake

I can't listen to Sinatra

I can't hold anybody's hand
I can't feel anybody's pulse
I can't see any old lady's hand veins
I can't take care of any living thing
not your dog, not your baby, not your mother, not you
I can't go into Shoprite
I can't turn over a bunch of asparagus
in a supermarket and scrutinize the cut legs
I can't shop
I can't watch ice-skating or Olympic gymnastics
or Judge Judy or The Price is Right or Family Feud
I can't wash windows
I can't put on the radio
I can't listen to soft rock
I can't listen to the Bee Gees
I can only sit where she sat
I can only sleep where she slept
I can't look at her white sneakers
I can't throw away the Brillo pads she cut in half
I can't cut a Brillo pad in half
I can't fold a napkin into a neat and caring triangle
I can't waste light
I can't thread a needle
I can't listen to Sinatra
I can't turn on a light or leave open the fridge
I am my mother now
I do what she does
I eat how she eats
I save electricity like she does
I save money like she does
I think like she does
words she'd say
hop off my tongue

I keen for Mom

Day 69

I TAKE HER INTO MYSELF. I can't believe she is gone. I go see my shrink and say: "I am getting exit cues, like I wanna get on a plane to Azerbaijan." I don't know why I say Azerbaijan, it just comes out. I get out of therapy and walk up to the Park Avenue Armory to see a show called, *The Occupation of Loss*. In the old army drill hall is an installation of eleven cement silos four stories high and inside each are mourners from a different country performing lamentations. In one silo are two women Lala and Haji Rahila, dressed in black chadors, sturdy women with thick strong work hands and booming voices. I stay with them for the duration of the event as they beat their chests and pound their laps in rhythm and keen. I repeat their rhythm with my hands and join in loud moaning and recitation. Our wails echo up the silo. This is the most intimate keening I've done, with women I don't know. When the time is up, I bow and thank them, and say: *"Shukraan"* and *"Alhamdulillah"* and "Welcome to America" and Haji Rahila with hand on heart says: "Azerbaijan."

I walk out of there stunned, the rhythmic keening echoing inside me. I am the silo now.

I am in a room of whispers

Day 83

being confided in
by angels. Winged wind

shadows at three a.m.
dust climbs up from the depths
with dreams

What is dust?
Cosmic and sacred
matter sloughing off itself

As matter turns to spirit
bits are left behind
trails of

dust
proof of spirit
flight

Angel on oxygen
poncho flowing
like wings

could that be you
atop the white staircase
built into the hill

or is every woman
on oxygen
these days?

All I Can Do is Cry

All I can do is cry
Since the moment you did die
All I can do
All I can do
is cry cry cry

All I can do is cry
Since the moment you did die
All I can do
All I can do
is cry cry cry

All I do is cry
There's no when where or why
All I do is cry
Don't know how to stop or try

All I do is cry
Since the moment you did die
There's no wonderin' why
All I do
All I do
is cry cry cry

Was There Room

Day 238

Was there room—in your eyes
the night—we sat by the fire?

Was there room—in your heart
when we started—to forge a love for life?

Was there room—in your soul
did'ja know—how far our love could go?

Was there room—in your thoughts
did'ja know—we belonged to the road?

Was there room—in your life
for one glorious mountain climb

Was there room—in your day
To say—I love you for all time

Was there room—in your night
for soft light—and plenty of wine

Was there room—in your smile
for your heart—to jump beats with mine

Was there room—in your soul
to be kind—no matter what life would throw

Was there room—in your nights
For your story—to be sung and told

Was there room—in your heart
When apart—did'ja find me in the moon?

Was there room—in your hours
D'jyou feel power—when we held hands tight

Was there room—in your stance
to take a chance—and speak all your truths

Was there room—on your lips
for a sip—of earth's greatest delights

Was there room—in your leaving
For believing—we'd connect after it all

Was there room—in your breath
for a death to come—and go

Was there room—in your eyes
the night—we sat by the fire?

O Mamma

O Mamma I love you, O Mamma I care
I'm here thinking of you, way up there

O Mamma can you hear me—way up above?
I want you near me—so you can feel my love

O Mamma I love you, O Mamma I'm true
Can't stop thinking of you. What am I to do?

O Mamma how are you? It's so hard to let you go from this place
I thank God you died peaceful, with a smile on your face

O Mamma can you hear me? Better now without ears?
Can you feel my heart beat? Can you hear this song?

There are things I'd do over, if I got the chance
but I tried my best 'cause, I knew life doesn't last

O Mamma I can feel your—arms around me
I wish you were here, so we could relax and watch TV

I know you had to go, everyone does
It's a simple truth, I'm filled with your love

O Mamma I'm crying, O Mamma I'm blue
Without you, I still I wake up, two a.m. like we used to do

O Mamma I hear you, in all I think and say
I do things just like you, I learned from all your ways

O Mamma I love you, O Mamma you're mine
Life is heartbreak after heartbreak. Still we must shine

I'm keepin' your house clean, just as you would do
Somehow it became springtime, tulip stalks tell me so

O Mamma can you hear me? O Mamma where are you?
Can you take me with you? Even if I don't stay?

There are things I'd do over. There are things I'd do
One thing I did perfect, was be in love with you

rain reminds me

of being thirteen alone learning
to turn a brass key

Now I know why the sky
is blue. The Madonna's robe
around us

Tonight I lift a paintbrush to a wall
paint light blue and purple stripes,
hang two shelves for my books
move a big antique round mirror.
it's like I am just moving in
though I've been here for years
it's all too late and I can't catch
my breath with tears

Some things are impossible to throw away.
Mom's old checkbooks. Years old.
Full of her full rounded penmanship
each check written to take care of her and me
to keep us warm and safe
checks for electricity, phone,
everything she paid for over the years
all I owe her: rent, my student loans,
electricity, gas, telephone, credit card, the dentist
the harsh realities of single motherhood
She was a master of home economics
coupons were money in her wallet
How did she cut soap bars and Brillo pads in half?
It's so hard to cut a Brillo pad in half, and with her arthritis?
How did she double the use of everything and halve the price?
Yes she knew the bargains, the three dollar egg special,
shutting lights, utilizing daylight, sewing by the window,
never splurging, never wasting,
especially the light of day

I am going back under

I want to stay under the covers
wrapped and warm

Fidel Castro died today.
He had the same birth and death years as Mom
and yet—what radically different lives.
Still, I can imagine a conversation between them,
an energy. My mother did marry a charismatic dictator
afterall. I wonder if souls swirl around each other
if Mom finds company in the other 2016 souls
some of her favorite stars she'd love to meet:
Pat Summit, Gloria DeHaven, Julias LaRosa,
Abe Vigoda, Gene Wilder, Muhammad Ali, Patty Duke,
Joe Garagiola, Zsa Zsa Gabor,
and others I'd love her to meet: David Bowie, Prince,
Eli Weisel, Michael Cimino.

Mom wanted her feet free
in her last days, free
of covers, heads, hands and feet free
just a light sheet, no heavy blanket

Me, I want to be wrapped
under something heavy
three blankets
a hat on my head
socks on my feet
and eye covers
I curl up
and go down
as far far as I
can go

Her Last Stand

Day 83

I have to write about my mother's hands
warm and wilted, I lift
to my face, cheek, forehead, lips,
lifeless but warm.
I am in pieces, just wanting to be held

in a way I can be put back together
Who can hold me this way?
Do I need to hire someone?
A "holder" a "hugger"

someone's arms I can fall apart in
without the hug being opened too quickly
like an oven door
when the cake will cave

The longest tightest hugs I enter come from Nick Medley
who works the welcome desk at Sloan-Kettering
where there's a basket of hard candy.
Nick hugs me the tightest I've ever been hugged
right into his heart and Nick doesn't let go.
Nick hugs until I say, "Okay okay easy easy easy,"
but I know I can linger, fall open

I hugged Mom so tight
the last time she stood up
I held her up as she cried
into my chest, just wept.

She held onto me, for dear life
for her last verticality
as I know she held me
the first time I stood up
I held her for her last
her last stand.

Exit Cues

Mom's watchband broke the morning she left home
for the very last time. We were going to her routine
lung doctor appointment. "Don't worry," I said,
"take it with you. We'll get it fixed in the city."
But leather wears out. Wristbands. Hearts.

I got rid of all the clocks within weeks.
The kitchen clock drove me crazy, a click a second.
I never noticed it before 'til the silence
of absence flooded and capsized the kitchen.
No more bang clang of pots and pans
open close of drawers and cabinets
no more Mom climbing up to reach the high shelves
no more running water, loud wrestling of paper bags
ripping of Saran Wrap and tin foil.

The living room clock never told time.
It was a faux antique that took the place of the old oak clock
Mom gave to my sister years ago after the brass pendulum
stopped at the hour my sister got married: 3:30.
I want the walls bare for now, I took all the photos down.
Time to clean up. Clear out. Time to go back
to my subculture, the theater, exit the suburbs
exit constantly going to doctors, exit the body
exit cues, exit exit exit everywhere I look are exit cues.
Mom's wristband. Time is up. Period.

Peaches came early this year. The baby tree
gave us two peaches July 4th. Never had the trees
given us peaches that early. We always harvested
on Grandma Rose's birthday September 6th.
But this year, this year only, we cut into peaches
the morning of July 4th and had a sweet breakfast.
Nine days later, Mom was gone. The trees knew.

The trees are in mourning also. Very few peaches,
instead, sap leaks out and congeals on the branches.
Wounds. Weeping.
Sweetness runs out
of life, clots on bark

Presidential Election Night, Tuesday, November 9ᵗʰ, 2016
Second Trimester of Grief, Day 120

HOW CAN YOU NOT BE HERE FOR THIS? How you loved this election saga! I wanted to vote for you! Election night, I don't want to be alone in the quiet suburbs on the couch with your absence. So I pack a day of pills, underwear, shirt, hat, scarf, stickball bat and head to the city. I park on Riverside Drive at the Jean d'Arc statue and walk—then jump a cab to Rockefeller Center. The cab driver gives me the update on the city. All closed by the Javits Center where Clinton supporters are. All closed by Trump Tower and the hotel where Trump is. New York City holds both candidates and their minions.

A security guard at 30 Rock sees my stickball bat and says: "I haven't see one of those in a long while!" I'm surprised he lets me in carrying a stick. I'm utterly alone in a crowd of tens of thousands. Everyone stares into their cell phones. I didn't want to be alone so I came to midtown —where I'm alone—surrounded by tourists. What brought me here? I saw on TV they were projecting a map of the U.S.A. on the ice skating rink and were set to project each state blue or red as votes got tallied. I wanted to see the ice, the spectacle, the giant map. But when I got here, I saw that the ice skating rink is walled off. I walk around, fighting through crowds. You cannot see the ice from any vantage point. It's all a TV shoot! Even the bunting on 30 Rock is fake, two-dimensional, painted as 3D, a piece of plastic printed to look like fabric. On TV it looks like real bona fide red, white and blue bunting. I'd be better off back home on the couch, where everything looks real on TV, but I am up close and see it's fake.

I get to a spot in the crowd where I can lean on a fence and have some space to breathe. To my left is a tourist who sits on the ground to eat her sandwich. We make brief eye contact to acknowledge that we are safe near each other. Another woman alone is to my side, incessantly texting. Impossible to make eye contact with. To my right are a pair of drunks, she keeps whipping her long hair over her head, and flailing about. Not safe. He grabs her ass. His eyes are glossy. They share head-phones and rock to the same beat. It is sex in public. I widen my stance so when she bumps into me she might contain her movement, but it does little good. She steps on my foot. As votes are counted, a red line is projected up the glass facade of a building. The red line is like a therm-ometer rising as Trump gains more of the vote. The red line rising is taking the temperature of the country and it is getting hotter and hotter and hotter. The drunks pull out long cigarettes and I leave before they light up.

I walk to Times Square. The map of the U.S.A. is giant across billboards. Again thousands of people, yet Times Square is incredibly peaceful, I even get a seat. The girl next to me wears a "Mount Holyoke Rugby" sweatshirt, which makes me feel safe. O! how I wish I was home on the couch with your commentary, Mom! What would you say as the map turns red, redder, reddest? "People are fed up! People don't trust her— she's a conniver. But God knows what he's gonna do!" I hear you loud and clear.

Twenty-five minutes 'til more polls close. I'm restless. Florida is too close to call. 9:42—Trump winning popular vote. Winning electoral vote. The half moon leaves Times Square. The rugby player leaves. A man sits down, stares past me. He hands me a piece of paper. "Bellevue" is handwritten on it. I point southeast toward Bellevue, to show him which direction to walk. As the giant U.S.A. map on the billboards gets redder, it feels like the whole country needs to be committed to the Bellevue Psych Ward tonight. I can't believe how lost and alone I feel in the world.

Where Will I Go?

If all I know is that you're not here tomorrow
Where will I go?

If all I know is that you're not here tomorrow
Where will I go?

Where will I go?
Where will I go?

If all I know is that you're not here tomorrow
Where will I go?

Where O where O where O where
Where O where O where

I want it to be as public as being pregnant

I'm three months in mourning
twelve weeks

an empty chair across from me

I sit in a vegan restaurant
still noticing everyone's veins
on their hands
and inner arms
I feel pulses and heartbeats

Since my mother died I am drinking more water
So much water, I can't even tell you
Quarts at a time
Maybe it is because I am crying it all out
It's like I'm at a new altitude
or in the desert
My body can't get enough
cold water

Hard Candy

Day 154

for our hoarse voices, hard candy
for our silence, for all hard things
that will never be spoken
hard candy to moisten our throats
sore from all that gets stuck
suck on this, hard candy to keep truths
sliding up and down, hard candy
to sooth the redness, hard candy
every old Italian lady carries in her purse hard candy
she's earned her spit, hard candy
ladies offer at home in precious dishes
hard lemon drops, hard butterscotch ball yolks,
hard *espresso* balls, hard orange,
hard tangerine, hard raspberry,
strawberry, coconut, cacao, hard anise, mint,
eucalyptus, hard black licorice, hard ginger.
Open your passages, hard candy, hard on the outside
soft cream inside, a reward for patient sucking.
Unwrap me and I'll give you a mouthful of truth.

All my life the first thing I did when visiting
an old Italian lady was dive
right into her hard candy.
Every old Italian lady in the Bronx
had a fancy candy dish full,
and so did every old lady in Italy.
Grandma Rose's candy dish was a cut crystal
rectangle with a silver lid that was magic to lift,
reveal all the Italian hard candy
and clink like a bell when you put the cover back down.
Sadie's was open golden glass on her coffee table
in front of the good sofa covered in plastic.
Lorenza's was a silver floor stand candy dish
upright beside her like a tall poodle
filled with butterscotch balls

next to her cherry velvet throne.
Zia Giuseppina's was porcelain in the corner
each candy gift-wrapped in Italianate metallic foils
gold and silver and red blue green.
Mary's was crystal with a crystal lid with butterscotch balls.
Mom had a wicker basket with mint green jellies
shaped like leaves tucked deep in her spice cabinet
and in her purse, hard peppermint candy, lemon drops.
Mom coughed up truths in *staccato* phrases,
would make herself laugh so hard
she broke into fits of coughing,
unwrapped another candy.
Preciosa Abbondanza carried her milk glass candy dish
to her lace front doorway in *Acquaviva delle Fonti*.
and held it out to me for my journey back to *L'America*.
That was the last I ever saw her, offering hard candy.
What's more beautiful than an old lady lifting a bowl
of hard candy toward you for your life's journey?
Hard candy for eternal goodbyes.
Hard candy for the taste of life in your mouth.
Hard candy to get through the priest's bad jokes.
Hard candy for *la dolce vita*. Hard candy to get
your juices going. Life is easier
when sucking on a hard candy.
Hard candy for hard times.

I remember Caroline Rose, going on three years old,
the moment she found my mother's (her great-grandmother)
stash of candy in the cabinet. Caroline Rose looked up
in amazement, in candy sisterhood and asked:
     "GG, you like candy?!"
     "Yes I love candy!"
Candy sealed their bond.

Hard candy hard candy hard hard candy I need
hard candy for the rest of my life.
Get rid of all bitterness.
Grazie a Dio for hard candy
old ladies need hard hard hard candy
somehow hard candy keeps everything

from heaving up and out of the guts.
And me now, my voice just cuts out on me.
I've been silent all week
eucalyptus and hard ginger candy—for my silence.
My one good vocal cord gets inflamed.
The paralyzed one is frozen in the 'on' position.
I am silent. I am silent. Drinking aloe
sucking on hard candy
but when I open my mouth
when my throat releases words
when my one good vocal cord vibrates
truth truth flows

Adult Orphan

Who knew it would be so sad
to fold a sheet alone or sip
a *cappuccino* or taste gravy?

I spread the sheet
white with cherry roses
across the bed, open my arms

wide as they can go
grab two corners
tears rise up, I sit down

My mother will always be
on the other end of every sheet
needing to be folded

I can still see her clenching her end
as the sheet snapped from Grandma's hands
to shoo away wrinkles

Mom dropped her end
Grandma grumbled: *"Mavatheen"*
In America we just didn't hold on tight enough

There was always one leader who snapped the sheet
and the other who just held on
I repeated this drama with Mom so many times

the flying sheet
out of my hands
it's hard to be ready for just how hard
that snap will be

the beat goes on

Day 156

I get electric shocks every day
as I get up from Mom's chair and my fingers
make contact with her lamp or the brass
doorknobs she turned for forty years
the whole apartment is charged
long leather fringe on my cowboy jacket
points out as if someone is pulling the strands
the air in the apartment snaps and sparks
as I move from room to room pennies appear on the floor
I keep sweeping up and pennies still appear
only high shine copper as if Mom
no longer matter
is now an electrical pulse
the pulse that left her heart
beats
in the atmosphere
invisible wings

Depart Soul Depart

164 days

Depart Soul Depart
Depart Soul Depart
It's time to rest for the heart

Depart Soul Depart
It's time to rest for the heart
Depart Soul Depart

Fly away
Fly away
to the great God beyond

Fly away
Fly away
Let us leave the body down

Depart Soul Depart
It's time to rest for the heart
Let us lay the body down—in the ground

Depart Soul Depart
It's time to rest for the heart
Depart Soul
Depart

Fly away
Fly away
to the great God beyond

Fly away
Fly away
Let us leave the body down

Depart depart depart
Depart depart depart
It's time to rest for the heart

Lilly O Lilly

I once had a Mamma—she was known as Sweet Lilly
prettiest girl in the Bronx.
As a kid she was crippled—cause she fell out a window
but her soul—you know was—strong as the rocks.

O! It took some years—for her to learn once again
how to balance on two legs and stand.
O! Lilly loved music—and with rhythm inside her
From that day on—you know—Lilly did dance!

O Lilly O Lilly—Are you near me Sweet Lilly?
Will you come for me when I go?
Lilly O Lilly—Can you hear me Sweet Lilly?
Will ya stay with me when I go?

She gave kind words, and haircuts, permanents and manicures,
Lilly held everyone's' hands!
While she spread beauty—she listened to everyone's ills.

O nothing was too hard as I held Lilly's soft hand in mine!
Through all of life's hardships, no matter what,
you know, Lilly's eyes sparkled and shined.

O Lilly O Lilly—Are you near me Sweet Lilly?
Will you come for me when I go?
Lilly O Lilly—Can you hear me Sweet Lilly?
Dontchya know that I love you so!

In life we can't save each other from sufferin'
but we can ease loneliness and pain.
The last time she stood up, she wrapped her arms around me,
I stood for her strong as a tree.

In the end—all there is to say is,
"I love you" and "Thank you, my dear."
I wish I could take away all of your fear.

O Lilly O Lilly—Are you near me Sweet Lilly?
Will you come for me when I go?
Lilly O Lilly—Can you hear me Sweet Lilly?
Dontchya know that I love you so!

We had a lifetime together, hours to do with
what we chose. And so fast it happened,
we slid into forever. At her grave you know
I tossed in a purple rose.

Lilly left with a smile as she took her last breath
and I felt her pulse come into me.
Then we dressed her in purple, covered her in pink roses
for her entrance to eternity.

Lilly O Lilly—Are you near me Sweet Lilly?
Will you come for me when I go?
O Lilly O Lilly—Can you hear me Sweet Lilly?
Now I look to the sky—for that face I love so!

With the sun in my eyes and Lilly in my heart
I heard all that she came to say.
"World Peace" she'd whisper in a demand
every night to God she did pray:

"World Peace! World Peace! World Peace Today!
World Peace! World Peace for everyone today!
World Peace! World Peace! *Il Pace per Il Mundo!*
World Peace! World Peace!
Give everyone in the world peace today!"

O Lilly O Lilly—I can feel you, Sweet Lilly!
Life with you—is all I've ever known!
O Lilly O Lilly—Rest in peace, Sweet Lilly.
Before you know it—I'll rejoin your soul!

We'll waltz through the Heavens
and we'll lindy through the skies
my sweet Mamma Lilly and me.
O Lilly O Lilly
O Lilly O Lilly
O Lilly O Lilly
Fly free!

Orange and Spice

I see a group of people I tell them
I don't know you, I don't know
what you're talking about!

"Next time they come, go say 'Hi,'" offers Audrey
The angels keep comin'
they come in and out!

I open my eyes, I am having illusions
A little girl's standing in front of me.
Do you see her? She's right beside you
I can see her—clear as can be.

"Is the girl in a dress," asks Jessie
Yes! I say Yes! I say Yes! Although
I feel so cold now I can't help from trembling.
My heart falls open just like an old rose.

Orange and spice, it's all very lovely
She sits by the fire with the girls in her eyes.
Orange and spice, it's all very lucky
She sits by the fire with the girls in her eyes.

Grandma is standing behind me with flour,
Behind the bed there, you see her Nicole?
Angels are comin'—this all feels confusin'
Where is my pocketbook? Let's go home!

Rosary beads and Ave Maria
The baby is hungry, I forgot to feed her!
Am I dreaming? The baby is screaming.
Who will take care of my baby for me?

I wanna stand up now.
What is happening to me?
Who will take care of you, Annie!

"Don't worry bout me Ma,
you gave me everything
You taught me everything I need."

Orange and spice, it's all very lovely
She sits by the fire with the girls in her eyes.
Orange and spice, it's all very lucky
She sits by the fire with the girls in her eyes.

"Will I get better?" I ask Dr. Stover
she looks me in the eye most seriously,
"You need rest Rachel, you need rest."
Ho capito! Doctor — *Capishe tutta bene.*
I need rest. I need rest rest rest you know
rest sounds good to me.

O! My blue pocketbook and my eyes they won't open.
The fentanyl drips when I push the button.
Thank you, I love you. I hear singing.
Get rid of the pocketbook. What am I going to do with that thing?

Annie, I just want to stand — Can this be all?
Let's go home and make meatballs!
Who'll take care of my baby without me?
I hear Annie whisper to me:

"May all your suffering cease — may your mind be at peace
May all your suffering cease — may your mind be at peace
May all your suffering cease — may your mind be at peace
May all your suffering cease — may your mind be at peace"

Orange and spice, it's all very lovely
She sits by the fire with the girls in her eyes.
Orange and spice, it's all very lucky
She sits by the fire with the girls in her eyes.

Holy water from Medjugorje
a high pitched sound and I'm on my way.
My blood is warm all over as I pull away

the body she stays down but strangely I am okay.
I am a spiraling whirlwind just like a tornado.
I am silvery gold light being sucked into the galaxy,

spinning so fast with the stars as my map
I hear Annie say, "Today's your big day.
Today's your big day!"
This is the week of Our Lady of Mount Carmel Feast.
July 13th I become an angel this day.

Day Count

Day 1—I cannot be touched, I cannot hold anyone's hand
I feel your pulse beating

Day 3—I am able to be touched

Day 8—Al gives me a dulcimer and I begin to strum

Day 14—I fall into the ocean, let the salt water recharge me.
The ocean is so loud I cannot think. The ocean is just the voice I need

Day 18—I buy twenty-seven blank notebooks

Day 19—I miss everything, your soft light quilts, your farina,
your half-bars of brown soap. It is overwhelming to look around
and not see your pocketbook, your gum, flashlights,
your crumpled tissues under couch pillows, your magnified mirror
where you put on lip liner and tweezed your eyebrows and chin

Day 21—I try to say goodbye to the things your body needed
on this earth: coats, blankets, curtains, your frilly bed skirt

Day 22—I cry into the couch, a giant sponge for my tears
that never end. The pearl rosary beads feel so soft
like your skin, your words, thoughts, prayers.
Why did Sinatra sing about dying in July?
It better be true what they say, that now you're watching over me.
It better be true. I want to go harvest in Italy.
Learn how to make *olio e vino*.
It is ridiculous how days stagger on. The relentless clock

Day 23—I have to look at the calendar
several times a day to know when I am, I am waiting
for you to get home. I pick a dozen peaches from Grandma's tree
and sit them on the kitchen windowsill. That's about all there is.
I am numb. Eating feels lousy. Everything feels lousy.
I am lost and alone. I open the mail by rote.
Not a big peach harvest this year. The tree mourns. The tree tells me:

"Go! Travel! Live your life! Don't stay here to take care of me!"
There's a gash of sap on the baby tree
A gash of sap

Day 133 — the tears come back, fill me, the tears come — fill — fall
O blessed eyes to release this flood
I look down at my hands and know
I will be done with this body one day
I've been avoiding doctors.
I am so thankful I don't have to go near a hospital.
Death shouldn't be in the hands of the white coats.
Death, and birth are sacred

Day 146 — I get up in the morning
say to the sky, "Hi Mom! *Ciao Mamma!*"
It's a beautiful world when the sky
is your mother

Day 170 — Your name is engraved on the stone
I run my fingers across all your letters
R A C H E L E   L A N Z I L L O T T O
I stand on the graves — of you, your parents, their siblings
I sing your favorite song, kiss the marble, do a twirl
crumble an apple turnover and crumb bun
for Bronx birds to feast on
head bent up to the marble sky

Day 176 — Your absence
has become
a presence

Day 202 — I join the cast of a play
I need to be with people
On the highway, I am driving. I say, "Ma, gimme a message.
I'm gonna turn on the radio. Gimme a message."
And I do. The song sings: "Leave this lonely life.
I wanna know what love is. I want you to show me."
That as your message.

You don't want me to be alone, your wish was to free me
You want me to move on. In my own way, I am.
I buy a *cappuccino*, walk into the acting studio
take off the woolen poncho you knitted for me
give a big hello to the others in the room
begin to stretch

Day 324 — I give a concert of all the songs I wrote for you
and play the dulcimer. The melodies carry me through

Day 379 — I listen to Sinatra
without falling apart. I am lucky though.
The Hoboken restaurant I sit in
is not playing your favorite songs

PART III:
Stage Light

"… losing a parent … you move up a generation …
The roof is gone. She will be with you in new ways as you go on."
—Joyce Ravitz
in a condolence card to me, 2016

I Wash the Windows

Third Trimester of Grief, Day 218

They don't come clear as Mom's
but I employ her tricks: white vinegar and water
crumpled newspaper, afternoon light
because direct sunlight splotches the glass as it dries.
Why can't I get the panes perfect?
She must have used a capful of ammonia to get that sparkle
on the glass, on the air, on the light
as it cut in through the house
but I don't want to breathe in ammonia.
I'd love to see that shine again
but I'm not gonna wheeze for it.
I choose to live without that flawless sparkle and sheen.
Mom's breathing problems had to be partly
from household cleaners: all the bleach, ammonia, acid
she used to get every surface to shine like her eyes.

When the house is clean, my mother is still alive.

The mirrors, I clean all of them but one
the big hand carved mahogany framed rectangle
I've looked into all my life.
This mirror held for Mom a beautiful memory:
On their first wedding anniversary, November 3rd, 1948
my mother and father picked out this mirror together
as a gift for themselves and their growing family
this mirror that miraculously has never been broken
this mirror that survived all the craziness
all the post-war trauma of things thrown, all our Bronx rage
this mirror that outlived my parents
Somehow they are inside this glass. I can see them framed here.
I remember my mother and father lifting me up to this mirror
the way adults hold babies for a first look at themselves
I remember my whole hand being lifted
with my father's thick index finger
I can see my mother and father waving their hands at the glass

teaching me how to wave my hand at my image
as my fingers learn to close then open
This mirror keeps the smudges and prints of time
the way old glass is a portal
for ghosts

Infinite Blu

O beautiful soul *Mamma!*
O anima bella Mamma!

May the blue of your eyes cloak us as the heaven
Può l'azzurro dei tuoi occhi ci mantello come il paradiso

As mother Mary's robe
Come la roba della madre Maria

As infinite blue love
Come l'amore infinita blu

Dearest Carissima Mamma

Day 216

MA, IF I COULD SIT WITH YOU AGAIN, for a *cappuccino* in a tall clear glass the way you liked it, and jelly donut cut in half for us to share, no doubt we'd talk politics. Me and you always voted together from the time I stood knee high and you held my hand in the curtained voting booth and let me pull the big important lever. I don't know how to tell you this. I can't believe you're not here for this. Ma, Trump won. It's a nightmare getting worse and worse. We watched this whole saga together and talked about how it would end, and now I had to watch the end without you. I wanted you to have your vote. Walking up to the voting booth, I kept thinking: "My mother voted Bernie in the primary, who would she vote for now?" The weeks leading up to election day, so much happened. Going through this without you right here to interpret stuff with—is horrible, unthinkable. You were smarter than anyone, saw the bulls-eye of issues the world spins around. I'll always remember your take on abortion rights:

"The rich will always be able to get abortions, they can fly wherever they like. Nobody likes abortions. Nobody wants an abortion. But if you take away the right, you're only discriminating against poor women."

And you're right. Who's more right than you? No one was ever more clear on how big issues boil down to poor women's daily lives and decisions. Senators can talk around that issue for a hundred years and I never heard a public figure attack the root of it the way you did:

"Taking away the right to an abortion is discrimination against the poor. Period."

Punto e basta!

We followed every beat together, every episode from *The Apprentice* to the primaries. Only you knew all the characters, all the moments. It was the prize fight you'd imagined. Remember last year you said: "Imagine if it's Trump versus Hillary? Oh my God, the country would watch every moment of every debate." The election felt like Americans choosing who's TV show would continue to air. All eyes were on him. All lenses focused. The Trump Show is the show that continued.

Remember the day he announced, June 16th, 2015, Bloomsday? It was one of our marathon out-patient days at Sloan-Kettering, the long days of utter exhaustion like healthy folk get after skiing for ten days—at the same time it's the opposite in every way possible—every muscle, the whole body needs relief, rest, to lie down, throw off gravity. The head can't be held up any more. You're drained of all your adrenaline, spent. When you're in Manhattan and you feel like this, where do you go? Restaurants—needing rest! The day Trump announced was so fatiguing, we decided we deserved a big dinner. A rare splurge. We went to V&T Pizza on Amsterdam at Ahun-tenth. I ordered steak *pizzaiole'*. You ordered *ravioli*. The restaurant's TV was mounted on the wall in front of our table. The Donald and Melania made their smooth entrance into history, down their gold escalator, his *deus ex machina*. Melania was the goddess in a white Grecian gown, floating down, on a diagonal, to the pink marble and gold trim lobby of Trump Tower. The Donald was just a step behind her. A God on a Golden Chariot. Drawn by horses, dragons. Slow, gold. The God stands tall, proud, deliberate, and is delivered down to the world; the entrance of savior. Here he comes. Here he comes. Slow, steady, gold. I hear *Bolero* playing. The country was mesmerized, the media could not take their lenses off him, as all await his landing, filming every beat. Riveted. Melania the stoic Goddess blesses the God's entrance. His feet don't meet the floor. He doesn't take mortal steps. The machine does it for him, the God's descent on the golden escalator.

New Yorkers couldn't believe it. We all started howling, laughing, talking. For me and you it was a needed respite, it was television, on a rough New York day, with our cancers at bay. We were amused. Better than a Broadway show. The couple at the next table were in amazement too, and we began talking, joking. New Yorkers needed each other that night. The waiter dripped *pizzaiole'* juice on my new blue hat as he swirled the plates to the table from overhead. What a fiasco. The couple witnessed this. We were all in a frenzy. The whole restaurant was laughing. That was a hundred dollar hat Audrey bought me for my birthday just weeks ago. A peacock blue fedora made out of woven paper. Why'd Audrey buy a hundred dollar hat? Remember? She said: "There was a sign in the window that read: 90% off everything!" "Yeah, sure!" you said, "that sign was there just for Audrey, to get her to walk in with the cash." I showed the boss at *V&T* the hat and complained about the *pizzaiole'* juice and he took ten bucks off our bill "to get the hat cleaned." *O madonna!* The things that make a night memorable.

I needed dessert. Me and you walked up the block to the Hungarian

Pastry Shoppe and got a sidewalk table, for *cappuccini* and *hamentoshen*. I yelled at passers-by, "Trump for President" and they yelled back, "Never!" "Are you crazy!" and "No F---Way!" Everyone on the street was laughing like it was a big goddamned joke. The couple next to us at V&T came and talked with us over *hamentoshen*. Everyone on the street was talking. We should have all went into Saint John the Divine and prayed at that very moment, or taken to the streets that night—instead of laughing, watching the grand performance of it all.

You know Ma, in the end, everyone we know who bought into the book and film, "The Secret" voted for Trump. Every single one. You remember when that book came out? Yeah the "the law of attraction" for folks prone to snake oil and big answers. Trump is the best snake oil salesman I ever saw. He is all sales. Everything I avoid. Price point. Point of Sale. Marketing. Lying. Manipulating. Business. Humans = two feet to sell two shoes to, one head to sell a hat to. Trump knows "The Secret," convinced himself he would win, picked off eighteen Republican competitors like a cowboy with a six shooter in a TV western. The news announcers didn't take him seriously. Remember? The best theory I heard was weeks later, some back door information from a bodyguard who told me Bill Clinton and Donald Trump played golf together and were overheard talking and Bill slyly coaxed Donald into running, as a Republican—as if that would make Hillary a shoe-in. I believed that moment. I pictured Bill and The Donald golfing. It was so natural. I heard Bill muscling information across, making himself understood, planting seeds, without really saying anything directly:

"The Republican party is wide open Donald, for a newcomer to take it by storm. Oh they're tired, believe me. The country wants to see another Bush in the White House like it needs another fad diet. You know Donald, it's a weak Republican field. I never seen such a weak field. All I want for Hillary is a worthy opponent, a contender. Someone to debate. To up the ante. Otherwise it's no fun. Lackluster. Can you see her debating Jeb? Boring as hell. No one would even bother turning on their televisions, let alone come out to vote. No lightning, no fire. You know, last time out, she got robbed. Face it, it was a beauty contest. The voters love stars Donald, and Barack, what he lacked in experience, he made up for in stardust. The voters ate it up. And Hillary, Hillary worked diligently, doggedly for decades, behind the scenes, you know, and all her experience was no match for pretty rhetoric with a preacher voice he called up when he wanted. But that's all ancient history. What she deserves now is a good opponent. A strong opponent. No one knows the world stage like her. She's been everywhere, knows all the players and all the plays. There's not a Republican that can hold a candle to her. But what I fear Donald is statistics and statistics say no party stays in office three terms, and that's what she's up against, statistics. It's a fickle electorate. All they love is—change."

I can see Donald swinging his club with all his might, his club arcing through the air and taking it all in and hitting the ball two hundred fifty yards and realizing this is his moment. And then Clinton's idea boomeranged.

O! Ma, remember that long long day at Sloan-Kettering we ended with Dr. Sun? Yeah the day he asked you to draw a clock. You were so frustrated. Ten after eleven. You got so confused. I don't think you ever had to draw a clock before in your life—maybe when you were five and learning to tell time. That friggin clock exercise got you all messed up and you lost confidence in yourself, like: "What is happening to me?" And whenever you asked: "What is happening to me," I didn't know it was steps down the path of death. For now it was just confusion about drawing the directions of the black hands on a white face clock. The short hand. The long hand. Which was which again? It was all so stupid. So out of context. You who could keep count of hundreds of knitting stitches in intricate patterns—you who could tabulate all your pharmacy receipts for the Medicaid spend-down—why did Dr. Sun ask you to do something you never did before? It felt like a trick question, like: "Tie your shoelaces backwards." What did it prove anyway, at the end of an exhausting marathon Sloan-Kettering day?

Dr. Sun asked you question after question. It was a draining interrogation. At the end of your long medical history, he said: "Is there anything else?" and he laughed, because there was already too much for one life time. And you looked at me, your eyes twinkling, because we always knew we got to this point in the story in every new medical interview, just when the doctor thought he had everything. After you told him about your Triple A: Ascending Aortic Arch dissection, colon cancer, bladder cancer, COPD, rampant blood pressure, heart failure. "What else?" he asks. "Is there anything else?" and he doesn't expect anything else and you look at me and twinkle and say:

"Well, when I was two years old I fell out of a window."

And we all laugh because it is just too much and we're laughing at God and we're laughing at life and we're laughing at miracles and we're laughing at suffering like dancing skeletons, we are laughing at the skeleton of the Statue of Liberty. We're laughing at America, we're laughing at medicine we're laughing at surgery and knowing that in any other time in any other place all of these survivings of yours would have been documented as Pope-verified miracles, *mirabilia verificatur*—or you would have died five hundred times—and I see you now as some sort of Bronx Italian Female Rasputin. And there we were with Dr. Sun after all his questions, after tests, after getting on the road by 6:30 a.m. to beat the traffic and get a quiet drive through Central Park as if we really were going somewhere we were excited to get to; some adventure, excursion, safari. And when you enter Sloan Kettering it is safari photos that greet you by the A-elevator near the garage; zebras and lions and rhinos and tigers and hippos—the big five. And you know you have made it. But first, in the garage there are circus posters of a lion tamer dressed in doctor white, with his black whip like a long stethoscope, and forty rabid lions like cancer cells. You walk up the ramp picturing your doctors as lion tamers and your cancer cells as ferocious lions that could turn on one another, destroy one another in a series of kills, and you see the zebras, and the lions, and you get into the elevator, tired from your safari journey but knowing you arrived at your destination, now you have to make it upstairs and strip for the lion tamer, and let him go on his hunt with his guns for the big game inside you.

And so we laughed, the list of catastrophes that you survived—inconceivable, the heft of your medical chart, "And that's not even half the story," you told Dr. Sun, because there's no room in the chart for your story, your escape from domestic violence, your life as a war bride of a sick marine.

Mom, I have to call your story, "Permanent Wave" or "The Permanent Wave" or "Her Permanent Wave" or "The Lady's Permanent Wave," not just because that was your career expertise, but because your life was a permanent wave. You never had a lake, you never had a calm sea. You lived in a permanent wave.

We left Dr. Sun's office exhausted from all his questions, all the tests, being shuffled from one doctor to another, exhausted from living in the wave. We drove to *Le Monde* on Broadway at Ahun-twelfth. I got you outta the car, outta the heat, with your oxygen tank, into the ground floor restaurant and we got our dark corner table. l leaned my head into my hands and covered my eyes. We took deep breaths, stretched our legs under the table. All of a sudden there was Dr. Sun's face up close, bending over our table, into our private rest space, and he says: "Do you have any questions?" And we both looked at him in shock and our jaws dropped and you shot back: "About what!" We both think: "What the hell is he doing here?"

No one can understand this, but when you leave Sloan-Kettering, you leave with the relief that they didn't keep us, the relief that we didn't die that day there, the relief they didn't tell us some dramatic test result, the relief of making it back out into the city's air, back out into the flow of traffic, the cars, the strangers, the citizenry, back out alive, to exhale with the wind, and when you discard the flimsy hospital gown you discard your vulnerability, you get back into your own identity as you put on your coat and step onto a Broadway sidewalk once again, and you don't expect Sloan-Kettering to infiltrate your world where you're just yourself, not a patient, not the victim of a mugging from some masked tumor, not Medical Record #00795424.

We were so startled out of a momentous rest where we had found calm in The Wave like the tunnel surfers find as the wave rolls over them and they are just ahead of the wake — as are we, just a step ahead of our own wakes ... And we looked at each other and said: "Oh my God — for the moment I was so confused, I thought that was Dr. Sun — I was so startled." But it was only the maître-d who ran away from our table apologizing: "I'm sorry. I'm sorry for disturbing you," and disappeared.

"He must think we're nuts," you said. "We must'a scared the hell outta him." We both laughed a laugh only we laughed together, knowing this flavor of post-traumatic stress all our own in a west-side cafe after an east-side doctor's day.

O! Ma, if I could sit with you, right now, over a *cappuccino* and jelly donut cut down the middle, here's what our talk would be:

"Happy *San Valentino*, I love you."

"Yes, darling. Happy Valentine's Day."

"Good *cappuccino*."

"The glass is just right — to fit in my pocka'book."

"You do it. I can't do it. I can take you some sugars.

So Ma, I can't process this. Trump won."

"Could you believe it."

"Ma, it's a nightmare fagetaboutit. They say the rich are building bunkers, and the working poor are trading in their dollars for silver and gold coins, so when the dollar bill devalues, they can run with their gold and silver across the border to Canada."

"Your father always believed in silver and gold."

"Yeah, they say it will never devalue—it's been around since before Christ. Always worth its weight. I should be worth my weight."

"You're looking good. Keeping the house nice and clean. I see."

"I'm trying. I try to keep it like you'd like it."

"I do. I love the new colors. The purple wall."

"The purple wall! You love it?"

"I love it! And the purple trim on the mirror! You can do anything! Anything you touch is professional!"

"Yeah professional. You know who's professional? Your cousin Rachel's granddaughter. She's working in immigration now. She passed the bar just in time for all the havoc. She's been sleeping at JFK helping out who she can, who's in detention. The airports are in such a frenzy people are walking on the Grand Central Parkway to try to make their planes. Cars can't even get in. Thousands of protesters. She's doing the good work."

"I wish I could make her a poncho."

"Yes, your spirit shields, yes she deserves one, she's a hero."

"She should be part of the Poncho Girls Club."

"I can't promise nothing. I don't know if I'm gonna do all that knitting. I'm writing like you knitted. Stitchin' words."

"Just don't forget to take a break. Some time for yourself. To enjoy."

"I know I know I hear ya. He's already being sued Ma, imagine, the President against the courts. They're saying his executive orders are unconstitutional."

"I remember when he made those comments against the Pope."

"O remember that! Right! The Pope said: 'It's not Christian to build walls.' And he said: 'Tell the Pope to live without a wall around the Vatican.'"

"Disgrace."

"I thought that was as low as he could go! He was just getting warmed up."

"And this Pope of all Popes!"

"O Ma, now he's against the judges. I'll tell ya, all Inauguration night I cried, cried like the days just after you died, cried. I miss your take on things, your quick witted critique. I miss watching this with you. I can't make sense of it without you. It's all crumbling. Remember what you said back in June?: 'Things are so crazy maybe we need someone nuts to be President. Obama was too much a professor.'"

"I miss watching it there with you!"

"I know Ma. I see your tears in the clouds. I get your purple flowers you drop for me."

"Good. Keep paying attention. Up here things are different. There's no weight. Once you drop the weight you're buoyant light. We're all light. It's all a matter of light. We don't worry. What a relief. It all seems so small now. You won't believe who I talk with up here. The other day I was talking with Muhammad Ali. He prayed for World Peace just like me all those nights of life. We have it here. World Peace. It's beautiful. Bright. Pure music."

"What does Ali think of Trump's Muslim ban?"

"Disgrace. Disgrace. It's all a Disgrace. He says their liable to detain his children at the airports."

"Yeah, I got your message. I saw the sign that read: DISGRACE, the night of the protest after the election, near Trump Tower. I asked you what you thought, and then I saw the sign, hand written, tucked by the stair railing down into the 6 train."

"Disgrace."

"Human folly. What would Ali do?"

"Speak out. Start a revolution."

"Fists in the air! I love you Ma."

"I love you too Darling. Now go! Live your life! I had my time. It's your time now. You hear me!? And promise me you'll take care of yourself. You need a good vacation. You were so tied up with me, now you're free. Buy new sneakers and wear them out!"

My Mother's Wooden Spoon

looks like a person by now
a friend my mother could talk to
strong, burned, worn by use
hard knocks against the rim of the pot
to shake gravy dregs

I turn to my mother's wooden spoon
after mine snaps at the stem.
I circled it too hard in my oatmeal
and the stem snapped at the head.

My mother's wooden spoon
has stirred all her gravies, soups, stews,
lentils, *past'n fazool*, chocolate pudding for icebox cakes.
Nothing could break it.
I don't know what kind of wood it's made out of.
Whose tree.
That spoon never got a rest
will never bend or break
outlasted her house
her marriage
her heart
breath
life

I still see her holding it
my mother's wooden spoon
inextricable from her hand
the way she stirred the world
so gently

Frankincense and Flowers

I AM NOT READY FOR SPRING, but when I stare at the daring purple crocuses that stab up through the cold hard ground with their announcement of change, I think, here we are, like it or not. I pray for more snow, more winter, more internal slowed time. Snow comes. More than before. I hunker down indoors, cook a *frittata*, get quiet in the whirling white snow globe world. I know the purple is just underneath the snow but I am calmed by the white everywhere. I take naps. Under the quilt, under the snow, under, under.

I have to be part of something. I want to be in a play but I'm not up to organizing. I see a posting from Susana Cook: "I need actors." Her play is called *Consensual Relationships With Ghosts*. Perfect. Exactly where I am. I feed ghosts like I feed birds. To the birds I toss Italian bread and they come. To the ghosts I pour *acqua* e *vino* e *espresso*, press my palms together, pray, ring bells, light candles. Mom is already here. Voice immediate inside me. No slippage of time. No call and response. I join the play. Susana Cook changes the name of the play to *NON-Consensual Relationships With Ghosts*, which makes sense but changes everything. Now I am with the living—which is way different than being with the dying. The living act as if they are moving toward more and more life. They study and make plans for a 'future' unlike those who smell death near. None of us know when the buzzer will sound, but it is time for me to pretend again the buzzer is years away. I bake chocolate cake and brownies for the Saturday cast rehearsals. Susana Cook gives us a wide berth for costumes, tells us to bring in colorful clothes that express some confusion, some gender-ambiguity or hyper-gendered-ness, as we wish. I pull out of my closet Egyptian funerary cloth I've had since my student days in Cairo. I know I've told friends along the way this is what I want to be wrapped in when I'm dead. It's orange and blue and green and red and vibrant and Egyptian cotton. I fold it into a cape, put on my white *galabeya*, and silvery gown I got off Ahmed at the camel market in Giza decades ago. I wrap my head in a pink turban with gold bangles. This is how I want to be in life and in death. I paint on a spiral moustache. This is my spirit creature; turbaned and bangled and moustachioed. This is me in the afterlife.

As the play opens there are a dozen of us dressed as ghosts, standing under sheets. We can't help but laughing because it feels entirely childlike to put a sheet over your head and identify as a ghost. We've all done that as children, pretend we were ghosts, and here we are, in slow movement, walking out of a backstage brick walled stairwell through a door one by one onto the stage, just as I expect souls enter and exit the earth one by one but en masse. We walk from the dark backstage lit by an emergency exit sign and a single white light bulb, into the stage light, bright as celestial light, blue. It's like walking through blue clouds. As a ghost, I can't see anything, just shapes to sense where I am floating to not knock into other ghosts who are near. The side light makes the sheet illuminate around me. We move individually yet as a group, sway with our breathing under the sheets.

Ghosts as we affectionately short-cut the play's name, has a run at La Mama. From the stage I can see faces of friends in the first row, then rows and rows in darkness. The separation of realms; backstage, stage, audience, feels like the separation I've been living with of the living and the dead, different realms at the same time, and yet together. Outside the theater is the street and the rest of the world. It's almost inconceivable how separate are billions of lives, yet how completely whole your one life at times feels. In the audience are my friends who were at Mom's bedside in vigil and at her wake, and now they sit, bouquets of flowers on their laps and smile at me and I feel Mom smile too.

After the show, Emily comes to me with daffodils, Rose with orange tea roses, Pedro with red roses, berries on branches, and orange tiger lilies, pink mimosas that wave to every direction. I bring the bouquets home and for the first time since Mom's wake, the apartment is filled with flowers and to me it smells like the funeral again. A vial of frankincense leaked in the car, it's everywhere I go, in the bathroom, on the back of my hand, frankincense and flowers. I look into a daffodil's open trumpet — its collar points in six directions and I feel my heart open and I know I am back — in myself — and it is my time, to jump, to sound my voice while I have it. My mother is inside me and all around. I went from her bedside to the stage as a ghost in a chorus of ghosts, bangles on my turban ringing, shimmering.

As the months go on and *Ghosts* has more shows at different theaters, my experience with these twelve ghosts deepens. I feel satisfied, like I am already dead and being in this play is heaven, and everyone in the cast and the friends who come back repeatedly are spirits that meet in heaven. Simba is there, Simba who sang to Mom in multiple hospitalizations and made Mom blonde for her finale, and Susana is there, and Rosette and Salley and Audrey and Jessie come and go and Moira is there and these other angels, who are new to me with sweet faces. I dream we go to heaven and we find out that we are all part of the same star. All together we make one star. Every star is made up of so many beings.

Closing night was at BAAD: Bronx Academy of Art and Dance, the old chapel of St. Peter's under the El, turned into a queer theater by ground-breaking artists Arthur Aviles and Charles Rice-González. As I drove down, I pictured us ghosts coming from the church cemetery between the stones from the 1800's, rising from the dead in the neighborhood where I was born and raised. 10461. Ghosts under the El. Instead, I got a text message from my beloved friend, author Edvige Giunta, to tell me that author Margaux Fragoso, her former student, died. Through Edvige's literary gatherings, Margaux had become a cherished friend of mine. I threw the car into park under the El, and climbed around the wrought iron fence into the church cemetery, to be with worn and tilted gravestones under big old Bronx trees—the life dates on many stones, not many years at all, like Margaux' thirty-eight. I felt a punch in the gut grief for young brilliant determined Margaux. On the uneven ground I walked, reading what I could make out on the stones, feeling the huge presence/absence of Margaux—how giant she felt to me, how precious the sound of her voice, the bright ring of her laughter, the words she asked: "Annie sometimes I feel like I belong somewhere else. Like I'm a light being. Do you ever feel like that?"

I ambled from grave to grave. One stone read: "In life she was respected, in death lamented." Another read: "The guardian of her dust." Antique phrases among the silence of the stones with the rumbling 6 train above us, dappled light through the tracks over Westchester Avenue. One stone was carved into the shape of an open book, low to the ground. Margaux had written a powerful memoir and a novel. This is what we authors leave behind—open books, open to be read, open to be witnessed, open for truths to be experienced as time goes on. Open. We open the material of our lives, cleave open our chests just the way a book opens anterior to the spine. A rough hewn stone, words long gone. A rock chiseled open into a book to mark a life. I prayed for and to Margaux, this one young woman's carved hewn bulk of life. The 6 train rumbled overhead.

I opened the red door to the theater, lay down on the black Marley floor, and stared up into the lighting grid as the actors rolled the piano into place and the disco ball snowed chips of light around the chapel. Red Edison light bulbs were turned on and off by a beautiful young lighting designer named Emmanuel who sat in the booth high up in the rafters. The name Emmanuel I knew meant something about the presence of gods, and I felt so happy hollering: "Thank you, Emmanuel!" up into the old chapel rafters. I loved staring up into stage lights, the blue and fuschia Fresnel lanterns, amber PAR cans, the white Source Fours, Emmanuel beamed down on all of us.

Mom where are you tonight?

IT'S ELEVEN O'CLOCK and I need to know. Bombs are flying. How dare the USA call their bombs, "Tomahawks." Even bombs' names are appropriated! Trump came on TV and talked of God and God's children and beautiful babies. They showed film clips of the missiles taking off in golden light in the black sky. It is too heartrending to even tell you. I am glad you are not here to see this. I shook all night in your chair. Remember when Rocco upstairs got a heart attack in his easy chair watching the news when Bush bombed Baghdad? I felt like that, in your chair. Trump bombed Syria. I thought of all your prayers for world peace for all. Truly, what could be more profound than the wife of a marine, survivor of domestic violence, praying for world peace for everybody? I know how adamant you were in your prayers. Why is peace such an unattainable ask? The intimate costs of war, have me sick. Alas, it's a baby boomer's yoke. Born after the war, raised in the PTSD aftermath.

The peach trees are in pink buds, ready to burst into our favorite season—pink. They will flower on Easter Sunday like always. The coat closet door fell off its hinge. I had to empty the wire shelving—I threw out all your CDs; Sinatra, the Bee Gees, the blind tenor that I could never bear the sadness of his songs, John Lennon, Dr. John, all your music. What's the use? I can't listen to your music—it shreds me: "Black Magic," "Luck Be a Lady," "Emotion," "Stayin' Alive," "Cabbage Head," "Imagine." My heart is already overflowing, so even one thing sets it spilling over all the edges. So, with the music in the trash, Trump bombed Syria, and I felt those "American Pie" lyrics "the day the music died." The next day people said the bombs could all be for show. A ploy. We are in a post-truth era. His press conferences are propaganda. Lies and misnomers are the norm now. I can read all the newspapers and watch all the news anchors and his press talkers and come away with nothing to ponder, just my baloney meter hitting its red zone. When I was a kid I remember Daddy watching the news about Watergate and Viet Nam, and coming away with an opinion, a thought, a way to think about things. Now that's all changed. Put on something light and silly," Aunt Lucy told me, "watch a cooking show."

I miss your commentary, your cut-to-the-chase boil it down perception. I remember Obama's last White House Correspondents' Dinner. It was April 30th, 2016. You had ten weeks left to live on this earth. Here's your commentary. Words from the wise! I know because I recorded you.

Remember? Here you are, word for word, and thank you, I am eternally grateful for all the times you let me record! You were a good sport.

> "I wanna know what this is gonna cost. I think if the women all donated their diamond earrings, they would feed millions of poor people to eat and take care of their health and pay for their medicine. They look like they all need a meal. These are the people that decide how much food stamps you could live on. Two dollars a day. Peanut butter and jelly. Yeah, their haircuts alone must cost five hundred dollars. It's a shame they're not all bald. Right or wrong? But tonight they got on their toupees. It's so crowded, I hope they all get the flu, and they can't eat the duck. How many ducks did they kill to feed them? It hadda be a mass slaying of all our poor animals, to feed these people, to eat duck. Go to a chicken farm, get the eggs and make them nice omelets! At least you're helping a farmer. You're killing all these ducks, fa' what? Let them live! Donate them for Mother's Day to all the poor neighborhoods. They used to give out boxes of cheese in all the poor neighborhoods. They can't afford that anymore. Because these people have to eat ducks! And all this other fancy dessert. They didn't even give us what the appetizer is. 'Til they get to the duck, they won't even know what the hell it is. Yeah, first they have to say hello to everybody. O hello hello. That's the new look—the straight blonde hair like they're scrubbin' floors. O yeah yeah. I'm fine, how are you? Look at those earrings. You see those earrings? Yeah fix your hair. Look at her necklace. Yeah. The duck's gonna jump right out of her plate, it's gonna be such a resplendent sparkle! They won't know what they're eating, there's so much jewelry, and so many diamonds that the dish is gonna be sparkling, they won't know what the hell is in the dish! Yeah they're taking pictures of one another. Yeah, sure."

What would you say now? You know what some in the Arab world are calling Trump? *Abu Ivanka al Amreeki.* It's affectionate: father of Ivanka the American. Long story short—he bombed the enemy of his enemy, thus earning affection from right wing radical groups, hence this newest term of endearment—too much to ponder. I've been speechless since I heard this. O Ma! O Ma! What would you say? *Ama Annie al Amreeki!*

I've been hand-washing and hanging dry most of my clothes. Today I rinsed out my bandanas. The lime green and yellow and baby blue and orange and pink swirling in the sink made me think of the women in colorful dresses washing clothes on the banks of the Nile. I am being called into the deepest part of myself, just standing with my hands in water, swirling clothes around the bathroom sink. Water and colors and hands and the swirling motion and the ablution and renewal of it all. The way cotton dries crisp. I thought to myself, in all my mother's life, she never once sent the laundry out to be done, not once—how did you do it? Every piece of laundry hung our whole lives? How is that even possible? I am sick one week in bed now and the fridge is empty and the laundry piled, and I am too dizzy on this Ceftin to take care of myself in all the ways a human needs. So I focus on rest. I am amazed how you kept a full fridge and an empty hamper forever. A mother's love is the greatest force in all the universe. Now I am alone, although all the Catholics I know tell me you are all around me all the time. I feel your spiritual force; thousands of tiny pink fists of peach tree blossoms.

The Green Mint Jelly Candies Shaped Like Leaves

THE GIRLS CAME OVER and I saw them through your eyes. Caroline Rose is making her First Holy Communion. She recited the "Our Father" and the "Hail Mary" with stops and starts. I remember how hard it was to remember all those words! She said: "Our Father, full of grace"—so cute. *Oh!* I forgot to tell you. Guess what Elizabeth Rachele wanted to be for Halloween? Are you ready for this? I never heard a six-year-old wanting to dress up as this. Okay. Salt. Salt! My guess is that she heard the adults saying you were in the hospital because you needed salt. You know kids hear everything. It must have stuck in her head—*GG needs salt!* They decided if one was salt, the other would be pepper—then they switched roles, so Caroline ended up dressing as the salt, and Elizabeth the pepper.

I got up early and made meatballs for them. Thanks to Rosette who brought all the groceries, *parmigiano*, a pack of eighteen eggs, everything. I've been too dizzy on Ceftin to drive anywhere, so I ate everything in the house and got creative with the reserves of food. I know I gave you a hard time when you'd make a pot of chicken soup and eat it for days. To me, it seemed like giving up—eh, I'll just have some chicken soup again and again. Anyway, this week I've been sick, so Monday I boiled chicken thighs with *finocchio*, carrots, onion, potatoes, and parsley that I'd previously washed, hung to dry, chopped, wrapped in paper towel and froze—just like you did. Tuesday I added *'scarole* to the soup. Wednesday I defrosted a couple of hamburgers and made the little meatballs and added them to the *ciambott'*. Thursday I added *cannellini* and a fresh boiled beet. So, Mom, just like you, I ate one pot of chicken soup all week, but kept changing it up each day.

The girls worked in your garden. They raked and lined up the bricks and replanted all the old peach pits they found under the trees. They wanted to plant flower seeds, but I couldn't find my envelope marked: SEEDS, so Rosette opened a papaya and collected the seeds, and got some lentils and some white beans, and the girls planted them all around the court. So who knows what's going to sprout! As a kid I could make a whole world in the dirt and mud with my fingers and a stick to carve mountain roads and tunnels. And now I gotta do that with my life. Imagine it. Carve it. Be in it. I oddly feel at home here, in your apartment, I can't say my apartment because you are still here with me, you're the water I swim through, you're everywhere. I found a penny on the bed today. The copper connection mystifies me. It makes sense because of the conduction properties of metal. It also demonizes mining and drilling ore from the earth. If copper and metals and gems are conduits for spirit and humans drill and gut the earth, then humans are fighting spirit, and *that* is the great war, human v. spirit.

After we sat at the table, dishing out macaroni and meatballs, the girls found your last bag of green mint jellies. They went hunting for them in the spice cabinet. Those green candies you cut into small pieces whenever I had to undergo an MRI, those candies that took away nausea and helped us calm down and sleep. I remember pressing the buzzer while in the MRI machine and asking the technician to put a few more pieces in my mouth. The candy got me through those long excruciating tests. Your candies helped me cope. I put one up on your altar for you.

I Saw My Smile, Mom

Nine months

OUR SMILE. SERIOUSLY, YOUR EYES. In the bathroom mirror, the new one over the sink. The sink is new too. Ah, but you know that, how the hinge of the medicine cabinet rusted and busted and one day the mirror, on its swing, came off in my hands. The porcelain sink was rusted at the drain hole. The landlord replaced all that. Remember how Hector discouraged you from getting the work done cause he'd "have to break the tile?" He made it sound like there'd be plaster and broken tile walls. I guess this job wasn't worth his while. Anyway he did the job and there were three little holes in the tile wall, not bad Ma, not big at all, not like he made it sound. You could stick a pencil in these holes, that's all. They were drill holes from bolts that held the old sink into the wall. So the new sink is in, and the new mirror, and of course Hector didn't bother to bring grout to fill the holes. So you know what he says to me? Ma, who would believe this. He says to me: "Some people stick flowers in those holes." I swear Ma, your voice jumped out of my mouth, Ma, your words, your brio, your sharpness. I started laughing, and I said firmly: "Hector, go get the grout to fill the holes!" I kept kidding him, "What people? Who? Who sticks flowers in the holes in their bathroom walls? You would never say that to my mother!" So he went and got the grout.

It's nine months today and my smile is back. I am sparkling like your eyes. Nine months and the peach trees are in full blossom, neon pink under moonlight. Nine months since I last held you while you breathed your last hour. It is 11:11 and you died at noon. It is Thursday and tomorrow is Good Friday and you died on a friday at noon and we washed you at 3:00 like Christ, and today I go decorate your grave. Today we go see your name carved into Grandma and Grandpa's gravestone, your full birth name, Rachele. Today I mourn in a new way, a bright way, a green and yellow way. My heart will open. I got my smile back. Nine months, a full pregnancy of mourning. Today Audrey told me: "Imagine what world she is being born into after nine months."

"Yeah," I say, "the outer galaxy." I breathe again and smile. We shout over all the gravestones. I set up your beach chair over your grave. I play on the dulcimer, the songs I wrote for you. We make garlands of flowers. Audrey pushes a spade into the earth and plants a purple hyacinth, a white lily, a red rose. My smile is back. I can feel it open and it feels strange like a quick bird I am glad is there and hope stays or at least comes back. My smile is visiting. The birds sing in my left ear and the highway traffic in my right.

Purple Firmament

Day 321

FOR A WEEK I LOST MY VOICE COMPLETELY, and as sometimes happens, already had an appointment with Dr. Stover just when I needed it. It takes months to get an appointment, so this synchronicity is helpful as it saves me trips through Urgent Care. I'd avoided going all year, back to my own ground zero, where so much has happened; three and a half decades of Sloan-Kettering. No matter who had the cancer at any given time — my mother was always with me. If we weren't in the car together, she was waiting by the phone anxiously, to hear how it all went, every test, every word from every doctor. Today was the first day she was gone. I drove down our same secret way, the route I mapped out so Mom would feel like she was going on a trip, enjoying the Hudson River and views of the Palisades, our peaceful ride down Riverside Drive where the road was always just ours with a couple of bicyclists. Down Broadway, where she'd people-watch the myriad that crossed in front of our windshield when we were first in line at a red light — all the different hair styles and fashions. I'd drive slow just so we could catch a red light for the parade of pedestrians. New Yorkers are always on the go no matter what — if they got no legs, they're in a motorized cart with an orange flag and doing vertical push-ups up out of the chair, radio blasting. Nothing stops a New Yorker. Nothing. You got no arms and one leg? Then you kick-push your wheel chair backwards through traffic. You keep going. That's a New Yorker.

Mom loved all the action. She looked for new styles, an old style coming back: "That's coming back!" she'd say. "Soon you're going to see _____ again!" Fill that in with different lengths of skirts, odd color combos, specific prints, fabrics, the shapes of collars or sleeves, the lengths of pant cuffs, the ruffled decorations down the center of shirts, the width of ties. She had endless comments on hair cuts, colors, lengths and styles. She was shocked when growing your roots out came in, bleached blondes with dark roots. During her career, the job was to meticulously touch up roots and give "frostings." I remember one glorious moment in New York street fashion when there wasn't a predominance of any one style. It was before shaving heads bald caught on, before the beard craze, and after the sensation of hanging pants below the buttocks waned. We were at a red light on Broadway and Mom marveled: "Anything and everything is in, nowadays." She was right. You saw styles from so many trends — it was a moment. Mom loved it and taught me to see it and love it. This swirls in my head as I drive to Sloan-Kettering, and later as I reflect and write.

There's no line to park the car in the Sloan-Kettering garage. For this, I am extremely grateful. The parking attendant who has taken my keys hundreds of times over the years, this time calls me: "Sir." On this particular occasion I am wearing a poncho my mother knitted for me and a New Orleans Saints baseball hat. I speak gently to save my voice: "Hey, I'll be a couple of hours."

I walk in, pass the lion tamer poster with snarling lions, the black and white zoo photos from the 1920's with the guy on the ladder feeding the giraffe and the fancy girl in a pinafore on the giant turtle. I walk up the long ramp and see in my mind the great paintings they took down that I loved walking by over the years, the clown juggling outside the *Arc d' Triumph*, the laundry hanging over the Mediterranean with wooden chairs and table on an open air roof. I pass the safari photos near the elevator and go up. All the collected memory hits every muscle in my body and I am glad I can cry. This is the last desk where Mom checked in the last time, this is the last chair she sat in the last waiting room, this is the free coffee machine that was broken then, now is fixed. "Look Mom, the coffee machine is fixed," I hear myself saying excitedly. I softly ask the Session Assistant: "Please page Sister Elaine."

"What's her last name?" she asks, looking in her computer.

"You don't know Sister Elaine? You're working here, you better meet her. You gotta know the Saints of Sloan-Kettering. Otherwise what's the point of being here?"

I stand over the same chair I last waited for Sister Elaine with Mom. When administrators say: "Have a seat," I wish they'd understand that sometimes you can't submit — to the energy of the chair, to the dropping down a level, you can't give up your stance, your power, your hope that you won't have to wait long enough to justify sitting, things will be moving along any moment now, you will hear your full name, or something like it, called.

I fussed with the coffee machine and took a few Graham Crackers to dunk and I was right back to the last time I was here. My mind sped through the details of Mom's whole last admission and I found myself talking to her: "I couldn't take away your cross, your pain, your suffering," and as soon as I say: "forgive me," I hear my mother say:

"There's nothing to forgive."

"Letting you go," I tell her, "calling off any more medical treatment, was the hardest most painful thing in my life. When the Rapid Response Team marauded us at 3:00 a.m. like storm troopers, and that Italian-American nurse practitioner barked orders:

"Get the ABG!"

I said: *"Whoa! Whoa! Whoa!"* and told her no one was going to stick you for anything. No intubation, nothing.

You looked up at me terrified: "Are they going to pound on my chest now?"

I can still see your hands push the air in front of you, and I told you: "No. No one will ever do that. No more needles. No nothing. I promise Mom. Not one more needle."

That nurse looked at me and offered intubation, saying: "Your mother's going to die. She's not moving air."

"You've seen this before?"

"Yes."

She was crystal clear. A captain. And when another nurse came in from the station saying: "Lanzillotto has a DNR/DNI," the team vanished as quickly as they had descended. She snapped the rubber gloves off her hands as she left your room."

I hear something close to "Lahnzehloo" called and I know it's me they're looking for. I walk to the back, into an exam room. There is a new painting. A sunset. The rocks are purple. The sky is striated pink. The crest of the sky is light blue. These are the colors I expected in the sky the night Mom died. Her purple and pinks in the sunset, with the light blue of her eyes. Here were her colors, in a frame on the wall in her last exam room. This is a painting by a patient. It's never been in this room before. Mom is here now, for me, in this sunset that I know won't be here a year from now when I come back, but somehow, at this moment on this day — is here. I feel a bit of magic. How can I explain to anyone the fantastic fact of this painting being in this room on this day?

Sister Elaine appears at the door, wearing a purple shirt and sweater. Mom is in the room. Again I am glad I can cry. Sister Elaine has super direct eye-contact. She doesn't sit, or expect to. I ask her: "How's the work of the Holy Spirit going?" She raises her eyebrows, in an expression that means — it's a lot of work — constant work.

"I saw forty-four patients today."

I am the forty-fifth patient. I ask her how all the patients are doing. She prays before surgeries, after surgeries, in recovery, in treatment, in the rooms. I clear off a chair for her and we talk of many things. Today I learn lots about her. At seventeen, she wanted to go to Hollywood. "I would have liked to, yes," she says, about being an actress. We talk and talk of the movie stars she admired and who I know in detail because of Mom's narration in my life. The eyes of Merle Oberon, the spunk of Barbara Stanwyck. I'm staring at the purple pink sunset and talking with her.

A doctor comes in. I don't feel like telling my whole story to a new doctor, so I say as little as possible. I want to see my doctor, Dr. Stover, the brilliant and compassionate giant of lung medicine. I ask Sister Elaine to stay, and she nods. While the doctor is listening to my chest, I point the purple sunset out to Sister Elaine. She nods. The doctor thinks it's a distraction. But really it's the main event. Not my lungs. Not today. That purple sunset is a memorial tribute to my mother, her presence in this moment. That is the Holy Spirit guiding several people's hands who think they are making random decisions. The male doctor is gone.

Dr. Stover comes in. She's who I wait for. She's in a class by herself. "I just learned something about Sister Elaine," I say, "when she was seventeen, she wanted to go to Hollywood!"

"I was gonna say — what, she was a movie star?" Dr. Stover says.

We all laugh. She sits, and the three of us women talk intently. These are power women I admire deeply. Career pioneers. Mission oriented Catholics. And they both showed love and compassion to my mother.

I ask Dr. Stover: "What's goin on?" and she tells us: "I just gave the commencement speech at my Catholic alma mater."

"Whadjyou tell 'em?"

"These are little kids. I told them they have to have a dream. Somehow I knew I wanted to be a doctor from the time I was seven. Someone bought me a nurse's hat. You know nurses wore the little hats. I was so unhappy. They brought it back and got me a little doctor's bag and plastic stethoscope. I was happy. I walked around the neighborhood thinking I was doing house calls."

Sister Elaine says: "My father told me to give nursing a try. I loved it. The community I was with said I had a vocation. I didn't think so. But I did."

"What is the order you are with?" Dr. Stover asks.

"Presentation of the Blessed Virgin Mary."

"I never heard of that order. I went to school with the Ursulines. When I went back, there's no more convent. It's so sad. They're just living in apartments wherever."

Sister Elaine commutes to Sloan-Kettering two hours each way, on buses, from four a.m. and stands the bulk of the day in prayer over scores of us. She is ninety, and stands straight as a sprout, with pure white curly hair. She encourages and prays over us at our most vulnerable times, pulls prayers out of the pouch around her neck, prayers she's written for every need.

Having an hour with these two women is a high point in my life. They exemplify spirit and service, kindness and brilliance and they truly help people which is a miracle to me.

I get back home, I take in the mail. A paper falls out, with the image of a gold heart against a purple background. On the heart is written in purple ink: "Life's greatest blessing is having you as my daughter." I don't know where this paper came from. It looks like a jewelry advertisement that fell out of some magazine. I don't get magazines. For me, it is a direct message from my mother. No clearer message could there be. She loved our mailmen. I could just see her saying: "Hey Vinny, move over—you don't mind I take this paper out of so-and-so's magazine and slip it into the mailbox for Annie, do ya? It's perfect! She'll read it and cut it out and keep it! The other person will just throw it out anyway."

to become best friends with your Mother

Day 339
for Meghan Flaherty

1. Mom let's make this together: a dress? a hat? a cake?
2. a long walk to collect shells
3. be her mother too, take the power, make decisions
4. tell her: "This is how it will be"
5. tell her: "I am making the decisions now"
6. you once were one
7. you are her she is you
8. when you are helpless she helps you
9. protects you when you are protection-less
10. she magically brought your soul into your body
11. who is she
12. who is she this person who brought you forth into the world
13. you are linked forever
14. she wants the best for you
15. you will not understand all her ways
16. you can always count on her
17. she will never turn her back on you
18. she will dish out the truth like no other
19. you both want the same things—for you to be happy and independent
20. she has already given you more than
21. she has already done more than
22. it is already given
23. it is already done
24. now is your turn
25. already
26. something in your directness is from her
27. something in the expanse of your smile
28. and her hands
29. let her do for you what you are uncomfortable with her wanting to do
30. the baby girl she once was
31. the high school girl with her friends she was sipping from a straw
32. know her dreams
33. know the history of her dreams
34. how she was treated as a child, know this too

35. learn every story she has to tell, memorize these, write these
36. learn everything she can teach you, even if it's something
    you don't think you have an interest in, whatever it is, learn it,
    learn everything, how a fitted sheet is folded by her
37. learn all the words to her favorite song
38. listen to the story of where she first heard it
39. blast it, hold her hands and dance
40. she gave you pulse and breath
41. eradicate resentments
42. thank god you made it this far
43. this is temporary
44. life will change everything
45. life is perfect just the way it is now
46. see everything as perfect
47. perfect in imperfection
48. relish every freedom
49. do things for her she will love
50. cook for her, bake every night
51. pour her coffee, her *vino*—don't wait for her to ask
52. bring her a glass of water
53. remind her of her mother in the way you hold something
54. roll dough by the window
55. let it rise
56. today you will look back on wishing to relive
57. sit and look her in the eye, hug her, hold her hand, go sit by water.
58. share something you are afraid to share
59. they say mothers are only as happy as their most unhappy child
60. she suffers your pain
61. you are her most precious
62. her voice is inside you
63. death will only make the echo of her voice inside you louder
    and more resonant
64. she has fears you don't know about
65. take her to visit the grave of her mother and grandmother
66. honor seven generations, from her great-grandmother
    to your great-grandchildren
67. plant a tree with her
68. gaze into roses

A lot of glass just broke
Day 314

Could it be Mom and Dad's mirror?
It sounds like that much glass
I don't think it can be anything else
I sit outside, ice my knee
listen to broken glass, the secret language
my father speaks to me in everywhere I go
glass explodes around me
This has happened since I was one years old!
The crash of glass makes me flinch
the sound of clattering clunks.
I know something has ended in glory
smashed into pieces, irrevocably ended,
shattered into light

The apartment feels like a sun-bleached shell
without my life with Mom inside it
there was once a life in there
a strong life — one mollusk after the tide.
shattered into light

It's over — the story of my parents
Time I continue mine, change mine, turn a page
The painters are finished
Everything is off the walls and piled in the centers of the rooms
The mirror is in a million pieces,
the mirror that witnessed all our lives
that framed my parents' marriage, held their hopes
and dreams and all us babies high in their arms
the mirror where we always will be
waving at our first glimpses
of ourselves, mahogany carved bows framed
us from 1948-2017. Now it's empty
a wooden rectangle spiked with nails.

shattered into light
shatter into light
shatter into night
shatter into day
shatter into bright light
shatter
into light

Fruit Weight

The thing about a year is it bends
back in on itself, the topography of a Möbius strip.
Upper respiratory infections, chartreuse
coated Azithromycin, my lungs creak open
damp basement doors, my expiratory wheeze
Xopenex and Ipratrobrium bromide nebulized
"Where the air is rarified," Sinatra sang and here I am.

It's not the air conditioner I need it's oxygen
after doctors lift and move stethoscopes like cranes
from spot to spot if only the stethoscopes could do something
spoon infection out of alveoli
calm the heart like the touch of a warm palm.

To Urgent Care I do not go. I note the date—July 2nd
I cannot go so close to the anniversary
of your last trip to the hospital Urgent Care like Calvary.
"It feels like a nail," you said of the needle in your wrist
the words cause pain in the back right side of my brain
the days of trouble keeping your head up
you held onto me, the walker, walls

salt crystals I placed on your tongue
like communion, you perked up
a flower drinking orange Gatorade
your determination to get stronger
stretched and flexed your fingers open into starfishes
tight into rose buds, grasped and clawed the air
with every muscle in your hand
to clasp life, the room air was a cliff edge

Two peaches last year
we ate off the baby tree on July 4th you and me.
This year the tree is so full the branches bend low
sweeping the grass and over the walkway.
I really need help roping up the peach tree branches.
Do you have extra rope?
All the branches are heavy
and pull to the ground.

Branch to Hand

It is still to you I say
"Good Morning," "Good Night."
No peaches are ripe yet,
that was special for you,
your last two days at home.
The trees interrelate with us.
The peach tree is your mother
who feeds you branch to hand.

I need to practice letting go
when it is holding on I do
in spite of all the facts.
Grandma Rose yelled: "Accumulation! Accumulation!"
at our American ways. I need to let go,
let go, let go again. Open to nothingness.
Be okay with the emptiness.

I cook stew, lentils, fill myself with *chicken parmagiano*,
heavy sustenance like I'm preparing for the hunt of life.
I notice sixteen things in every situation
that could go wrong and I make adjustments
to keep whoever is around me, safe.

Our last year together, it was like carrying two bodies,
and now as your one year an angel day approaches
it is to the cemetery we will go
and to the church to light a votive candle.

I am learning to survive, Mom
I am learning your wisdom

Sunset: again I heave heavy breaths
overflow with tears

Nightfall: I feel things
are possible again

One year ago, on Jesus' lips

I put your A+D ointment.
This year I went back to the *basilica*
to touch his lips again
Jesus in his mother's arms
the sculpted Pietà.

But the *basilica* has been renovated
a rectangle of neon lime green light around the altar
racks of pushbutton faux candles
the room of saints cleaned
the Pietà nowhere to be seen.

"Let's pray," said Audrey but the throng
pushing singles, fives and twenties into the hands
of Saint Francis next to his sparrow
up the the sleeve cuffs of Saint Anthony
into the slit of the coin box next to *La Madonna di Carmine*
was too loud and conversational. I couldn't focus.

I looked up at the ceiling murals:
St. John the Baptist stands next to Jesus in the Jordan River,
Angel Gabriel kneels his "Annunciation" to teenage Mary,
Over the altar, Mary with the sun behind her
hands the brown scapular to the crescent moon

On the way out of church
I stepped towards the bathroom
a line had formed into a hallway
and right outside the bathroom
the Pietà!
too high up to touch the lips of Jesus.
All I could reach was his foot.

Mary gazed down at Him toward
the brown wood bathroom door
a plastic sign: "lavatory"

I feel Mary's look of pity
on all of us
all of us

Morning 362

I dream you are in the hospital
the doctor stands over you saying:
"You need chemotherapy. You will be fine."
The doctor walks out of the room and you look to me
for an interpretation: "What kind of chemotherapy?"

"He said you're fine Ma, if you want I can go ask him.
If you don't want any more chemotherapy, that's okay too.
We can just live it out, have fun while we can."

You nod and smile.

I open my eyes
put my feet into slippers
slide down out of bed and stand.
I squeeze a lemon into a tall glass of water
I have to tell myself—This is real.
I cut yesterday's half peach and apricot
and over it drizzle maple syrup.
I am so glad, so glad today
we are not in the hospital.
I put two eggs into the pot of water to boil.
I stir the oatmeal with flax seeds and peanut butter.
There's enough for two.
Your portion I'll set aside
to eat tomorrow

Ancestors' Kisses

Day 365

On the first anniversary of your death
the topmost branch of the peach tree split
in two places. The second tree—the little tree
which gave us two peaches last year
the last peach you tasted

This, day 365—it was hot, the air heavy with humidity
the wood flesh exposed like a striated muscle
I knew I had to take care of this branch, so I
stepped into the brush and stretched to cut it

but first I just stood there, under the tree, red peaches
all around me, a waterfall of fragrance, branches bent
to the ground. I felt I was being kissed all over.
Each peach a sweet little red kiss, your kisses,
on my cheeks and forehead, hand, all over my head.
Kisses of love and thanks. So many kisses.
I picked as many as I could, three at a time
into a brown paper shopping bag.
Giddy with peaches and an abundance of love,
I remembered you saying:
"On Grandma's tree the peaches
grow in bunches like grapes."
Now I say: "Thank you Mamma,"
as you said: "Thank you Mamma,"
when you picked peaches
from inside your living room window.

Each peach like a rosary bead, I count
one by one, knowing nobody will believe me
when I say: "Hundreds of peaches from one branch alone."
So I count. Guess how many?
How many peaches from this one split branch?
How many peaches made it into the kitchen?
Two hundred and forty-five peaches!

Two hundred and forty-five red sweet kisses!
Plus the many that had fallen on the ground
the many the neighbors took home,
the many the workmen ate
All together—a peach for every day of mourning.
This is my communion now,
sweet peach nectar and flesh
fills my mouth, peach after peach,
la dolce vita of it all
To be part of the ancestral flow
out the window
I spit pit

Mother and daughter lifting *cappuccinni*,
Annie and Rachele in *Ferrara, Italia*.

How can time end. It doesn't. We Do. Songs Do. — Without — no one by me we go — though while we were here we hold on to the chains of the swing

AT the Apex of — AND A CHEST PAIN COLD AS AN GRAVITY

WHEEL FOR A moment WHERE we'd see how FAR we COULD GO

A WELL of tears inside me — I WAIT IT OUT —

got you now NO SIGN ON EARTH BEFORE FALLING AT ANY MOMENT

we FLY SURE we'd BRACE. TIME IS A masked marauder AS we PUMP to REACH THAT MOMENT

The universe is Reached, Double-barreled

A DILIGENT ATTEMPT where the ink finds its page the words haven't trusted us to not get old or — SCHOOL ON ZEREGA — FOCUSED ON COMPLETING the TASK AT HAND AND the illusion of being left [lost] to have OR wander the illusion of being left [lost] to have enough to dream to a kindred state rippled into the NIGHT WHERE FLYING is its own pattern SWIRL SOUL up into the NIGHT letter + departed phrase the PRINTED I HAVEN'T been with a PAPER + PEN like I did in Catholic the Painted STROKE, I HAVEN'T been to Reach out through hundreds of years here now where the ink finds the line on the page is a blessed place. STAYING within the line. AND the ink AND making

the branch needs to be cut - but the earth - dry - over your grave ... the essence ... the flag ... three ... short earth ... I pushed the spade within heart

LABOR PAINS — love to hold all that in the daylight where others can foster the LABOR PAINS — peach the LABOR PAINS — ... IT IS LABOR

All the song + poems + stories + foster flex faith ... all the art? All the branches bend + too ... of the branches. And the ... of the fruit is too heavy ... SAP FLESH the wood waters LIKE TREES FLOW SAP FLESH CONSTANTLY BEING BORN in new forms ... the weight of the FRUIT is too heavy ... crash ... FLOW

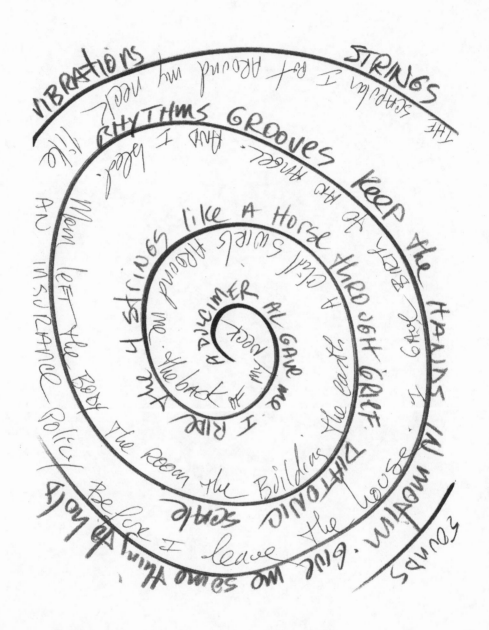

VIBRATIONS ... STRINGS

The scratches I get Around my neck. like

RHYTHMS GROOVES keep the HANDS iN motion

gave back of ho Anecc. And I bled

AN INSURANCE Policy Before I leave the house

Mom left the Body the room the Building the earth

DIATONIC scale

Blue me some thing Holy

sounds

like A Horse thro

4 strings A dulcimer swirls Around me. the back of

I Ride the A DULCIMER AL GAVE me my neck of

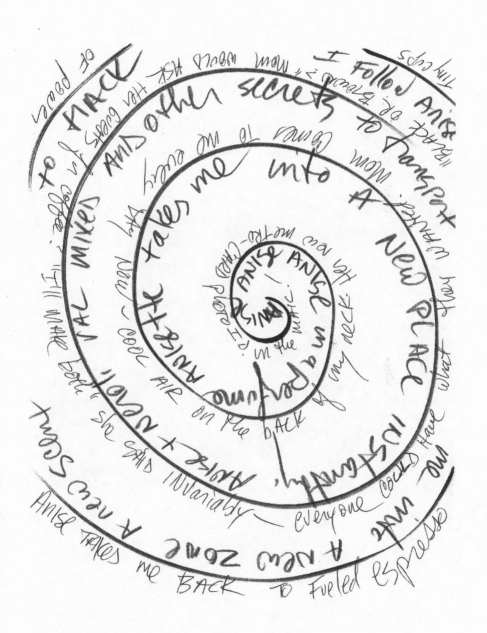

Annie and Rachele, daughter and mother, in their backyard, 1968
2433 St Raymond's Avenue, Bronx, New York 10461

Praise for *Pitch Roll Yaw*

Punk and pathos, spit and spirit, the no-holds-barred and the word unheard. There is a commitment here to barreling beyond the page — into the embodied realms of performance and the blues and an oral-scriptural recoding of personal and social history — but one that is rooted in the possibilities of poetry as "a system of meaning that honors the word." Lanzillotto's bold queering of form yields everything from hearty yet unsettling list poems and how-to poems (about lovers and family, about cancer and the city), and from experiments in Italianglish to elegant and luminously funky villanelles and triolets whose dark light rhymes with Dante. Remembering and remapping homes, from the native Bronx to the Christopher Street piers, Lanzillotto's is also poetics of the tribe (or rather many tribes), summoning what Diane di Prima calls in her *Revolutionary Letters* "an organism, one flesh, breathing joy." This one's for those other bodies of ours: the ethnic, the working class, the immigrant, the queer, the painfully racialized and gendered and medicalized bodies that somehow find their flight in song, in what Lanzillotto calls "stories birthed in light." *Pitch Roll Yaw* is rich soul raw. Prepare for liftoff!

— **URAYOÁN NOEL**, New York University,
author of *Buzzing Hemisphere/Rumor Hemisférico* and
In Visible Movement: Nuyorican Poetry from the Sixties to Slam

Explodes across the page packed as they are with joy and grief and love. The voice of the poet, recognizable and true, forces us to listen and admire the poet's willingness to risk vulnerability. Like Whitman's barbaric yawp she rails against loss and suffering, refusing to give up, to give in. The poet grabs onto life and bites into it as if she were biting into one of the peaches from her grandmother's fruit trees. She refuses to let go without a fight. Amazing poems by a poet who plays with language and form, but ultimately elucidates in narratives what it means to be human. Brava.

— **MARIA MAZZIOTTI GILLAN**,
winner of the American Book Award
for *All That Lies Between Us*

A butch Walt Whitman dressed as a queer nurse appears at your bedside and hooks up your I.V.. Poems flow into your bloodstream in long flowing lines, lyrical and sensuous giving you an instant rush of hope amidst illness, lust, abandoned love, and an unsolvable longing for a lost and gritty New York. Lanzillotto puts you under with lasagna dreams and Bronx swagger. You bliss out on the concoction, a litanic potion of the medicines she's taken, the sex she's had, the street lingo she spits, her love-wrestle with *la famiglia*, and the steaming plate of lasagna that in her weltanschauung means all is well. When you re-awaken after having experienced the full dose, you know that a world inhabited by such a passionate Whitman-esque nurse — wait a minute, that's Annie Lanzillotto! — all is alright!

—**STEVE ZEITLIN**
author of ***The Poetry of Everyday Life:***
Storytelling and the Art of Awareness

Pitch Roll Yaw

Guernica World Editions 1

Pitch Roll Yaw

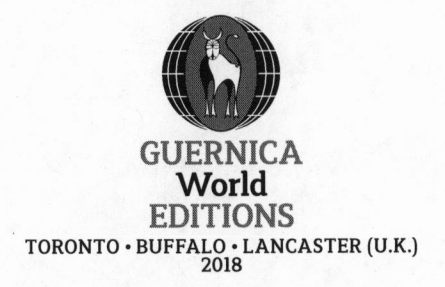

Annie Rachele Lanzillotto

GUERNICA
World
EDITIONS
TORONTO · BUFFALO · LANCASTER (U.K.)
2018

Michael Mirolla, editor
Cover design and interior layout: David Moratto
Cover Image: Annie Rachele Lanzillotto
Guernica Editions Inc.
1569 Heritage Way, Oakville, (ON), Canada L6M 2Z7
2250 Military Road, Tonawanda, N.Y. 14150-6000 U.S.A.
www.guernicaeditions.com

Distributors:
University of Toronto Press Distribution,
5201 Dufferin Street, Toronto (ON), Canada M3H 5T8
Gazelle Book Services, White Cross Mills
High Town, Lancaster LA1 4XS U.K.

First edition.
Printed in Canada.

Legal Deposit—First Quarter
Library of Congress Catalog Card Number: 2017955488
Library and Archives Canada Cataloguing in Publication
Lanzillotto, Annie Rachele
[Poems. Selections]
Hard candy : caregiving, mourning, and stage light ; Pitch
roll yaw / Annie Lanzillotto. -- First edition.

(Guernica world editions ; 1)
Poems.
Bound tête-bêche.
ISBN 978-1-77183-305-9 (softcover)

I. Lanzillotto, Annie Rachele. Pitch roll yaw. II. Title.
III. Title: Pitch roll yaw.

PS3612.A73A6 2018   811'.6   C2017-906462-2

This book is for Rachele Clare Petruzzelli Lanzillotto,
my mother, who at eighty-nine, when I asked her
what was on her bucket list, said: "Good Italian bread."
So we stopped at the best pork store around
and I got three Bronx baked Bastone seeded loaves,
roasted red and orange peppers,
mozzarella knots fixed with parsley and olio d' oliva,
marinated artichoke stemmed hearts, Pugliese green olives,
and returned to our apartment which had no heat
or hot water in January.
After our feast, we each slept,
her in the stratolounger, me on the couch,
for three hours.
It was the closest to Heaven we'd known.

Acknowledgments

PATERSON LITERARY REVIEW (PLR), Maria Mazziotti Gillan, Executive Director and Editor, Paterson, New Jersey, sponsored by the Poetry Center at Passaic County Community College. In #45, 2017: "There's nobody left to talk to," "Diminished Capacity: an indictment" (2016 First Prize Allen Ginsberg Poetry Award.) In #44, 2016: "Salút!" "God made air blue," "A Confession Unheard," "My Grandmother's Handwriting" (2015 Honorable Mention Allen Ginsberg Poetry Award.)

Philadelphia Poets, Rosemary Petracca Cappello, Editor, Philadelphia, Pennsylvania: In Vol 23, 2017: "Holy Cards," "Palm Trees in Caution Tape," "Caput Mundi." In Vol 22, 2016: "Two Moons" and "Kindred." In Vol 20, 2014: "Tip the Pallbearers" and "Church Bells and Block Ice."

Hedgebrook Cookbook: Celebrating Radical Hospitality, by Denise Barr and Julie Rosten, edited by Liz Engelman, She Writes Press, Berkeley, California 2013: "Her Giant Silence."

Streetcry Inc. for recording: "Two Pound Jude," "My Soul's Gonna Go," "Losin' Ground" and "Mother Cabrini Throwdown" on the album Swampjuice: Yankee with a Southern Peasant Soul, Annie Lanzillotto and Washbucket Blues. www.annielanzillotto.bandcamp.com. Lyrics, Music, Vocals by Annie Lanzillotto. Production, Music, Guitars, Bass, Recorded and Engineered by Al Hemberger at The Loft Recording Studios, Bronxville, New York 2016. Flute, Tenor sax by Rose Imperato. Blues Harp, Tenor Sax by Bobby LaSardo. Drums by J.T. Lewis. Executive Producers: Ron Raider, Ellyne Skove, Audrey Kindred.

Notes

ↄ

"Binocular Song" and "Listen to the Loud Ones Too" are in honor of Steve Kindred, May 14, 1944—December 9, 2014, "irrepressible American radical—student and anti-war activist, socialist, and labor organizer ... a legendary amongst Teamster activists."—Dan La Botz, *Jacobin Magazine*.

"Cowboy Coffee" is for Al Hemberger, beloved guitarist and sound engineer of The Loft.

"Two moons" and "Halo, Whisper, Shadow Echo" are for Dr. Murk-Hein Heinemann, who understood my strange desire to keep my cataract as long as possible for an impressionistic look at the world.

"Cosmology of the Sun Ball" is for Steve Zeitlin, Founder of *CityLore*, author of *Four Corners of the Sky: Creation Stories and Cosmologies from Around the World*.

"Birthed in Light" is for teachers Rhonda Einhorn and Belinda Healey, Principal Frank Geiger, and all their seventh graders at Columbia Middle School to whom I had the privilege to teach my signature workshop "Action Writing" over the course of seven years.

The last word in the poem, "Palm Trees in Caution Tape" originally was "morning." When my mother read a first draft of the poem, she said, "How do you spell morning the other way? Spell it that way." And so I changed it to "m o u r n i n g"—one month, to the hour before Mom died.

"Holy Cards" I wrote and mailed out to *Philadelphia Poets* lit magazine on July 4, 2016. Two days later I took Mom to the doctor, never to return.

Table of Contents

Introduction:

"Tuck this Accent Back into the Bronx Earth":
Annie Lanzillotto's Language of Sopravvivenza

IN HER POEM "Trach Kit," Annie Lanzillotto tells of buying some equipment she may need to save her own life. Lanzillotto is a cancer survivor who's been in and out of hospitals for over three decades since being diagnosed with Hodgkin's disease during her freshman year of college. One of her surgeries for thyroid cancer has left her with a paralyzed vocal cord, and untold hours of radiation have incinerated her breathing apparatus. "The way things are going dying of a closed up throat feels increasingly likely," she writes in the poem's prosaic meter and matter-of-fact tone. She's heard of a fellow cancer survivor, a man suffering from a similarly irradiated neck, twice saving his own life with a steak knife and Bic pen. She opts instead for the "expensive toys," a Quick Trach kit and LifeStat keychain tool. "They're sharper than steak knives. You just puncture, not slit. Puncture is easier."

Lanzillotto has a specific problem calling for a specific solution. When an allergic reaction or infection leaves her clutching for air, people shouting "Are you alright?" are of no use whatsoever. How, then, to help? Lanzillotto instructs in five crisp bullet-points: "1. If you hear me choking, don't question me; 2. Bang me on the back; 3. Get water quick; 4. Heimlich only if I've been eating and no air is getting through at all; 5. Help me puncture an airway." For her own part, Lanzillotto promises: "If you're the one to choke out in public, you'll be lucky if I'm around to pop a hole in your Cricothyroid membrane and blow."

"Trach Kit" is a startling poem, not least because it unsettles our assumptions about what a poem is and what it is supposed to do. Much as we may believe in the life-affirming properties of poetry, we are not quite prepared in reading a poem to receive instruction on how to respond in an actual life-or-death situation. We may treasure poetry for its intensity, immediacy, and intimacy, but we do not expect to be implored to assist in puncturing the poet's trachea, or to imagine the poet eager to

return the favor. We may be so broad-minded as to entertain any and all rhetorical styles as eligible for poetic discourse, yet still be brought up short by this poem's clinical, in-your-face bluntness. We may even be familiar with theories of literary pragmatism—Kenneth Burke's definition of literature as "equipment for living," the disarmingly anti-romantic idea that poems are basically just strategies for dealing with everyday situations, or Gilles Deleuze's kindred notion of the poet as a "physician of culture" rendering diagnoses of life's illnesses so as to move us toward better health—and still not be ready for the slashing but salvific body blow that is the experience of reading Annie Lanzillotto.

What Lanzillotto in this poem calls her "survivalist journey" is straightforwardly literal, a matter of simply "wanting to breathe." But the whole of Lanzillotto's remarkable multidisciplinary oeuvre—poems, essays, memoir, performance art, music, short documentary film—may best be reckoned as an evolving survivalist treatise, a practical guide and philosophical reflection on the fragility and tenuousness and (for that very reason) intense ecstasy of life. In *Pitch Roll Yaw*, as in all of Lanzillotto's work, we bear witness to the ravages of the diseased body (her own, those of dying kin, friends felled by AIDS) and horrendous violence (the casualties of the 2016 Orlando gay disco mass shooting memorialized in "Palm Trees in Caution Tape"; the policewoman who "pulled her last trigger on herself" in "Retired Bronx Cop"; the 9/11 victims whose names Lanzillotto solemnly touches at the Ground Zero memorial in "Onyx Abyss"). And yet, paradoxically, there's an extraordinary vitality to this work, a sense of teeming possibility and rapturous overflow bursting out of even the most dire and gloomy situations. The writing is exhortative, a call to action, a Nietzschean insistence on the pursuit of an ever-ascending mode of existence, a Jamesian will to believe in the infinitely regenerative power of life itself: "Ignore the blackened hands of the clock/ Inspire children with song and poetry/Read voluminously, write, create songs/Tend the earth, garden, forage. Grow, grow, grow/Listen inside your ears/Commune with the mentally ill, the imprisoned, the dead, the ones without homes,/Save all strays! Be useful!" (46)

The seeming paradox of a survivalist ethos tethered to a life of amplitude and lusty exuberance took root at an early age. On her first day of kindergarten, as Lanzillotto narrates in her stunning book *L is for Lion: An Italian Bronx Butch Freedom Memoir*, her father sent her off with these words: "When you sit down in class make sure you don't sit near the windows. A bullet coming in through the bottom of the window can cause the greatest shrapnel effect" (*LL*, 4). Good for a kid to know. Lanzi

spent his teenage years in the 1940s fighting in Okinawa. His war never ended; the field of battle just shifted from Japan to his own mind. "Your best friend's your worst enemy 'cause he's the guy you trust" (*LL*, 37) is the kind of oracular wisdom Annie receives regularly from her Marine father. Lanzi's post-traumatic stress disorder, paranoia, hair-trigger temper, and capacity for volcanic rage rain chaos and destruction on his family. He bunkers in basements and boiler rooms—oil heating is his trade—communing with his punching bag, his hardware ("... buckets of copper wire, bolts, ironings, hinges, U-clamps, flat head screws, nuts, drain plugs, thermostats, faucets, nozzles, magnets ..." (38)) and his binders full of meticulously arranged horse-racing statistics. Annie learns as a child to listen for the signs of his ascension from below, the imminence of his threat to her mother. Years later, long after her parents' divorce, visiting her father's apartment, Annie feels like "I was in a Marine camp on the edge of a jungle" (*LL*, 189).

Five terse lines in "Trach Kit" scrape the knife's edge that separates absolute security from acute vulnerability in the Lanzillotto domus: "A Marine will take action/Marines don't just stand there./A Marine will save your life./As long as they're not battering you/they will save you" (118). Fiercely protective of her mother (and passionately invested in the traditional maternal domain of kitchen and family table), Annie nevertheless feels the primitive allure of the jungle, not just its wild refulgence but also its power as a space of primal knowledge. There's a certain exhilaration that comes from being the only kid in the class who knows that the school "could blow at any moment," the kid whose father drives the family car "like a tank in enemy terrain/cigarette smoke out double-barreled nostrils ... butts flicked at the asphalt to crack into explosions" (39). Joey Lanz is proud of the way Annie attacks a T-bone steak ("... bone in my mouth and meat drippings all over my hands" (*LL*, 70)), while she revels in the way he grinds out his cigarette butt in the meat fat left greasing his plate. This is life lived close to the bone, life lived hungrily through the body's nerve endings. When Lanzi teaches Annie his method for testing battery power ("You gotta focus the tip of your tongue on the cathode to taste if there's a charge there" (*LL*, 19)), he inadvertently trains her to be "a lesbian lover of the most sensitive caliber" (*LL*, 197).

We laugh at this line as we often laugh when reading Lanzillotto. With *Pitch Roll Yaw* the laughter commences at the book's dedication page, where we meet Annie's mother, Rachele Clare Petruzzelli Lanzillotto, the kind of valiant and spunky woman my own mother (an Italian American of almost exactly the same age and disposition) liked to

call "a real pip." Here we are amused to learn that Rachele's bucket list consists of just one thing: "good Italian bread". The laughter ratchets up with the poem "Butch for Hire," where we're informed that a butch woman makes for an excellent home care companion: "Butches cook and clean as good as any femme," "A butch will watch *The Price is Right* with you/Keep the conversation light/Play cards," "butches do wound care," and, best of all, "A butch will stuff your peppers!" (29). What's uncanny is that we also laugh at "Trach Kit," and at many of the passages in *L is for Lion* about Lanzi's vexing ailments and acute behavioral problems. The reason is the sheer incongruity, both tonal and situational, between Lanzillotto's language and what that language describes. Just as a poem is not the place where one expects to receive emergency medical training, a kindergarten send-off isn't the usual time for discussion of shrapnel physics, elder care (Lanzillotto's of her own dying mother, no less) is not the customary occasion for droll musing on butch excellence, and who could possibly imagine a battery cathode having anything to do with sexual technique? For that matter, who else but Lanzillotto—to call out another of the audaciously antic items in the present collection—writes a poem/song called "Mother Cabrini Throwdown"?

More than just mordant wit, such writing betrays the underlying mechanics of the writer's mind: a rare brand of super-keen pragmatic intelligence, an ability to size up scenes, situations, problems, and challenges —to *capishe*—with stunning acuity. This can be chalked up in part to Lanzillotto's jungle survivalist skills, her Bronx street smarts, her paternal training in constant vigilance. But it also points to something Kenneth Burke associated with the very best thought and art, a property he termed "perspective by incongruity." Our creative breakthroughs come not by recognizing familiar arrangements and patterns—"trained incapacity" Burke called that approach—but by pairing up things that are not supposed to go together, the better to see what these things really are and what else they could be. Lanzillotto's humor is a blues humor, a tragi-comic humor of incongruity that insists on the redemptive possibilities of suffering, the expressive freedom enabled by constraint, the lyricism borne of catastrophe, the highest joy wrested from the deepest sadness. As in the bittersweet bardic tales spun by venerable Mississippi Delta and Chicago blues men and women, this humor is clear-eyed and piercing but never judgmental or self-righteous, never smugly certain of right and wrong, good and bad. Even as Annie candidly chronicles her father's done-us-wrong behavior, she stays lovingly and productively

bonded with Lanzi, tasting his pain in order to drink in his wisdom, learn the lessons, get on with it, survive, thrive.

The key dynamic here is the play of difference, the generative dialect of opposition, and this is not unrelated to Lanzillotto's outsider class, ethnic, and sexual identities, her masculine femininity, her self-description—writing in *L is for Lion* of her ball playing years—as "a Bronx Italian dyke who identifies as [Yankees catcher] Thurman Munson" (*LL*, 193). "All of a sudden I was a tomboy with the most gorgeous pocka'book on the block," she writes in "Spaldeen Prada" about a luxury gift from an Italian relative she ends up using like a gym bag. "I have a classy Italian pocka'book/and the pink rubber soul of a Bronx street kid" (101). We hear the wondrous street vernacular in "BronxSpeaks" ("Then this scooch walks by actin' like he's in cahootz with the whaddyacall" (108)), latest lesson in the ongoing tutorial on New York City gender-transcending expressive culture Lanzillotto inaugurated with earlier poems such as the now classic "How to Catch a Flyball in Oncoming Traffic." Throughout *Pitch Roll Yaw*, we see and feel the tomboy in action—we ourselves become part of the action—as we ride the "See Saw" concrete poems (poems typographically configured into the shape of a see-saw) that open each section of the collection. Urayoan Noel nails it when he lauds Lanzillotto's "bold queering of form"; I will go further and suggest that Lanzillotto's work represents a bold working-class Italian Bronx butch queering of the world. I don't want to shortchange Lanzillotto's sexuality—not with her poignant lament in "The Underfucked": "What happened to my one night stands/'gainst bathroom walls and beer tap eyes?/More doctors' now than lovers' hands"(33)—but I will use "queering" here in a broader sense inspired by Burke's idea about transformative knowledge and creativity: queering as the heightened vision—the clearer understanding of what things really are and what they might be—that comes of living with and through incongruity.

In *L is for Lion*, some of the funniest and most poignant passages—perhaps especially for those of us who were or are first-generation college students—come when Lanzillotto arrives at Brown University. "My father's into oil and horses," she deadpans when the research scientist who becomes her mentor asks about her family background (*LL*, 190). In Dr. Senft's lab she studies schistosomiasis, a tropical water-borne parasitical disease that eventually takes her to Egypt for field research. Meanwhile, on the home front, Joey Lanz (whose un-credentialed intellect Annie knows to be no less formidable than those of her professors) continues to fix oil burners, wager on the thoroughbreds, and chronicle

in a handy breast pocket notebook his "battle with my phlegm" (*LL,*151). For many of her classmates, the Ivy League was the natural expression of class privilege they never had reason to question; for others, it means the pious pursuit of the American Dream, the promise of upward mobility. No doubt the admissions office saw Lanzillotto as fitting the latter category. Maybe her family did too, but they had a different way of putting it. "Since I got into Brown," she explains, "my family treated me like I was 'made.' I would be an earner. I would be protected by being part of an institution, a system, a bigger-than-you place" (*LL*, 103) Never has a truer thing been said about the Ivy League: stripped of its aura and pretenses, basically it's a straight-up protection racket.

The figure of the outsider who *capishes* better than the insiders resonates with Italian Americans' self-image, one of the reasons some of us, to the endless consternation of the tribe's ardent anti-defamationists, are flattered by fictionalized Mafia dons who master and re-write the codes of capitalism even when we despise everything else about them. Writing about Frank Sinatra, Dean Martin, Frankie Valli and other Italian American entertainers, Simone Cinotto observes how "a charmingly outcast identity, a characteristically plebian cunning, and a certain dose of clannishness ... coalesced in their attitude about *working the system*— i.e. getting the most from the dominant economic/cultural complex in terms of material rewards and recognition, while resisting being absorbed into its foreign values and codes of behavior." For her part, Lanzillotto's working-the-system cunning is more impressive—nobler, one might even say —for never being about economic enrichment, only her survival and her survivalist art. When Hodgkin's hits, she's an intellectual gangster seizing control of the cancer knowledge trades. At Brown, she creates her own class, then her own major, a multidisciplinary inquiry into the science and culture of cancer from hematology to support group social work. At Sloan-Kettering she secretly sits in on her own Tumor Board meeting, armed with a speech that begins, "Linked to this mediastinal mass is a mind. A mind which needs to understand." What she understands best of all is that she's a survivor. "I was the daughter of Rachele. I knew how to bounce back. I was Joey Lanz's daughter. I could summon all my powers of public speaking. I was [debate coach] Sister Raymond Aloysius's protégé, and she was tougher than any doctor." (*LL*, 151)

It's one thing to survive by dint of outsized toughness, as Lanzillotto has done time and time again as with the thoracotomy she insisted on undergoing against the judgment of brutally candid Tumor Board naysayers ("Fagetaboutit, this one's a goner," shouted one when shown

the X-ray films). It's another to *live*, to live freely, robustly, and usefully. This kind of living, from the ecstatic and transgressive to the everyday and obligatory, permeates Lanzillotto's writing. In *L is for Lion* we learn of the artist's love of flying small planes bombardier-style, the breathtaking rush of a dramatic nosedive, the plane's wings "at such an angle that they sliced the air backwards"; it gives her life "the feeling of being in a perpetual bank turn." (*LL*, 182-183) That feeling intensifies in this collection's title poem, its words gripping the page in the shape of a curving whoosh across the sky: "I want to do in my body/what I can do in a single-engine Cessna/turn on three axes and come out of my skin/ pitch: pivot up/to the beating white sun/roll: tilt into a bank turn/over the ocean rumble/yaw: rotate side to side/along the horizon curvature"(24). Images of movement, metamorphosis, transmutation, defiance of time and space snake through these poems. "Do not honor time/Beat time./To the hoop, to the hoop, to the hoop," run key lines in "How to Fast-Break" (24). In "10/4," Lanzillotto and a college friend skip their organic chemistry midterm and light out for the territories, two "spiritual trippers" who end up in a Sante Fe prayer mission: "We looked up at each other from our textbooks/agreed to take a study break, got in my '64 convertible/push-button transmission Dodge Dart with the Slant-Six engine/popped our favorite Saint Francis cassette in the deck,/unhinged the top and let the driving wind whip it down./We sang and cried in the rich velvet blue night a smattering of stars overhead./We wanted to feel alive, not stuck in a book" (75).

One might say the same of these poems: such is their aliveness that they seem to liberate themselves from the page and take flight out into the world. For Lanzillotto, written language is not inert inscription; words are breathing, sounding, touching, and moving things. They do not signify the see-saw; they *are* the see-saw. The sentient energy—the animal realness, the fleshly presence—of words first struck Lanzillotto in childhood while listening to her older sister type: "Rosemarie's typewriter makes its own rhythm, like my mother's sewing machine, or my father punching the speed bag in the basement, or me bouncing my basketball against the cement. We all make big noises. With Rosemarie I learn that words can appear and disappear on pages of paper, and that strands of words can be perfected" (*LL*, 59) In the fifties and sixties, Beat and Black Arts Movement poets privileged live audience oral performance of the written poem ("How you sound??" asked LeRoi Jones/Amiri Baraka), often in conjunction with jazz, drawing not just on that music's hip rhythms but also its grounding in call-and-response performer/audience

connectivity. In recent decades, spoken word performance and slam poetry, allied with hip-hop, have popularized the idea that versifying should be public, performative, and interactive. Lanzillotto is down with these practices; she's nothing if not a mesmerizing performer vigorously engaged in public outreach, inclusivity, interactivity, collaboration, cross-cultural dialogue and community-building. Her verse is musical in the most essential way, the same way in which ancient Mediterranean bards, Scottish and Irish balladeers, African and Caribbean griots sang their tribe's stories in catching meter and enchanting melody. She's a walking minstrel, a mediator of community speaking and listening, ever involved in activism, protests, occupations, daily struggles of living and surviving in the city.

And yet Lanzillotto's poetics go even further in underscoring the material aliveness of the word. She's coined the term "Action Writing" for her public performances of real-time spontaneous writing on large scrolls of paper. The term recalls Action Painting, the practice allied with Abstract Expressionism in the fifties. In both cases, attention is focused on the act of creation (painting, writing) *itself*, with the effect —as art critic Harold Rosenberg theorized—of highlighting the "objectness" of the materials (paint, words) at hand. Other of Lanzillotto's creative practices further insist on the material objectness of words. In 2013, in a site-specific interactive work called "Blue Mailbox Book Crawl," Lanzillotto led her audience on a processional walk through the East Village, stopping every few blocks to hoist herself atop mail collection boxes to deliver stories from *L is for Lion*. Between these orations, the assembled pilgrims read aloud from text (passages from the memoir, private family letters, immigration documents) that a fellow activist-artist projected onto neighborhood buildings using the same equipment he and his crew had used to illuminate "99%" on city structures as part of the Occupy movement. So it was that on a warm, beautiful May evening, the living words of Lanzillotto and her ancestors optically materialized in the cityscape, the poignant realness no less than when—in "My Grandmother's Handwriting"—she tells of seeing evidence, just a few lower Manhattan blocks away, of her grandmother's flesh-and-blood hand on her naturalization papers in the National Archives (98).

In his book *Walking Blues*, Tim Parrish offers a compelling interpretation of Ralph Waldo Emerson's famously cryptic remark, "language is fossil poetry." "The poet," Parrish reasons, "is a kind of archeologist-artist, his pen also a pick, working over the materials that have already been shaped into prior forms. The poet inherits his language, but none-

theless creates a new language by excavating the remains ... With each new cycle of creation, the poet's new work still bears an imprint of some other work's remains." Lanzillotto's pen/pick bores all the way down to the geological substrate, up into the earth's agriculture, out into the human languages of work, food, sex, love, grief, and loss. Her first poetry collection, *Schistsong*, took its title from the metamorphic bedrock—"the very alive bone marrow of this earth"—undergirding Manhattan island, hard and durable enough to support skyscrapers reaching to the heavens. As it happens, the Bronx is built not on schist but on gneiss, the same substrate that lies below the mountains that rise up on the American continent north and west of the city. Gneiss is coarser-grained, with thicker and more irregular layers, and more distinct foliation—not unlike the cast of Bronx characters brought to life in Lanzillotto's verse and prose. The geological term for the rock's cross-hatched layering is *Gneissic banding*. Lanzillotto, when all is said and done, imagines herself (her voice, her words) crystallizing into the next band of the bedrock: "I'll be buried in the Bronx/have to build a box to put myself in/at the end of the day tuck this accent back into the Bronx earth/oxygenate the soil catalyze tectonic plates crashing up into mainland mountain folds./ Where d'ya think a Bronx accent goes?/To the gneiss baby, into the bedrock./Hey baby how ya doin? Yo! Whatssupp man" (114).

Meanwhile she continues excavating the remains of her glorious but embattled heritage, an Italian American culture she fears has forsaken its Italian soul, its ancient wisdom. "We've lost the language/of *sopravvivenza*," she laments, italicizing the Italian word for survival, italicizing also the larger historical contours of her survivalist journey (40). This is also *our* survivalist journey, and I don't mean just Italian Americans. When Lanzillotto nourishes the familiar romance that figures Italy as at once an Ur-Mother breastfeeding us straight from the earth and as a culture of surpassing beauty founded on its ethic of dedicated workmanship, she's delivering a universalist manifesto for our time. When she gathers with family and neighbors every September to celebrate the harvest from a tree her grandmother bequeathed by throwing a peach pit out the window ("May all creation/marinate in chianti, drink the elixir/ sap be sweet/for all life/then becomes trees/May all creation/be sweet as peaches/for eternity" (78)), or when she pines for "my father's hands' knowledge, pipe cutters that they were,/leaving the precise shine of fresh sliced copper on all us" (112), she's outfitting all of us in much-needed equipment for living.

Annie Lanzillotto's is not the first organicist jeremiad in this age of

automation, plastic, fake food, gluten-anxiety, and ubiquitous Purell. But it may be the most powerful by virtue of its voicing in a pungent Bronx accent that ricochets off the gneiss with the impact of a properly deployed Trach Kit. "Steam the carpets. Steam the couches/Sanitize! Clean! Clean! Clean!/I wear flu masks routinely,/beg for purification!/They answer the call. Relatives visit/touting bleach wipes/Clorox by the gallon, tubs of hand sanitizer/Gone is the old school crumb bun visit/casualty to gluten and carb minds/you can't even enjoy a bite anymore" (44) Lanzillotto once said of her mother, "[she] doesn't just clean, she purifies." (*LL*,15). But back then it was Rachele's soaking tubs full of white vinegar, clothes bleaching in the sun on a silver pulley clothesline out the kitchen window. Back then it was taking the hungry body's word against the doctor's—like "Uncle Frank who without—geezus what organs did he have left?—still he ate/sausage and peppers 'til he sweat, hot cherry peppers, fork in one hand, white hanky in the other" (112). Back then it was Rachele herself, barely surviving an exploded aorta, spirited by Annie to the Arthur Avenue Retail Market, sucking on a slice of *sopressata* and changing back into her old bargaining, arguing, flirting self, savoring all of the salty, fatty, chewy flavor of life (*LL*, 239-243).

This is not winsome nostalgia for a disappearing ethnic "identity"; this is pragmatic instruction on the *practice* of survival. This is a Heimlich maneuver to evacuate the toxic garbage in our system. This is knowing how to eat and live with bottom-of-the-pot gusto. ("You must learn to desire to live more than to die./Take. Eat. You must accept it. Take this. Bite./Eat everything in the garden, the cherries and the onions./Hot peppers at the stem. Everyt'ing" (71)). This is puncture, not slit.

—*John Gennari*
Burlington, Vermont
July 2017

Professor of English and Critical Race and Ethnic Studies
at the University of Vermont
author of *Flavor and Soul: Italian America at Its African American Edge* (2017)
and *Blowin' Hot and Cool: Jazz and Its Critics* (2006)

Author's Foreword:

See-Saw Poetry

PITCH ROLL YAW is organized into fourteen stations each beginning with a *See, Saw* poem—one line of two phrases separated by a fulcrum: comma, caesura, spondee, dash, or backslash, with a quick shift in weight and change in meaning. The two phrases shift the physics of the line. The line is laid out on the page at any angle that a see-saw can go. My childhood experiences of see-saws are the inspiration for the poetic line. I remember scooting my body forward or back by increments in relationship to the weight and bounce of whoever was on the other end of the board to find our equilibrium. We hung suspended, balanced, horizontal in the air. We stood and walked on the board toward the fulcrum with bravado. We rose high to the sky and at the board's apex lifted up out of our seats, holding onto the steel handle. We banged the board down onto the cement at the bottom to jolt the kid on the other end up to the sky. By the end of the line everything changes. A dramatic shift has occurred. The reader is bounced or lifted or dropped or leveled off magically suspended in air.

—*Annie Rachele Lanzillotto*
Yonkers, New York
2015

See, Saw 1:

for her the bullet was not aimed but the sky refused to take it this time

Binocular Song

for Steve Kindred.
May 14th, 1944 — December 9th, 2014

I almost remember
conversations we had
the rush of voice
loud break of your laughter
your willingness to extend the evening
to its max, but the words
the words don't fly back to me
The words are gone, black specks in the sky
on rooftops, gables, branches
quivering

Listen to the loud ones, too

Their incessant rants you're sick of hearing
will one day cease, and you'll wish
you could hear them just once more

I saw a spotlight

for my Aunt Laura Catherine Lanzillotto Gatto
November 2, 1927 — Saint Ann's Feast Day, Friday July 26, 2013

from the clouds the night you died
you told me to shine

One diagonal beam of gold white light
out a doorway

in a cloud I was sitting
on a bench staring upward

surrounded by flowers
There are roots there are huge blooms

stems like straws with capillary action
Nutrients move upward upward up

Hydrogen yanks oxygen by the hand
Plants beat gravity

Anything that goes up is a triumph of soul
blooms high in the wind

trampled under hooves
I was thinking of Bronx miracles

how you survived a truck
running over you as a child

how at your wake your eight children
celebrated that finally you were reunited

with your one unborn son and could hold him
in your spiritual arms

We rise rise
all earth rises

into sky
to bloom

Kindred

At the memorial for my ex's uncle
I realized how much love I had made
not just with her, but with a whole family.
The dead who swirled around the whole affair:
her grandmother with rows of cool porcelain dolls
her stepmother's soft fuzz and sweet love overflow post-chemo
her stepmother's mother who talked brusque as me
shot out to Vegas every chance she got, swore loud
made me feel at home in Ohio!

All the spirits I met only in stories:
her grandfather preacher who bellowed Iowa sermons
now boxed in her father's attic
her uncle's wife's brother—
arrhythmia ejected his soul from the car

A collection of flesh:
the father and uncle's good heads of hair
the uncle's defining white shock parted to the side
his pro-union politics
his wife's feet sinking in the spongy ocean
while she bends to lift shells
the ocean floor like injera
floating within us, whole fried onions
fingers licked to laughter, long nights
waiting in line for hand pounded globes
of ice-cream in salty air
beach pit fires under moonlight year after year
the uncle heaving buckets of ocean water
into the fire pit at night's end
after the full moon ascended out of the ocean
leaving its bright roots coming for us across the waters
        "I forgot you were there that year,"
the uncle's wife says to me, "that year I didn't see
the moon come up at first just the whole ocean glowing orange
like it was on fire, like a UFO had come. What a city slicker, huh?"
the uncle's wife's other brother on the guitar around the fire
now eulogizes the ocean
recedes, winds change
direction the twin ponds calm

We lifted a sail to many a wind
I watched my lover's sailboat disappear
into the horizon as the thick gray arm of the storm
reached down from the clouds, made a fist in the ocean
three hours I waited on a drizzling dune
staring at the last point on the horizon
for the triangle of the white sail
with the one diagonal navy stripe
to reappear, struggling to stand against wind

We shared books with our feet shin deep in the pond
skipped over poison ivy on the trail
made the hours last through amber tumblers of scotch
cold *Pinot Grigio* in warm ocean breeze
taught the boys how to fly
balsa wood airplanes with rubber band powered propellers
hold their breath in their cheeks underwater
we rowed across lakes
dove to find the claddagh ring the girl lost underwater
dug in sand, built our dreams
watched each other's get dismantled
got caught on one side of the tidal flood at Lieutenant's Island
and talked for three hours, the talk of a lifetime

freckles, pathologies, back stories, breast contours
wet fingers crack open a lobster
tantrums, rants, belly girth
voices' call, whisper, cry, rage, pray
things only tribesmen know
I had loved them all and lost them all

I pressed palms around the crowded memorial
in the union hall on 43rd Street, hugged goodbyes
took the elevator down out of the building
caught a glimpse of the flashy socks
with Turkish orange geometry
of my ex's newest lover

yes the strangers are all here too

But it is the flesh
of the dead
that is gone
still

See, Saw 2:

the language of leaves I struggle to read, I promised a tree yet gave you a weed

if flowers had minds

if flowers had minds they would open like hands
to the five directions if flowers had minds
they would stand and reach for sun
if flowers had minds they would grow as tall as they could
if flowers had minds they would spiral
into the core of themselves in tight red buds
and hold their power until they could bring it forth
if flowers had minds their petals would fall
where they stood and beautify and refurbish the earth
if flowers had minds they would find a way
to make love in wind if flowers had minds
they would spread seeds to the winds for the next generation
if flowers had minds they would burst
color in sunlight: striped red and pink and orange and yellow
and blue and purple and all possible combinations
if flowers had minds they would work nights
to bring oxygen to the world
if flowers had minds they wouldn't judge themselves
if flowers had minds they would grow where they lay
if flowers had minds they wouldn't damage the earth
they stand on if flowers had minds
they wouldn't destroy themselves with inhalation
of toxic poisons if flowers had minds they would climb trees
if flowers had minds they would overtake ruins
if flowers had minds they would find cracks
in rock to spring up from if flowers had minds
they would open and close
with the day with the sun and the moon
if flowers had minds they wouldn't think
they weren't as beautiful as the next kind of flower
if flowers had minds they wouldn't beat themselves up
if flowers had minds they wouldn't prick
themselves with their own thorns
if flowers had minds they wouldn't eat their neighbor
if flowers had minds they would stay together in groups
if flowers had minds they wouldn't each strive to be different
if flowers had minds they would bring creatures

toward them with their own nectar and fragrance
if flowers had minds they would be
the most beautiful creations on earth
if flowers had minds they would plug into the earth
conduit the sun, re-charge the lithosphere
green lightning bolts in soil
if flowers had minds they would wave green seats
for the sun in the wind, catch carbon, hydrogen, oxygen
if flowers had minds they would reach down deep
into soil for nitrogen, phosphorous, potassium, iron, zinc,
calcium, magnesium, sulfur, manganese, boron,
copper, cobalt, chlorine, molybdenum
if flowers had minds they would stay above the earth
while their roots clawed down deep dark earth
if flowers had minds they wouldn't uproot themselves
separate out from the source of their sustenance
if flowers had minds they would stay where they were
not seek to change places on earth
if flowers had minds they would come back year after year
if flowers had minds they'd live out their life in peace
if flowers had minds

And then God made trees

to be
our homes breathing homes,
strong flexible ironwood, cherry, maple,
tulip, oak, ash, fig, elm, peach, olive, apple,
willow, redwood, sycamore, date palm, umbrella pine,
cypress, palm, birch, poplar, linden, alder, mahogany, padauk,
baobab, and if you can find one to climb, a dragon blood tree.
Our homes radiate out from a center strong trunk, grow ring by
ring, give shade, offer air, shelter, dapple sun, elevate us from
predators, enemies, floods, grow with us over generations,
grow around us and our riggings: floors, walls, decades.
Our tree brings all our mistakes into structure. Our tree
and bones emulate one another, give us ways to rise.
What could be better than a breathing home
against wolf and tornado bite?
An anchor
to earth
to ride
out the
storm,
a bunker
with inter-
connecting
escape routes
lattice of branches
interlaced roots.
Trees provide all.
Peel your medicine.
Listen to your ancestors
whisper night. Trees provide
all from mashrabiya   to totem
trees veil and reveal   lift honor, sun arc
cradle night, moon star   one tree for each to nest
hive, burrow   a breathing home wood spiral
grow with us   for generations elevate
us by increments   through decades lift
us toward   our final home
as we ready to find   a high branch in the sun
sky molecules   breathe out
lift

God made air blue

Man makes air black
God made earth green
Man makes earth black
God made coral pink
orange teal moonstone vermillion lime malachite
amaranth amber azure violet cerise titanium
A man dives into the reef
weighted by a black hammer and crow bar
sinks his body swiftly to bash bludgeon and reap
the bounty of the ocean floor

Where are the kids who colored outside the lines?
Where are psychedelic streets and trestles?
Where is coral left to live and protect shorelines?
Where do beings create a world
as beautiful and sparkly as the gods?
O gardeners, graffiti scribes, tree planters, river keepers,
Sabato Rodia, Wangari Maathai, Kipchoge Keino,
restorers, artists, pressed earth architects, conservationists
All revved souls! Can we be saved from this spiritual crisis?

Fears are doors
with burning doorknobs
the brave open
open quickly
My grandmother knew how to become a peach tree
I don't know how to become a bee
I've stopped vibrating at that frequency
of pollination, of work, of service.
So when I die, I don't know how to become a bee
or a tree or a speck of wind.
That's the problem. Upon death we must know
how to become sweet, otherwise
what do New Yorkers turn into after we die?
Traffic?

A walking skeleton with fire in her eyes
a jacked-up heart
quick-draws her tambourine
at the end of the night
as the F train threads
the setting disk
of sun

Winter comes, bare

Novembre branches tip red, vulnerable extensions
Febbraio frozen branches — ice chandeliers in moonlight
under snow *Marzo* swells buds
shoots up strong verdant green
pink *Aprile* bursts open a thousand flags
Maggio peaches tiny as pussy willows
Giugno hangs low juiced life sap flow birdsong suns
Luglio wasp nests wrap stone turbans wound round branches
Fruits fall and start trees of their own
Agosto hundreds of pounds of peaches
pull branches to the ground
on Grandma's birthday the sixth of *Settembre*
the peaches we pick and bake into pies
Life is the weave of time
Ottobre I prune her wood
Gennaio snow makes me know
gods talk
wine blood mingle
thoughts tonight
before bed
Dicembre
Grandma's peach tree
is my calendar

Her Giant Silence

A mother owl behind the woodshed
dropped down from the pine
flapped a great silence above me
and flew off
changing her direction four times
before disappearing from my sight.
I was stunned by her giant silence.
I walked back to Oak Cabin and lay down.
The kitchen that night was suffused
with the smells of creation
the sweating goddess in her long black apron
smiled and stirred, opened the oven door
lifted out a dessert with a French name
filled with raspberries.
The farmer earlier that day taught me how
to pick nettles and whack my knees
to help the arthritis. But for tonight
I put all stinging cures aside
calm my mind from my torrent of words
open my mouth for the raspberry and cream
light a fire
hum
the moon looks sideways
rests on her elbow
a slow blue
moustache wafts by

Two moons

with one eye I see
O what a beautiful cataract
glimpse through a wet glass
Features out of focus but auras
spin round heads and hearts
kaleidoscopic magnificence
Who knew the world is a Cezanne
as you age who knew as senses dull
what comes into focus is tight to eternity
voices chime words without edges
leather hearts hold beat and sway
clarifications fade
Two moons with one eye

Halo Whisper Shadow Echo

Don't get distracted by details
the cataract says to the right eye
Look at the souls of things
how the sun ricochets auras of light
off chrome car fenders
how street lamps effuse into the atmosphere
how sky is ocean and ocean sky

Don't bother with the man on the grass
or what he's doing with his hands
See the glory emanating around him
how he blends in, darkening a patch of grass
You can see that too, the void
of energy waves, the absence
of bright auras, dark matter
Absence is visible too

Don't mess around with personalities
see right through to emanations
the patterns of energy that unite
what matter seems to separate

Halo, whisper, shadow, echo
obliterate projected energy
that would otherwise be cast upon you
Emanate to combat projections
fears, desires, needs, thoughts, shooting at you

See the harmonic blend of energy
vibrating waves into matter
See the waves of matter
see waves

This is the message of the cataract:
Matter is energy, wave patterns, light
spiritual brilliance — an impressionist's still life
the energy of the thing and not the thing

All exists as vibration
Matter is moments
become this one
glorious moment
now

Failed Haiku

for those who can edit this down to 17 syllables

After you get your cataract done
the day the eye patch comes off
you must, must! walk by The Chrysler Building
on a clear morning while the sun on a slant
splashes against the silver arcs and spire
which prick the blue sky like the needle
with precision you saw come toward your eye.
This is your reward for vision.
The fish is on the hook.
You will stand amazed
curves, lines, edges, steel miracles.
You have never seen this clearly in all your life
as this moment
and never will again.
April!

the moon's coming round through a pocket in the sky—a silver coin in denim

See, Saw 3:

Cowboy Coffee

Coffee used to be so simple
John Wayne over a fire
a canteen and wolves
howling a spiritual elixir
the aroma of horses
in desert winds
sarsaparilla pines cry.
Now it's a pushbutton
pod computer chip got it all
down to a science froth
plastic foil cup
enterprise barista world
with names no one understands
and prices with variables.
I just can't picture John Wayne
gunslinging in Starbucks.
Can you?

Bronx Cosmology of the Sun Ball

Dawn
The giant pink Spaldeen
bounces up off the grey concrete
sidewalk into the sky
That's how the Bronx sun is born

Dusk
The sun ball rolls down
into the corner sewer grate sea on Zerega Avenue

Nightfall
The goddess child untwists her wire hanger
lays on the curb over the corner sewer
listens to the rainwater ring the iron pipes
hooks the sun ball with the crook of her hanger
hurls the sun ball down at the pavement
The sun ball bounces so high it sheds stars

Dawn
At the stoop she throws
hits the point of a step
The sun ball accelerates
across the street
over the roof
into the atmosphere

Daylight
is one pop fly
in a blue lane of traffic
the chrome grill of a car
noses the sun ball
slowly westward

Made of Rubber

Where O where
can our lost Spaldeens be?
On rooftops, in gutters, sewer pipes,
attics, basements, Westchester Creek,
Pugsley Creek, Bronx River,
East River, Harlem River, Bronx Kill,
from sewers to rivers floating up out of muck
into the Atlantic where they bob up and down pink
in the ocean, travel the seven seas
wash up along barrier reefs
ricochet off ribs in the bellies of whales
along shores, dikes and beaches in faraway lands.
There's an island out there somewhere
where tens of thousands of Spaldeens rest
in the shade in crevices, caves
settle in nooks, rock crags
You know
how they love to hide
behind car tires
just out of hand or leg's reach
you know they love the dark
you know they bounce ricochet ride
every possible hard surface
All our old Spaldeens
are out there
you know
living
forever

Bedford and Barrow

for Audrey Lauren Kindred

Who makes blue glass?
Men along the Nile
In Baghdad Americans break blue glass
with bombs dropped out of the blue sky

Glass thrown in early mornings
makes me shudder
truck down
one last cobblestone corner
swallows glass this century
my body seizes the bed
over the old speakeasy

Ice, the large spinning block
ocean waves, heart waves
my blue eyes you've looked into for decades
the sometimes blue glass Gull Pond

The blue cold leg we brought to a pulsing red
taught us that we too, have the power
to change
even us
blue jewel power
heart artery oxygen
O precious breakable relationship
irreplaceable

Pitch, Roll, Yaw

Echo Tango Foxtrot
 I want to do in my body
  what I can do in a single engine Cessna
   turn on three axes, come out of my skin
    pitch: pivot up
     to the beating white sun
      roll: tilt into a bank turn
       over the ocean rumble
        yaw: rotate side to side
         along the horizon curvature
Romeo Zulu Lima   Stand on air
 Top off fuel in both wings   in the steel-tipped
  Tap the body all around   sky before I
   Climb into the cockpit   fall
   Get the tower's clear
   for takeoff. Line up the
    nose with the runway
     centerline, Full throttle
      Thrust lift leave the ground
       and everything human sized
      We are sky
       Pull up your flaps
       Aim for a cloud
      like a tunnel
       Holler joy
       at the sheer silliness
       of finding yourself
      alone in a
     cloud

     O how thick is this sky
    and unending
    You can almost stand
   on sky once you feel it
   you feel wings
   once it pushes
  against
 you

The Living Drum

We
are
all
drums
which play our own beats
Billions of drums with or without feet
Bash, bam, weave, bop, electric syncopations
All together we add beats to earth, water, sand, sky
our sacred ministrations

We are
standing drums
winged drums
finned drums
slithering drums
drums with spines
pitter pattering drums
thunder drums
tiptoeing drums
burrowing drums
grinding drums
whispering drums
floating drums
drums with tentacles
hibernating drums
crawling drums
sleeping drums
flowing drums
drums with roots
falling drums
drums that gather force bash
then fall back and recede
sucking vortex drums
opening drums

A silent drum swoops down, hovers, beats,
feather rakes the indigo forest sky
and is gone.

We are all drums
which play our own beats
Billions of drums with or without feet

What because I'm a girl! — I gotta hold my urine?

See, Saw 4:

Butch for Hire

for Mary Cuffari Capotorto, 1/18/1924—12/23/2014

If I was a little old lady
    I'd want a butch caregiver

Butches are vigilant as German Shepherds
    sleep with their ears cocked on call 24/7

follow you to the bathroom in the middle of the night
    clear your path. You are Queen.

A butch will tuck you in at night with a well-spread blanket
    say prayers in whatever language you speak

hug you, rub your back and feet
    keep your toes from curling up on one another

straighten each toe, kiss you on the forehead
    get up the moment you open your eyes

cover your shoulders when the blanket wanders low at 2:43 a.m.
    offer the strong crook of an arm for you to latch onto

be your walker, tote your oxygen tank
    support you out to the car, help you breathe

Open the windows, open the jars, take out trash
    coax you to eat, make coffee, toast your raisin bread

close the windows
    deflate and pull out the old catheter

surprise you with early morning pancakes, organize your meds
    adjust the BIPAP so it doesn't cut the roof of your nose

beg your permission then make the decision to call the ambulance
    when you say, "Just hold me. I don't want to go anywhere."

Coordinate your doctor appointments
    decant your oxygen, humidify room air

uncork your red wine
      fluff pillows under your neck and legs

keep your feet higher than your heart
      turn you side to side

revive you with peppermint
      lotion on the soles of your feet

administer Sub Q injections in the early morning
      wearing a head lamp so you sleep undisturbed

A butch has the know-how to schmooze
      with your docs' secretaries

bull through red-tape circumlocution
      when protocols blindfold and spin you with paperwork

A butch will take you to all your doctors and celebrate each day
      wait for you to apply your Pink Lightning lipstick

stir the oatmeal with a slow wooden spoon
      Escort, Chauffeur, Chef

A butch will stuff your peppers!

And butches do wound care.

A butch will walk in front of you
      when you're coming down the stairs

behind you when you're walking up
      on the curb side when you're next to the street

switch side to side
      when you're in a big parking lot

A butch will hold your hand
      tell you you're gorgeous

warm up the car, have a wool lap blanket
      in your favorite color on the passenger seat

click your seatbelt
    scent the car with rosewater

play Sinatra "Lady Luck"
    cruise you all around town

A butch's car is your private bassinet.

Butches cook and clean as good as any femme
    do windows — white vinegar'd newspapers crumpled in fist

open doors, garden your pathway all the purples you love
    make chicken soup the way you make it

chop the Holy Trinity
    celery carrots onions

give baths with water the perfect temperature
    scrub your head and back

A butch has access to women's bathrooms
    but will usher you into the men's room without thinking twice

A butch knows all the shortcuts
    drives any kind of vehicle — wheels, wings, sails, motors

Butches are good with drills, saws, shovels, picks, awls,
    screwdrivers, hammers, nuts and bolts, needle-nose pliers,

All kinds of wrenches.

Butches will let you try to teach them
    to sew, knit, crochet, iron

A butch will watch *The Price is Right* with you
    keep the conversation light, play cards

A butch will catch you when you fall.

Yes, if I was a little old lady
    I'd want a butch caregiver

And I'd give my butch time off, a door to close
     a day to stay under the covers to cry and just feel safe

Caregiver. Caretaker. Caretaker's a telling word.
     There's the one who gives care then there's all the takers.

Vultures on the sidelines, ready to swoop down
     to pick the carcass of the house, the plot, the very gneiss

you built your life upon, antiques, rings, Lionel trains
     Hummel statuettes, pennies in tin Band-Aid containers

Butches give
     And a butch comes equipped

Her neon orange belt doubles as a
     harness to support you when you walk
     catch you when you fall
     weapon to keep your attackers at bay
     flag to swing in the air to mark your location
     whip to make a perimeter when you need space to breathe

A butch can snap you back to the present moment
     when you lose your train of thought
     or are tempted to float   away   away

Bottle openers on their key chains, pocketknives, all in one tools
     Some butches go further, with belt loop clip-on brass
     Emergency Trach Kits. A butch will open an airway
     when you can't breathe. Screw the two brass fittings
     together, wipe a little spit or Betadine
     Puncture the crichothyroid cartilage, then blow.
     You should all know where this place is.
     A little piece of cartilage the puncturing of which
     can save your life. Feel for your Adam's apple.
     Just below there's an indentation.
     This is where you go in.
     This is where your life will be saved.
     Hand sanitizer is just the beginning.

A butch can break a pill exactly in half
    carry pink pills to settle your nerves
    blue pills to lift your spirits
    green herbs to open your lungs
    sterile oxygen tubing, universal keys
    to open all oxygen tanks
    yellow flu masks for when you're around anyone
    who coughs, and hard Italian candy
    to swallow all that won't be resolved this lifetime.

And butches do wound care.

A butch will catch you when you fall.

Shut off the TV. Yes Death is when you shut off the TV.

Stand behind you on your deathbed
    Call and sing the *"Ave Maria"*
        palms open
            as your skull portal opens
                your soul revs and spirals
            the silver helix soul!
        soul pull   soul pull   soul pull

Call your name
    when your last breath's gone.

Call your name
    when your last breath's gone
    through the Bronx
        you
            leave
                behind

The Underfucked

What happened to my one night stands
'gainst bathroom walls and beer tap eyes?
More doctors' now than lovers' hands

around my chest and down my thighs!
On skin the stethoscopes pry still
and I remain without big sighs

of ecstasy release and thrill.
The Underfucked! The Underfucked
am I! Awash in memory a mil-

-lion lovers' nights I prayed with luck
we'd sweat for hours not coming up
for air each other's cunts we'd suck

like oxygen masks, nebulized rare
flaming tongues defied all reason
to catch a glowing stranger's stare.

And now it's passed, pink blossom season
branches weighed low with green fuzz fruits
aloof to aged body's treason

upon the spirit shank of youth.
Days through the park my boy-dog galloped
for sun-gilt she-dogs in heat and truth.

He ran for lust in a dolphin's scalloped
wave 'til she splayed belly-up at his feet
hip pistons mounted wet walloped.

A fuck cannot make the heart replete!
My two-legged girlfriend became his *amor*
his seventeen years, we shared love complete.

And when I die and they open my armor
after all wind blows, my heart has landed
a paw print they'll find, pressed with ardor

upon my dead heart muscle stranded
his paw print, my heart branded.

No I never made love to a woman

I never made up songs in my head over a woman
never felt the first time her tongue broke through
entered the cave of my mouth
I never felt her bite hard
I never joined breath or darknesses
never felt a woman give me her weight
take my weight
hips rock, I never
touched a woman's fingertip with light
sucked nipples, bit into neck's curve like a lambchop
I never made love to a woman
nor jumped a fence
or worked my fist inside her
my tongue flipping her clitoris
I never lay in the small of her back
motherchild
sistersister
loverlover
felt her open wide
roar "Aw!"
of the primal earth
I never held
a woman cry
felt her hair
like breath
or the pond
deep inside
sap
lifted her
lifted her
No!
I never
made love
to a woman

he's softer now that he's half what he once was

See, Saw 5:
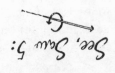

Hundreds of Blue Pills

Mr. Coffee stays in the basement next to the furnace
takes things apart, leans into light bent over his workbench:
a sawed-off chair. Screwdrivers, pliers, an awl, hang in dowel holes
as he sorts organ by organ into ritualistic containers.

Mr. Coffee assigns new purposes, high heels
are now earrings of Cinderella's mask, the ocean her eyes.
A toilet seat lid printed with the silhouette of lovers
hangs on the wall, a secret porthole to youth vast and clean.

Mr. Coffee is now a grandfather clock. Memories are coins
in slots, dollar bills are rolled up socks, dollar bills
are elbow pipes, dollar bills are rolled into a medicine vial
and stuffed into a length of copper pipe. Hot water is diverted
from the furnace into a Styrofoam cup of Sanka he stirs.
Wall tiles soak like so many teeth in buckets of acid.

Mr. Coffee is thorough. Adult diapers he cuts into strips,
wraps plaster owls as gifts for his children.
Owls need new perches and children need eyes on them.
He sorts through buckets of copper wire, bolts, ironings,
hinges, U-clamps, flat head screws, nuts, drain plugs,
thermostats, faucets, nozzles. Magnets he gives
for things they will never be able to collect, gather or name.
Answers in a black box, an airplane on the bottom of the ocean
distant as a kite in the night sky. If the string would only break
we could forget our hopes of recovering a recognizable piece of the past.
The pieces, cruel as they are, find their own uses, scatter
with the currents in the vast clean sea. By the beach we wait
stand at the water's edge, hope that in the moment we let go
what we've been waiting for will wrap around our ankles
like the pair of tortoise shell green lens sunglasses
that grabbed Mom's ankle at Orchard Beach in 1969.

Mr. Coffee stays in the basement next to the furnace.
When a visitor carries in tiger lilies like debutantes
in a vase, cut for their presentation, he hollers:
"What are you bringing me flowers for? I ain't dead!
Bring them to the lady upstairs!"
An old hand who makes sure he takes his pills on time.
His pockets she never checks or she'd find his resolute deception.

Twelve Bells

I ain't never gettin' in his car ever again.
As a kid I always got carsick.
Once that car door was shut
my girl body inside the hull
back to World War II all over again.

Our car he drove like a tank in enemy terrain
cigarette smoke out double-barreled nostrils
smoke infusion
cigarette butts flicked at the asphalt to crack into explosions
out the window wrist hinging
cigarette lectures on how to shut ya' mout'
chewin' secrets of la famiglia
'til I asphyxiate
a trap of locked doors and controlled windows
one-armed steering limp over the wheel
noxious incessant monologue
terroristic turns
for the race we are in
curb jumps, muscling out other cars
swerving, cutting people off
coming close as possible to bikes and pedestrians
threatening other drivers
overtaking cars by the right lane
taking up as much of the street as possible
riding in two lanes at once
curse shrapnel
enough for the windshield to snap

but the glass held firm
to contain in private
tobacco drenched rant
menacing glares
hard stares
philosophy that life is one bout
twelve bells
and you're left with either your fists in the air
or your cracked jaw and smashed nasal bone
on the blooded canvas

Diminished Capacity: an Indictment

It's not that my Mom and I get along better than any of you with your own mothers—really that's not it, I know it seems that way. You don't know how many times I hear from you all: "You have a special relationship with your mother," and it's true of course, we do, but we make it that way—we jump a lot of hurdles to get to where we are, and that's what I want acknowledged. Don't call me special if it exonerates you. I believe you can do it too. You can create that relationship with your mother.

I am as full of rage and resentment as any of you—or I could be, or I have been, in the past, in fact perhaps worse, I mean, I lived alone with my mother since I was a teenager. She was mother and father. We had fights fagetaboutit. I hated living in Yonkers with her. I still do. It's dead up here. We're on a 'dead end' street. Every day I see the word 'dead' and 'end' coming home, and it does a number on me. Then I come down the hill to the courtyard where we live and the sign says, 'odd.' They meant it for the house numbers, but it makes no sense. So I see 'dead' and 'end' and 'odd' and that's my story—at the same time that's the story I fight against. I was miserable and lonely and isolated so much of the time. My Mom came up here to create "peace and quiet" for herself, but what I needed was culture; a piazza, to hear a piano being tuned and a guitar played by a lady sitting by a fountain. I'd shoot water pistols at my mother's cigarettes. She tormented me, smoking, while I had asthma, lymphoma, she kept smoking, smoking. I was miserable. But I've expressed so much of it through art through writing through therapy through songwriting through performance-art, I've told my whole story or enough of it anyway. I gave the rage a place on stage. I straightened it out in my psyche. I blame art. Capital A Art can be held accountable for whatever healing I've done.

And now I've come to see her for the eighty-nine-year-old woman she is, with chronic heart failure, who survived more than most people ever will, the ascending aortic arch dissection—nobody survives that! She survived it! The colon cancer, the bladder cancer, the bilateral segmented pulmonary emboli, the COPD, man these things, fagetaboutit, you're talkin' death stop death stop death stop death. All the way back from the time she was two and fell three stories out the window into the concrete Bronx alley. She was a cripple through her childhood, then the young battered wife of a marine, I mean *holy cow!*—what she's been through! It raises the compassion hairs along your arms! We gotta feel

for our mothers, down our spines! You gotta get over whatever it is you're accusing your parents of not having done for you. That's the only thing to do. Loosen yourself from your accusations. Yeah I know your father didn't take you to one single baseball game, your mother made you slave as a kid, taking care of the younger kids, your father won't leave even enough money to bury himself so it all falls on you, your mother fed you too much and now you overeat, bread and butter bread and butter bread and butter, at least it was the best bread and the best butter. You know what my poor mother told me when I complained to her: "I never had my own room!" She answered me: "I never did either." And she was right. That shut me up from my whining. Me and her share one bedroom and one living room and we usually sleep in the same room because we can only cool off or keep warm one room at a time, plus I can respond quicker to her needs. At eighty-nine, she's a baby now. A baby who needs saving. All my life I never thought, *geez*, my mother doesn't have her own room, no, I only thought "me." That's the privilege of being selfish. We can't see over our own nose. I'm grateful my mother answered me so sharply, because in that answer she freed me from my lamentation.

You all better hope and pray your kids don't hold against you your lacks and acts, in your dying hours, the way you hold it against your parents. You know what my Mom told me today? She was on the nebulizer and out of nowhere, she says: "Your father and I adored each other. We just felt right together." You know how shocking that was for me to hear? I mean they'd split before I was born. I never saw an inkling of that affection. Do you remember some affection between your parents? If so, then their love built your self-esteem. That gives you strength to persevere. To work. To earn dough. To feel your worth. I never saw it. Never saw her hand held, never saw her sit on his lap, never saw a kiss or a hug. The opposite. The smacks. The tears. The screams. The police barging into the kitchen. I was born far too late for the first years of affection they had together, the first years with vacations, *ah*, there I go again, counting my lacks. What's the sense? If I think about it from her point of view, then she's been hug deprived and more, for a very long time. Poor woman. *Geez, Madonn'*.

She told me this story while she was on the nebulizer today:

"You know I used to take care of the phone. Your father used subcontractors. So one calls, he says to me: 'I hear you're really a beautiful woman. Word got around you're a real knockout.' So I says to him: 'Really? Did ya hear what a knockout my husband

is?' And when your father came home, I told him. That's how
naive I was. Who knows what was going on around in his mind."
When you're just sitting, breathing together, all kinds of reflections
come out.

My Mom and I have grown our capacity, have worked at it. You know,
once I got to read the vows at a wedding, not the vows, the Saint Paul.
It was my goddaughter's wedding. I read it in Italian. Saint Paul does not
use the word *amore* for what gets translated as love, but *carità*, which
translates as charity, as in 'care' as in *all* kinds of love and not just for
humans, no, *carità* is not species hegemonic. *Carità* is for the land and
the air and the water and all plants and animals and all all all. It's the
way my grandmother Rose was with every thing that grew in the fields.
The way we need to learn to care for one another and the world. Tak-
ing care of my mother is growing my capacity for *carità*. I'm so thankful
I get the privilege to walk her to the commode in the middle of the
night, to sleep at her feet on the couch when she is too panicked to be
alone, to hold her vigil as vigils must be held, not on banker's hours, to
take her straight home from hospital stays and keep her out of rehab;
rehab — if ever there was a euphemism for courting death, it's rehab! To
calm her when she panics. It's my privilege it's my blessing being the
baby, the one who cares for the blessed Mother, to give back for the
thousands of hours she nursed me back to life to give back to the one
who gave me life.

My Mom and I both have developed the capacity to help one an-
other, to heal one another, and this has been hard work and lots of strug-
gle and misunderstanding and discussion and runs counter to the ram-
pant materialism that warehouses the elderly who are drugged up to
be cooperative so they don't shout for cups of tea at two in the mor-
ning, just sit nice'a-nice in their chairs in nursing homes marveled at
by visitors for table cloths, cloth napkins folded into formations, river
views. *Dio v. Cesare* still holds, materialism is endemic and filters down
through the generations. There's a diminished capacity. Is it that people
haven't suffered enough? But everyone suffers in one way or another.
Haven't been nailed to the cross enough? Haven't had lives ruptured
enough? When you go from one privilege to the next, there's no clue, just
a rushing around to earn a million useless dollars. Shop. Press a button.
Have strangers take care of your babies and elderly. Who can cook to
heal? Garden to heal? Tend the lambs? Soak and brush Mom's dentures?
Change her diapers? Irrigate her wounds? Cream the cracks of her skin,

the heels of her feet? Carry her to bed when her legs fail? Our mothers have already done all of this for all of us ten thousand times and would love to again if only they had the stamina! Our mothers have suffered our every loose tooth and bowel! Every fever and seizure! Every cut and scrape! Every babble and irrationality! Every bedridden sleepless eternal night! Every bad decision! We've all lost all the ancestral tongue from language to healing to growing fruit and vegetable to twisting a chicken's neck to slashing a goat to survive to *carità*. We've lost the language of *sopravvivenza*. People think *miracles* are supernatural but miracles are work—hand in hand with faith and vigilant action!

I've taught myself a smidgeon of it back. It's taken fifty-two years. A smidgeon of how to help things and people and animals and the earth grow and be cured. A smidgeon of Italian and Italian history. A smidgeon of our culture. When you say "I don't speak Italian" you should also say: "I don't speak olive trees, I don't speak earth, I don't speak fig trees, I don't speak grapevines. I don't speak hearth fire. I don't speak zucchini, I don't speak *apizz'*. I don't speak *olio*. I don't speak *vino*. I don't speak *aglio*. I don't speak divining water. I don't speak healing. I don't speak spirit. I don't speak dreams. I am a deaf mute. I speak money I speak money money money speak me. I speak politeness. I speak comfort. With my indoor voice. I speak office. I speak new shoes. Everybody speaks life and death.

God help me when the day comes I need more than money God help me when the day comes I have to take account of every deed and word God help me when the day comes I need someone to wipe me and I can't do for myself God, help me now. Death doesn't have an indoor voice! If you don't have the inner capacity that comes from having a crater blown through you—to nurture to love to mother your mother, to hold your ancestors to your breast to nurse to take off your mother's MaryJanes one at a time every night and put them back on at two a.m. and three-thirty and four-o-five when she has to go to the bathroom, then find it. You see, it's not that my mother and I get along so well, it's that we've developed our inner capacities and bridged the gap. I can rage as good as anybody. You should have seen me that month hyped up on Welbutrin, slamming my mother's oxygen machine down in and out of the car, throwing doors closed, cutting off taxis on Avenue A, mouthing off to cops, making my own lanes.

Diminished Capacity: a Plea

Neighborhoods are disappearing but that's the least of it.
La lingua, i dialetti, le canzone, la poesia, la pizzadolce
la pizza rustica, la conoscenza, a way of being
a way of surviving, a way of telling a story
the way of laughter, *sopravvivenza*, a talent for life.
Let's talk about the disintegration
of the Italian American mind.
Our minds before our neighborhoods are in disrepair.
This is the infrastructure that needs to be rebuilt, buttressed.

Wealthy healthy idolaters wait in lines around corners
to celebrate births not of saints but the new gizmo.
Calendars revolve around cycles not of planting, but shopping.
The Farmer's Almanac is replaced by a fashion catalogue.
Rituals celebrate not miracles but products and seasonal sales.
Vehicular cult worshippers perpetuate the infestation of cars.
Soul is slain. RSVP'd to death.
Death disrupts the well-laid plan.
Death is when you shut off the TV.
Dogs are pocketbooks, adored and shown off
until an anal sac lets loose.
Steam the carpets. Steam the couches.
Sanitize! Clean! Clean! Clean!
I wear flu masks routinely
beg for purification!
They answer the call. Relatives visit
touting bleach wipes, Clorox by the gallon,
tubs of hand sanitizer.
Gone is the old school crumb bun visit
casualty to gluten and carb minds
you can't even enjoy a bite anymore.
Stop all kissing. Stop all hugging.
Freeze a good two feet away from each other
at salutations and valedictions.
Don't spread germs. Don't shake hands in church.
Don't sip the chalice for the blood of the Christ.
Did the priest wash his hands before handling the Host?

Stash away wise old women in nursing homes
mute as geraniums erect in chairs
money stacking no good no good at all
passed down to jackass generations
who pray at corporate altars in business-speak
lie polite sport logos to announce their tribes
forget ancient wisdoms, savor bottom lines
numb the soul into amnesia
blow-up at the slightest rupture in the conversation
blame the poor and the sick as if being poor and sick
is a lifestyle choice, forget syllables by Jesus
every potent utterance, blame the imprisoned
and the homeless then give money to the church
stuff those envelopes velvet lined baskets
coin boxes at the feet of saints
send business shirts out to be ironed but forget
the one pocket placed squarely over the heart
the only pocket that ever does any good.
Vote for anemic glazed-eye heads of state who stare blankly
at *jihadi:* "They blow themselves up—what can we do?"
Bitter edges hide beneath shadows.
The mystery remains. How to take care of oneself?
The sick and the poor, shut-ins and agoraphobes,
roll off couches on the exhale, isolated in the struggle
for food, medication, housing, transportation, unsolvable
mysteries all. Pray through night. Pull curtains closed
in daylight. All is night.
Sopravvivenza svanisce
but for the field sparrow who weaves chest hair
into a spring nest from the man
who shaves outside his neighbor's window
and violinist whose soundwaves
ride *l'armonia celeste.*
Cittadini e non-Cittadini pur!
Ignore the blackened hands of the clock.
Inspire children with song and poetry.
Read voluminously, write, create songs.
Tend the earth, garden, forage. Grow, grow, grow.
Listen inside your ears.
Commune with the mentally ill,

the imprisoned, the dead,
the ones without homes.
Save all strays! Be useful!
Hold dogs in loving arms
until *l'ultimo respiro*.
Saint Mark and Saint Luke had it right—
the worth of the mite in the hand of the beggar widow.
Calmati!
The rage that settles in fists—shake it off.
Money decays like any green, rots.
Cities crumble. Paint falls off.
Hinges that held the weight of doors
for decades in one motion
open and shut, in their final opening
like our minds, just
snap

il vento e te, accanto a me

the wind and you, beside me

See, Saw 6:
←

Tip the Pallbearers

Tip the pallbearers and the gravediggers and the priest
Away from the grave walk last
Hallelujah soul's released

Bow your head when the casket is lowered then go to the feast
Drink to the dead! To all who have passed!
Tip the pallbearers and the gravediggers and the priest

Laugh with the living as if your days will never cease
Answer all the children's questions whatever they ask
Hallelujah soul's released

Laugh for the skeletons wearing their favorite hats in peace
Pray for those left standing their hearts' pain vast
Tip the pallbearers and the gravediggers and the priest

Nights say thank you, I'm sorry, I love you, forgive me please
Applaud setting suns free souls paint pastel contrast
Hallelujah souls released

Head impetuous into the wind, pursue caprice
Laugh. Cry. Love. Breathe deep to the last
Tip the pallbearers and the gravediggers and the priest
Hallelujah souls released

Church Bells & Block Ice

Church bells at Melrose and Ahun-fiftieth ring, "Here Comes The Bride"
Same as eighty years ago when the smiling iceman was a boy
Block ice down splintered wooden chutes slide

Wagon of ice the white horse pulled down Melrose with her jutting stride
The smiling iceman at eight, was old enough for his father to employ
Church bells at Melrose and Ahun-fiftieth ring, "Here Comes The Bride"

In '41, Japan bombed Pearl Harbor, over two thousand died
The smiling iceman at eighteen was a marine waitin' to deploy
Block ice down splintered wooden chutes slide

He kissed a Grand Concourse beautician, two Bronx hearts did collide
Two years she waited to walk down the aisle full of joy
Church bells at Melrose and Ahun-fiftieth ring, "Here Comes The Bride"

Perfumed letters in foxholes, her photo he passed 'round with pride
The smiling iceman came home from war, shell shocked vicious paranoid
Block ice down splintered wooden chutes slide

War was declared over but in his grey matter enemy did hide
Their house, kids and marriage his rage would destroy
Church bells at Melrose and Ahun-fiftieth ring, "Here Comes The Bride"
Block ice down splintered wooden chutes slide

Third Eye Sword

Immediate God, adorned and ready, I see you I rush forward.
Ocean salts recharge my poles, be a harbinger for my soul.
Spirit shield protect me, keep sharp my third eye's sword.

Attune me to cosmic harmonies, every resonant chord.
Protect me in city streets that exhale fire and gnash at human control.
Immediate God, adorned and ready, I see you I rush forward.

Keep me safe and separate from my protective veneer vizard.
Heal me as I walk forward—given all the city stole.
Spirit shield protect me, keep sharp my third eye's sword.

I've lost my home, I've lost my mind, watched my family subtly slaughtered.
On hot curbs I lay smoking in a haze of old lyrics of rock n' roll.
Immediate God, adorned and ready, I see you I rush forward.

My saints all dead, I look to others instead, the humbled and the augured.
Naked in rain and in traffic I stumble, I forget when I last felt whole.
Spirit shield protect me, keep sharp my third eye's sword.

I hammer ink down in a system of meaning we call words.
Knowing life is a *passeggiata*, one sweet promenade stroll.
Immediate God, adorned and ready, I see you I rush forward.
Spirit shield protect me, keep sharp my third eye's sword.

Poetic Mead

On the moon I bleed.
O! Blue moon soul!
One more swig of Poetic Mead.

Creek bends 'round the cabin where I write and read.
Moon reigns tug silver blood right outta my hole.
On the moon I bleed.

Rest your heart's ache when your soul has the need.
Stave off death's scythe swing, of which we have zero control.
One more swig of Poetic Mead.

Lancelot pounds in on his muscular white steed.
Pen tracks life on paper, one magnificent scroll.
On the moon I bleed.

Earth spins so fast we can't feel the speed.
Heavens pass overhead, generations roll.
One more swig of Poetic Mead.

The city stands up to heaven on the good welder's bead!
Citizens slow down to pay the toll.
On the moon I bleed.
One more swig of Poetic Mead.

Death at Birth

Death at birth
The heart hears an endless baby's cry
Mamma's been stripped of all but mirth

Tears shine her cheeks, she wants to leave this earth
Mamma's feet shuffle in a haze as she wails, "Why"
Death at birth

What does a god think a life is worth?
Eight minute baby life — all too quick to die
Mamma's been stripped of all but mirth

Empty dank womb, deflated girth
again try again say try again try
Death at birth

Mamma's feet don't leave the floor, she curses church
Undrunk breast latte sours soon gone dry
Mamma's been stripped of all but mirth

shriveled seed root egg Mamma feels the dearth
ripped out her needlework, not a knot she'll tie
Death at birth
Mamma's been stripped of all but mirth

Birthed in Light

Each year I teach the seventh grade
To open stories birthed in light
As paper rolls the poems are made
Each year I teach the seventh grade
Hearts rhyme these days I'd never trade
I write with all my might my might
Each year I teach the seventh grade
To open stories birthed in light

See, Saw 7:

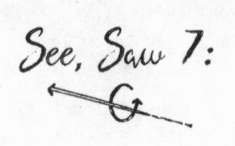

"Rumors are worthless, but become very costly," Mom.

Palm Trees in Caution Tape

*for the victims of the gay night club "Pulse" massacre, on Latin Night
June 12, 2016, in Orlando, Florida*

if only the prick went in there with his fists
for an old school barroom brawl
if only anyone in this land had the gravitas
of Gandhi whose hunger
stroked 'til all weapons were laid down
if only our gay bodies weren't veritable targets
for boys who thought they were straight
—testosterone rage
if only estrogen shots were given
as loading doses to straight boys in rage
if only trigger action could be jammed
by an app if only I could design that app
if only the word of God
was not heard: "Murder"
if if if
all these strong twenty year old boys in rage
had somethin' better to do
all these boys their fathers say were good boys
"he called to say hello the other day"
if only we really knew one another
if only rampage could find something else
besides skin to shred
if only blood could stay inside
corpuscles capillaries veins arteries hearts
if only everyone understood that gay clubs
are churches shrines, green zones
and that this is a church massacre
if only beautiful young queer bodies
did not have to be carried
out and named
if only hatred had no ammo
then we'd have a chance
in this sunny blue skied
mourning

Retired Bronx Cop

It would have been easier if we'd been born boys
rather than butches. If we could have gone shirtless
in sunshine rather than barrel strap on strong white bras
and walk around the Bronx tight
as cement in designer jeans.

Now a stone angel weeps over the thin blue line.
A good cop pulled her last trigger on herself
leaned against a fence, a sidewalk hoses down easier
than a rug. That's a good Italian American butch for you
showing consideration for the cleanup detail
even in her your most tortured hour.

In your prime, your backseat was a make-out haven
baby blue plush velvet sprayed with perfumed
seductive forethoughts, armrests that pulled up
for leaning over bench seats. Your smile lasted longer
than anyone's, wide enough to fit a cigar into
right there, in the corner of that big proud Italianate smile.

You stood formidable in the New York City crosswalk,
ushering the throng marching against war,
a sturdy cop, keeping tens of thousands
in line across the avenue
hand on hip, herding the mob between barricades,
third baseman alert, formidable, nothing got by you.

How could the earth
have offered a bit more gravity
to survive the wince through time?

Souls are mercurial
the soul we don't know
how to look after.

Your soul I honor
on this one
laser printed page.

Onyx Abyss

Post root canal
the numbness slowly wears off
my cheek as I stare transfixed
at the square hole
the onyx abyss and the waters
rushing in fifteen years of numbness
wearing off
this city
this bigger than
all of us place
this grid of grand dreams
astonishes as it heals me tonight at sunset
I ask a guard: "Who polishes all the names?"
      "One worker."
      "The whole thing? All these names?"
      "Well, I only see the south side,
the south tower, but I think so."
      "With a buffing rag?"
      "With a rag and blowtorch—
gotta regain the shine from all the touches,
all the scratches."
      "What time they start?"
      "8:45 nightly."
      "Now that's someone to talk to.
I gotta come one night 8:45."

8:45 a strangely precise time to start a work shift
8:45 with blowtorch and rag
8:45 is the time in the morning
the first plane hit the north tower
8:45 thousands of names now
burnished by blowtorch and rag
I cry tears over granite
I touch the finality
of smooth fonted names
eternal font
carved into black patina bronze
I touch as many
names as I can

This Literal City: Twinkie

The statues have all turned to flesh
and are hiding in the doorways
There are thousands of them
adorning this city
At Ahun-sixteenth Street at the far end
of the subway platform under blankets
on benches in Abingdon Square
mounted in Grand Central Station under the stair
case brass railing where they are cast
in Tompkins Square in tents
at the base of the Manhattan Bridge in boxes
under awnings of Small Claims Court
and all along the streets
on the church steps on 1st Ave at 67th
over the heat of the grate on Greene Street
in the center of the Williamsburg Bridge
inside four cinderblock walls
rectangles cut as windows
in tunnels, along train tracks
under steel girders
beneath the mammoth trestle on West 133rd
on the corner of 6th Ave at Waverly
as the next wave of headlights pass
her shadow splashes up onto the wall
of the bank her back is against
then flattens out again across the pavement
when the light turns back red
She's there every night of the week from nine to two a.m.
"Twinkie's the name," she says.
I can sit and talk with her but I gotta ante up
into her fluted paper cup
cause if I talk to her it costs her money.
"I gotta appear alone to rake in fifty bucks on a Friday night."
One night I take her into a deli. "Buy whatever you want."
A six ounce apple juice only. She's fifteen. A lefty.
Just a girl child. On the run
from some landlocked familiarized hell

allured by anonymity and sea air,
New York and its harbor
the possibilities of river movement, ocean currents
and the feeling that from here you can go
anywhere.

Telemusha

for Simba-Nyota Wa Katolo Mwangala Bushiku
Ina Banza Wa Lubu Sandra Yangala

The hardest working American
braids hair seventeen hours, eats on a dime
made it to this country where she heard
you could ask the telephone operator anytime
you needed help, picked up a subway payphone

somewhere not over the rainbow rush hour D train
skip stop underground maze clicked through and heard:
  "How may I assist you?"
To which she implored:
  "Help me, I'm lost. I don't know how to get home."
Alas! the operator was of no use and the D train
took her all the way back to the end of the line
right to the ocean she just escaped over.

We all have gotten lost trying to find our way home.

Simba ran
out of Zaire.
Born in Lubumbashi in the province of Shaba
her parents were of warring tribes
father — Muluba Katanga, mother — Muluba Kasai.
Neither tribe would accept or protect young Simba.
  "If you live in the province of a tribe at war
  with your blood tribe, they slash your head off,
  or they do *telemusha*. That's when they don't kill you,
  but they kill you. They don't kill you but you die.
  Telemusha means sliding to your death, slipping away.
  You are kidnapped, trapped on a train,
  with no food for thousands of miles.
  You die along the way."

Simba ran.
Her family all ran
in different directions.
    "I ran to the nearest city where there was no shooting.
    Kinshasa. I was fifteen."
Northwest   Simba ran
toward America   Simba ran
clear across the Congo   Simba ran
A thousand miles   Simba ran and ran
    "I don't know how many miles. I never stopped running."

Now she's the most popular nanny and teacher
to a generation of children in the same Brooklyn neighborhood
where she first asked the operator for assistance
when she found herself lost
sings the sweetest lullabies in seven languages
Lingala, Tshiluba, Wolof, Swahili, Kiluba, French, English
and after eighteen years in America
is still in constant threat of being deported.

Losin Ground

for the suicides of 1899

Waters arisin—Cajun Coast slippin away
Oil wells havin their way—with the bay
Nouveau riche asleep—on Bowery and Vine
With my songlines erased—I can't navigate time

The bridal dress—swept out to sea
When the waters rise it's a—larceny
Venezia will be a—scuba tourism
N'awlins a Disney—exhibition
Mannahatta's already a mall—without distinction
Neighborhoods—extinction
Civilizations come—civilizations go—Ask Pompeii—Hell, ask Plato!

Losin Ground—Losin Ground. Turn around baby—Losin Ground

John McGurk stopped me and—asked for directions
I waited a while to listen to—his reflections
I'd never seen a ghost before—lost in New York
Slow and limpin, one eye closed—I wanted to hear him talk

I lost my scent, said he—It all smells so damn flowery
Whatever happened to 295 Bowery!
I'm lookin for my old haunt known as Suicide Hall
but all I see is this shiny green glass and steel mall.

Losin Ground—Losin Ground. Turn around baby—Losin Ground

O! Mortar and bricks—held our stories and tricks
So soon the past they erase—this could be any old place
A hundred years ago—there wasn't a sailor on either side of the equator
that didn't hold 295 Bowery as his destination—sooner or later
But surely there's a sign somewhere to honor all who don't last?
Why does New York City obliterate her street life past?

Yo! Can you do me a favor—kind walker of the night?
Remember our backroom girls, the suicides of 1899
C'mon honor their plight

By the times these girls had found me you unnerstand
far too low she had sunk. A shot of acid in her cup
she swallowed easy when she was drunk
I never gave a girl a hand up—but never knocked one down
Each made her own fate workin her youth and looks
with sailors in town

Harbor towns got power you know—you never know
who washes up ashore. These ladies at least for the night
the sailors did adore

Blond Madge Davenport! Big Mame! Jenny Kellar!
Tina Gordon! Deaf Lilly!

Losin Ground—Losin Ground. Turn around baby—Losin Ground

Ghosts don't have—no where to rest
We're birds on wires—without no nest
Takes supernatural endurance—to endure this plight like
Paolo e Francesca—endless flight

It all goes down river—your rotten dreams
Above ground bones—your stillborn pleas
I can't help thinkin—what a we gonna do
We're so rooted in place—but the places move

Losin Ground—Losin Ground. Turn around baby—Losin Ground
Losin Ground—Losin Ground. Turn around baby—Losin Ground

From Ramses Two to Trump
we built obelisks and towers
So all could read our names
and see the size of our powers
While riches we are rakin
The poor live in jails—not of their own makin

I wasn't much better—I took my cash and ran
All the way to California—to cure who I am.
But I died anyway—with the brokenest of hearts
Two thousand miles wasn't nearly enough—for a fresh start

Losin Ground—Losin Ground. Turn around baby—Losin Ground

Hey! Mamma Earth will shake us—off her back
'Til there's nuttin to hold onto and no turnin back.
As ice melts all waters rise
Remember all truths—forget all lies.

Accept destruction. Accept decay
Remember the names of those who've gone astray
Take care of each single one
And while you breathe in this town—have you're say

Remember the past—It don't last
Live for today—Have your say
You can't guess tomorrow—what horrid things will
replace your sorrow

I walked away from my meeting with McGurk
I got no where to live—I got no where to work
I thought about the things McGurk had said
How tired he was—in his haunted head

I walked through the night 'til morning came
and shook the city bright—I wasn't the same
I thought about the scent dogs need like ghosts
to find their way home—aromatic signposts

Losin Ground—Losin Ground. Turn around baby—Losin Ground

I wondered where I was—to what century I belonged
Where I might go—to who I might sing this song
What to do with the names he told me
'cept pass them along to every listener's memory

Blond Madge Davenport! Big Mame! Jenny Kellar!
Tina Gordon! Deaf Lilly!

All the suicides of this town
through all the centuries
They say if you make it in New York
you'll make it anywhere
but what if you can't
what if you die without a name!

and I heard the Devil say:
Turn around, baby, turn around
Turn turn—Around around
Turn around baby
Turn

If you try too hard, it's harder.

See, Saw 8:

←

Bronx Grotto

Go down tree fo blocks
take a left on Allerton, a right on Matthews
and ya right there at da corner a Mace.
Dey got everyt'ing ova dey
whateva dey got in France at Lourdes
we got right ova hey
Saint Lucy with her two sets of eyes balls
yeah two on a plate, two in the head
drippin wet Madonnas we got
fagetaboutit, all the saints
you name 'em they're standing dere
but ya gotta get dere early ta bless ya car
it's late now, ya gotta wait on da line
faget the feast days—
then ya really wait fagetaboutit
ya got a coupla of buckets
basins what-have-you?
Otherwise ya gotta go back n' fort'
'n wait on da line all over again.
If ya continue on Allerton 'n hook around on Mace
dere's da johnnypump dere
ya can pull over right dere or double park
dat's where da line forms, ya better off
then ya go in behind da gate wit' ya buckets
and fill up on da Holy Water comin down da rocks.
You'll see it.
Folla' the pilgrims dere.
Take all da Holy Water ya want.
Ya gotta drink seven glasses ta cure anythin.
Oh sure dere's lots a stories.
Who couldn't walk walks.
Who couldn't see sees.
Who couldn't talk talks.
One lady I know started gettin letters
from her husband who was killed overseas!
Yeah, when I ain't thinkin straight
I put my whole head under the flowin water

stay there an hour. Drink seven glasses.
Ah, what's the sense of talkin — when I was younger
at night I hopped the fence a coupla times
my old man was botherin me
'n slept among the saints. It felt wonderful.
Man I looked up, dere's Saint Michael with his sword
keepin guard over me.
Dere's the Blessed Virgin with da full moon
around her like a mink stole. Beautiful.
The howlin dog feedin Saint Rocco a hunk a Italian bread.
Ya feel protected ya know?
Like ya got bodyguards galore. Spirit guards.
I wear my scapular, dat's my insurance policy.
If I die wit' it on, I'm all set. Dat's the promise!
San'Antonio. San'Francesco. San'Giuda
dose my three point guards.
Dey take care a everyt'ing.
Yeah we got everybody dere, whoever ya like.
Da Monsignor Pasquale saw to it.
Gino cut all da rock himself.
I pray to dem too, dese guys,
dey made all a dis for all a us.
Once a year I climb da Holy Stairs
on my bleedin' knees *La Scala Sancta*.
Dat's another story.
What? I'm gonna live and die
by what da surgeon says?
I don't think so.
I go to my grotto.
Leave nuttin to chance.
Remember seven glasses.
Somethin in dat flowin water
takes care a everyt'ing
flowin through
dem billion year old
Bronx rocks.

Salut!

I am grappa
People can only take me in small doses
a coupla drops in a glass the width of their thumbs

I am grappa
Around me
they start acting crazy
the three year old drunkenly spanks the parmigian' shaker
the bull charges me across the beach
the baritone dog barks endlessly
the six year old yells a free-fall scream into the telephone
the catatonic bursts into song

I am grappa
The love of my life can only take me once a week
otherwise she starts bangin' her head into walls

I am grappa
clear as water
but watch out

I am grappa
Crowds pay to hear me for an hour on stage
sure they'll be the stronger for it

I am grappa
Vinaccia distilled in *il bagnomaria*
skins pulp seeds stems

I am grappa
Made from scrap

The Woman Who Knows How to Eat

Tell me somet'ing'a new my love.
I have all day. *Vino e sangue*
Grapes and first oil. *Vino e sangue*
Don't give me water, give me the vine.
Water sinks the ships. *Un poco di vino per favore.*
I'll tell you when to stop pouring.
Vino e sangue Life is divine.
Long paths between fields of fig trees, sweet trees.
Drink the sap. Take it inside you.
Twigs roots seeds stems
acquavite di vinaccia, everyt'ing'a that's left.
Sure today they tro' away tro' away
the strongest bottom-of-the-pot life force.
Tro' away tro' away
buy everyt'ing'a new, new, and fa'what?

You must learn to desire to live more than to die.
Take. Eat. You must accept it. Take this. Bite.
Eat everyt'ing in the garden, the cherries and the onions.
Hot peppers at the stem. Everyt'ing.
Look at the lonely man who sells hearts
wraps intestines and parsley
around the lungs of kid lambs
soon his foods will only be found in a museum.
Pig tongue, calf hearts, eagle stew,
sweet and crazy pigs' liver
kidneys, rock partridge with ham, stuffed pheasant
salami du nord, south galantine chicken with capers
twenty-seven kinds of sausage, cardoon soup, veal rolls
with *fagiolini. mortadella di Campotosto, mozzarella in carroza,*
favi dei morti, pane di morti, involtini, shimeril, cevelade.

Today you spread butter on toast.
Yesterday we spread marrow.
You know what I hope for you?
I hope you live a life as good as I.
I walk in the middle of the road.

I'm not afraid of my own strength.
I led a full life. I created. I gave birth.
I spit pits onto the earth and trees sprouted.
I grew all the fruits. All the vegetables.
I knife the earth to mine bitter greens,
and the sweetest *i fiori di zucchini* lightly battered
lightly fried, light as wings.

I fed all living things to living things.
Birds the seeds, fish heads to the grapevine,
milk to the babies. I made love. I gave birth.
I mothered. Drank the grape.
Ate food straight from the earth.
Buried my dead deep.
I worked hard, earned these aches and pains.
My fire-escape garden fed *insalata* to a family of four.
I woke up and saw the moon go down.
Do you know what it is to wake up
and see the moon go down?
To be up working before the world awakes?
It is to feast on the succulent rind of day.

With this holy oil I anoint you so the devil's grip slips

See, Saw 9:

What Saint is that

side saddle on a white horse?
What saint is that
arms open to the sky
three gold shoots coming
out of her head?
What saint is that—halo hovering
while she holds open a book of light?
Who's the saint in the white suit?
Who's the saint all bejeweled and robed?
How many robes is she wearing
and why does she wear a crown?
Who's the saint holding the baby?
Who's the saint with the sword and shield?
Who's the saint with the cut knee?
Is he feeding bread to the dog
or is the dog feeding the bread to him?
Why does she have light pouring from her palms?
Who's the tall one with the beads?
Who's that with the thorn in the middle of her forehead?
Who's she with the bruised cheek?
Who's the one with the white book?
And her with the visible heart
is she looking at me?

10/4

Saint Francis makes me crazy
the way he follows sparrows across gables.
Saint Francis makes me crazy
the way he strips off his clothes in the piazza
hands them back to his father
and says: "Here. Here is all that belongs to you,"
in his Umbrian tongue
Saint Francis makes me crazy.

The night before my Organic Chemistry midterm
I sat with Dana Littlepage at a long table
surrounded by portraits of historical men
of Brown University. The table was polished
to a mirror shine. Big, oval, stately.
The Electron Microscopy building on Brown Street
walls so thick they held silence.
We looked up at each other from our textbooks
agreed to take a study break, got in my '64 convertible
push-button transmission Dodge Dart
with the Slant-Six engine, popped our favorite
Saint Francis cassette into the deck,
unhinged the top and let the driving wind whip it down.
We sang and cried in the velvet blue night
a smattering of stars overhead.
We wanted to feel alive, not stuck in a book.

The chorus sang:
"Lord make me an instrument of thy peace.
Where there is hatred, let me sow love.
Where there is injury, pardon.
Where there is doubt, faith ..."
We drove north.
Near Boston, I said: "Wanna go to Logan
to watch planes take off?"
The progression was natural, the call of the road
the crying and singing and laughing, the questions:
"How much you got in the bank?"

"What's the next plane out?"
the easiness of emptying our bank accounts
to hop a plane to anywhere.
Albuquerque!
We got to Santa Fe and just started walking,
the sun a guiding thumb on our foreheads
to St. John's Church where we stayed three days
for a community prayer mission.
We walked right in and felt at home
got on a first name basis with everyone we met.
Littlepage and I were both wanting to do good
to be of service, to feel alive. We were spirit trippin'.

I knocked my flesh covered skull
against the red hard cover
of my Organic Chemistry textbook I carried everywhere
praying my brain would unlock
the relationship of every atom
in the universe to every other exchanging shapes
becoming combinations of elements.
I was nuts on the other side of the glass.
I meditated on the teachings of one dedicated professor
who stayed with a group of us students long afternoons
into evenings until we *capished*.
She held up plastic models of atoms. Spun them around.
Spoke emphatically in her German accent, repeating repeating
until one by one we opened our mouths and saw in a flash
what the hell she'd been talking about.
Revelatory moments! Atoms, all things,
interact, exchange, combine,
shake hands, change through interaction.
Bashed awake, my brain opened, an old waterlogged door.
Dr. Morse, legendary dedicated genius.
She deserved a portrait painted of her and hung in that room.

Saint Francis makes me crazy
the way he understands chemistry and the elements
the way he says the wind is our brother, the moon our sister.
I look up at the voluptuous moon riding clouds.
You are my sister, moon, I say.

Death our sister. The sun our brother. Illnesses our sisters.
I telephoned Dean Donovan and told him:
"Saint Francis makes me crazy. I had some kind of breakdown
revelation. No money to come home.
Have to reschedule my Orgo midterm."
All the while, through the desert
I carried the red Orgo textbook, bigger than two Bibles
and sung the Saint Francis song as I hiked along the Santa Fe River
uphill, intent on finding its source
but it dried up along the way
into dry rock and sand creek beds, and that's how
Saint Francis taught me the word: *arroyo*

The Making of Madonne

This is how a *Festa della Madonna* is born.
One day an old lady in a new country
throws a peach pit out a window.
The old lady dies and the pit grows
tall into a tree and births thousands of peaches
and scores of baby trees.
Each year friends and neighbors come
on the old lady's birthday, the sixth of September
to harvest the peaches with her daughter and granddaughter
bake pies, eat, sing, breathe together in the peach fragrance
that fills the house, laugh, talk about the year that's past
wonder about the year to come.
unveil soft sweet pink gold peach flesh
with their teeth, tongues and fingers
fuzz, perfume, essence,
this ephemeral "being together"
soft prayers spoken
each time a peach skin breaks open
sweet flesh glow forth.

May all creation
marinate in *Chianti*
drink the elixir sap—be sweet for all life
then become trees

May all creation
be sweet as peaches for eternity
Possa tutta la creazione sarà dolce come le pesche per tutta l'eternità.

Spiritual fortification. Spiritual resistance. True Freed Om
La Madonna delle Pesche, Madonna of the Peaches
her feast day named and tradition begun
as another *Madonna* rises

The Saint of Clotheslines

From the second story dining room window
to a pole over the garage
for twenty-five years that white rope held our clothes
in our backyard on our block in our parish
in our neighborhood in our boro in our city in our country
in our world on our planet in our solar system in our galaxy
the empty rope I hung my childhood imagination on
as I watched my mother snap and hoist
wet white shirts socks green work pants out the window

After forty years I return
to 2433 St. Raymond's Avenue
to the triumphant white vein
horizontal flagpole to my mother's labors.
I open the squeaky gate
step over the scar on the sidewalk
from my father's daily kick to the gate
and walk into the yard as if I still live there
the great maple tree friend of mine that towered over the house
is a cut stump now

One word: S T A R T is still there
engraved in block letters in the cement
where my father made me my very own hopscotch board
there it is without a crack forty years later
I see the words Art and Star
within the word Start
and all the numbers one to ten
boxes in perfect symmetry
I jump in all the boxes

S T A R T
One
foot
two feet
one
foot
two feet
one
foot
two feet
one
foot
Turn

A man came out my mother's clothesline window
and yelled, "You're trespassing!"
I looked up and saw our kitchen ceiling behind him
that my mother painted with Q-tips up on the ladder
to get white paint into the concave pattern of the recessed tin.
"This is private property," the man yelled down on me.

And now sitting here writing, I think:
"Don't trespass on my memories, man.
My memories are private property"
where my mother pinches wooden clothespins
to clamp our socks to bleach in the sun
the silver pulley hangs on the painted hook
drilled into the exterior wall
my mother leans half out the window and all over the world
wet laundry drips down onto cement
over yards, on rooftops, between alleyways,
across canals in the sun
women, stories high, window to window,
building to building
as clotheslines lace us all together

And as an answer from the Saint of Clotheslines
as I drive off the block
and turn my head for a parting glance
my mother's clothesline drips

with fresh wet shirts and socks
polka-dotting the concrete below
sleeves like windsocks
the Bronx breeze
waving

Two Pound Jude

for Robin Jude Cole Henderson

Two Pound Jude!—Two Pound Jude!
Daddy didn't know no—Saint but Jude
Two Pound Jude—from New Orleans
Where everything was pristine clean—in her house!

Two Pound Jude!—Two Pound Jude!
Daddy didn't know no—Saint but Jude (so she's)
Two Pound Jude—from New Orleans
Where everything was pristine clean—in her house!

Born a coupla months—too soon
Arrived on the scene—like a Brigadoon
Momma tripped and fell—over the cat
Baby Jude was comin' and—that was that

Way down Houma—the bayou town
Werden't no hospital—that far down
Doctor's office—would have to do
The great Alan Ellender—to Jude's rescue!

Two Pound Jude!—Two Pound Jude!
Daddy didn't know no—Saint but Jude
Two Pound Jude—from New Orleans
Where everything was pristine clean—in her house!

Two Pound Jude!—Two Pound Jude!
Daddy didn't know no—Saint but Jude (so she's)
Two Pound Jude—from New Orleans
Where everything was pristine clean—in her house!

Daddy 'n Aunt Rosalie—the nurse
wrapped Jude in a shoebox—hell it coulda been worse!
and ran her up—Highway Ninety
to the city hospital—called Charity

The second oldest hospital in The — United States
Just after Bellevue — Could they save Jude's fates?
Momma knew — just what to do
poured milk into an eyedropper — for baby Jude!

They named her Robin — but someone said
"You need a Saint's name — to bless that baby girl's head!"
Daddy didn't know no — Saint but Jude
And that's how she became —

Two Pound Jude! — Two Pound Jude!
Daddy didn't know no — Saint but Jude
Two Pound Jude — from New Orleans
Where everything was pristine clean — in her house!

Two Pound Jude! — Two Pound Jude!
Daddy didn't know no — Saint but Jude (so she's)
Two Pound Jude — from New Orleans
Where everything was pristine clean — in her house!

Daddy's little girl — O he did adore!
Gave her pencils, crayons, chalk — so she could draw
She made her first mark — 'fore she could walk
Daddy showed her just how — to grip the chalk

Up in the crib — you know Jude stood tall
Made her drawings — up on the wall
Life came to Jude — drop by drop from birth
Jude drew her pictures — for all life was worth!

Two Pound Jude! — Two Pound Jude!
Daddy didn't know no — Saint but Jude (so she's)
Two Pound Jude — from New Orleans
Where she mixed Terracotta — and Capri Green (in her house!)

Two Pound Jude! — Two Pound Jude!
Daddy didn't know no — Saint but Jude (so she's)
Two Pound Jude — from New Orleans
Where she mixed Terracotta — and Capri Green (in her house!)

'Twas a fine day — she wed the sculptor Antony!
Then the great storm came and — swept out to sea
Her bridal dress — and all their things
Yes the storm picked the lock — left them with nothing
but their collection of blessed rocks
they picked up in their travels
Rocks people gave to them over the years
Can you imagine you come home
you open the door and everything's gone
except your collection of rocks?

In the wake — of that fateful day
The hospital called Charity — was washed away
And remains abandoned — to this day!

Two Pound Jude! — Two Pound Jude!
Daddy didn't know no — Saint but Jude (so she's)
Two Pound Jude — from New Orleans
Where she mixed Terracotta & Capri Green — in her house!

Fibonacci guides Jude's dreams
Zero, one, one, two, three, five, eight, thirteen!
Paint on canvass — Jude's blues and greens
Creation of a world of peace — serene

Two Pound Jude! — Two Pound Jude!
Daddy didn't know no — Saint but Jude
Two Pound Jude — from New Orleans
Where everything was pristine clean — in her house!

Two Pound Jude! — Two Pound Jude!
Daddy didn't know no — Saint but Jude (so she's)
Two Pound Jude — from New Orleans
Where everything was pristine clean — in her house!

Mother Cabrini Throwdown

Mother Cabrini walked here
Mother Cabrini walked here
Mother Cabrini walked here
and threw down
and threw down
and threw down
Mother Cabrini Throwdown
Mother Cabrini Throwdown
Mother Cabrini Throwdown
aThrowdown
aThrowdown
Throwdown

Everywhere she walked
Everywhere she walked
Everywhere she walked
Mother Cabrini threw down

She asked to go to China to serve the poor
but the Pope said, "I'll send you where they need you more.
Go to the U.S. of A. Help those Italian-American immigrants
and all the wretched strays. Go to the U.S. of A."

'Twas 1889 when she landed in New York
English, the Italians could barely talk.
She got street smart, rolled up her sleeves
Her secret power was she did believe!

Il Cuore Sacro di Jesu
gave her the power to create and do.
She founded her own religious order
Thousands of sisters to work across all borders!

She founded organizations.
How many!? — Sixty-seven!
Her deep devotion made earth a Cabrini brand Heaven.

Everywhere she walked
Everywhere she walked
Everywhere she walked
Mother Cabrini threw down

Schools! Homes! Hospitals! Orphanages!
Schools! Homes! Hospitals! Orphanages!
Settlement Houses! Classes! Programs!
Training Centers! Nurseries!
Micro-business in embroidery!
Schools! Homes! Hospitals! Orphanages!
Schools! Homes! Hospitals! Orphanages!

Le Sorrelle di Cuore Sacro di Jesu!

Think a' the trend nowadays, they're tearing down hospitals
all for what the landlord craves—puttin' hotels in their place!
They turn cathedrals into condominiums.
The priority?—Private wealth
instead of community spiritual health!
Church bells ring no more
tuning the souls of the rich and poor.
O! Church bells ring no more! Church bells ring no more!
Church bells don't ring in condominiums, that's for sure.

Mother to all
Mother to all
Mother to all
Be a Mother to all
Everywhere you walk
Everywhere you walk
Everywhere you walk
Be a Mother to all!

Give 'em somethin' to eat, give 'em somewhere to rest.
Give the poor and the sick, and the lonely and the disinherited
and the jailed and the orphaned and the ones with no where to be
Mother them! Be a Mother to all!

Everywhere you walk
And she walked
And she walked
And she walked
And she walked
Everywhere she walked
Mother Cabrini threw down!

Mother Cabrini Throwdown
Mother Cabrini Throwdown
Mother Cabrini Throwdown
Spirit throwdown
Spirit throwdown
Spirit throwdown
Throwdown

Do the Mother Cabrini Throwdown, for goodness sake,
everywhere you walk, leave good in your wake!

Be a Mother to all
Be a Mother to all
Be a Mother to all

as you walk
as you walk
as you walk
as you walk
You walk
you walk
yeah you walk
you walk
as you walk
and walk
and walk
and walk
and walk
and walk

Mother Cabrini Throwdown
Mother Cabrini Throwdown
Mother Cabrini Throwdown
and walk
and walk
and walk
and walk
Camina, Camina
acamina, acamina
Camina Mahatmamamma Cabrini
Camina Mahatmamamma Cabrini
Camina, camina
Mahatmamammama
mamamma
mammama
Mahatma Cabrini
mammama, acamina, camina
ooo camina
Mammamamma Cabrina, camina, camina
ooo sciamaninn!

My Soul's Gonna Go

If you see me out late—You know that I know
One of these nights—My soul's gonna go
Gonna take my soul—One day when I don't know
My body and me—My soul's gotta be free

If you see me dancing wild—With a big smile
You know it's cause I know—One of these spirals
Gonna take my soul—One day when I don't know
My body and me—My soul's gotta be free

Tonight might be the night that I die—Let's keep it real
Tonight might be the night that I die—But it's alright

If you see me drive fast—You know it won't last
One of these days—My life will be past
Gonna take my soul—One day when I don't know
My body and me—My soul's gotta be free

If you see me jump high—Up to the sky
You know it's my soul—Just waving hello
With the wind in my hair—You know I feel free
My soul's gonna fly—Away from me

Tonight might be the night that I die—Let's keep it real
Tonight might be the night that I die—But it's alright

If I kiss you too many—Times or too deep
Don't you know one day I won't—Wake from my sleep
If I hug you too hard—Or hug you too much
Don't you know one day—I won't be able to touch

Return to the sea—My soul away from me
Return to the sky—My soul must fly
Return to the earth—Place of birth
I know one of these days—My soul's worth

Tonight might be the night that I die — Let's keep it real
Tonight might be the night that I die — But it's alright

One of these days my — Heart will stop its beating
One of these days my — Mind will stop its cheating
One of these days my — Bones will break
One of these days — One of these nights
One of these minutes — I can bet my life
My body and me — My soul's gotta be free

Tonight might be the night that I die — Let's keep it real
Tonight might be the night that I die — But it's alright

Tonight might be the night that I die — Let's keep it real
Tonight might be the night that I die — But it's alright

See, Saw 10:

_G⟶

"I'm sure she's as good as anybody else, they all say one thing and do another."

Mom, verbatim, on Hillary Clinton's announcement
of her second bid for the U.S. Presidency, June 2015

For the old

woman in Bedford Hills Correctional Facility
who sits stationary as the pines
weaving the silence around her
with a metallic green crochet hook
linking bright yarn through all the colors of the rainbow
to protect as many women's heads
as she can cover—in one life of time

I wear your rainbow beret with the blessing
with which you arranged it on the crown of my head
your aged wise eyes brown with a ring of sapphire
a soft halo of white hair
against Bedford Hill's yellow cinderblock halls
so narrow you can't help but walk right smack into trouble
even when you need to walk the other way

Cinderella cinderblock yellow brick
yellow yellow brick blocked road block
geese, cardinals, sparrows, red-winged blackbirds
never knew you were caged
just that concertina wire curled bright silver with burning razors
under the icy Westchester sun
rambling clouds the sky beat down

I arrest society here and now for cutting
you out of itself, for withering women
behind bars, hurt girls hurt early
with early girl hurt girls hurt
locked in cars by perpetrators
girls names in blurred ink illegible
slip through the god's list
'spose to be consecrated oil keeps babies slippery
at Baptism from the Divil's grip
'spose to be you can outrun the Divil
get a move on, but behind bars where's there to run
only one direction to walk in, stay in line
babies not 'spose to slip through the gods' hands ever

All the forgotten women I remember
no public protest movements
chant for your release

Caput Mundi

Iranian President protected from a glimpse of the goddess
where The Temple of Jupiter stood, 509 BC
on The Capitoline Hill where elephants raised torches
in coiled trunks as Caesar walked, 44 BC
where the magnanimous bronze balls
of Marcus Aurelius' c. 175 AD horse were not covered
by a loincloth when Iranian President Hassan Rouhani
sat under him in the Capitoline Museum, 2016 AD
No
the white plywood coffin-like burka was reserved for Venus
the Roman Aphrodite; Goddess of love, Goddess of sex
Goddess of fertility, Goddess of beauty, Goddess of pleasure
Goddess of victory, Goddess of procreation
Goddess of prostitutes. Goddess of—Goddess of—
her flawless Parian marble complexion cool as flesh
coursing with white marble blood.
Venus, Venus, V—
Let her be known!
The Capitoline Venus—consecrated by the bloodshed of soldiers
enclosed in a burial cabinet so as not to offend politicians
while the horse's balls big as cannonballs hung in plain sight!
Venus behind wood veils. Venus who stands in a nook of her own
her hand covers her vagina, her hand rises to cover her breast
as if just for this visit this January moment, demure
as delegates traipse through her corridors to make business
deals worth seventeen billion Euros.
But what is seventeen billion Euros to the eternal Goddess of love?
What danger to these men could a glimpse of the Goddess possess
as she steps out of her ancient bath, out beyond the Gods
of her invention, beyond the sea foam from which she sprang?
This week the Goddess is called just a nude amongst nudes.
Yes these were the statues craned into bomb shelters in WWII
while flesh and blood boys were sent into shells' way.
Free all nudes now—the nude female form exhume
from insufferable white coffins on pedestals

out in the open for all to see the blank boxes of walls
that men build proudly in the *Caput Mundi*, the head of the world
up on the *Campidoglio*, the crown of the *Caput Mundi*
where Michelangelo oriented Marcus Aurelius so the palm
of his right hand opens over the city
his horse's rump to the ruins
of the empire's past.

Flat Earth

No land. Move on! Move on!
We sailed off the flat earth like a shelf
gushing flat earth ocean waterfall
masts sails clouds ocean arms legs decapitations
there was no Asia only silence
wet roar black gaping ocean mouth
Admirals Log: You don't know the sea 'til you fall into her
my crew thrashed in sky
Ahoy! Freedom from the tyranny of caged souls!
masts snapped as the earth jumped up to meet our sails
in clouds the sea rose for a laugh
we fell nose down into a gravity-less vortex
bloody night, bloody night
the sea reared up from under us
we flew into a stone ocean
continents with wings, chew and snap
grinding earth, bile earth bile mother
interminable belly abyss
plates melting crashing
hell molt core hot core molten core
No land. Move on! Move on!
blood mother monstrous umbilicus
mortal morsels
Yamo' Nina Yam'
earth's black hunger
crust into hot belly
crush bloody melt blood earth
stars on reigns abuzz hot glitter
shattered stars shattered stars
waters swollen moonlight
just where the charts ended
heading south by southwest
the waters fastened to clouds
No land. Move on! Move on!
my charts were exact
ocean levels fell, wash the heat from my rock skull
bruise bone flesh steel blood rain guttural volcanic frozen

there is but one imperative: change
sew the continents back together, build for a while there
have your lifetimes of sufferings, fight for what you can
we fall faster than we want
down into blinding fountain of shattered stars
shattered night

See, Saw 11:

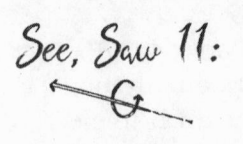

I need to be around people who don't have all the answers, just questions

My Grandmother's Handwriting

I went to the National Archives at 201 Varick Street
to find my grandmother's naturalization papers.
When the clerk handed the paper to me
and I saw her original signature, I cried.
She'd died a few years before
and the sight of her signature in blue ink
by her hand, the fact that she had signed this piece of paper
eighty-seven years before, pressing the pen sure and hard
the sight of her inked lines and shaky letters opened my heart.
My grandmother's handwriting has a special effect on me.
She wrote slowly and deliberately, one hand steadying the paper
the other hand guiding the pen—this American gadget.
When did she first encounter a pen?
She'd gone to grade school up to the second grade
in *Acquaviva delle Fonti, provincia di Bari, Italia.*
She told me that at eight years old she'd learned enough
she had to help the family work the land.
They didn't own land, they worked the fields
owned by a *padrone.* This is a common story.
How the *padrone* squeezes the workers of the land
to produce crops, how there is not enough access to water
for crops, how field hands' goats get taxed more than the cattle
of the *padrone.* How the *padrone* extorts gifts and favors
from the field workers. I don't wonder why my grandmother
wanted to take a chance, get on a boat, come to *L'America.*
I do replay the scenes in my mind.
Scene one: Her mother Rachele looks over her four daughters
and decides the youngest, my grandmother Rosina
will go instead of her older sister Maria.
Rosina will go with Lucietta.
Scene two: Maria alone. She capishes
The Great War is now over and in the interim years
she lost her chance to go to *L'America.*
Now she is twenty-three, too old to start a new life.
Scene three: Rosina is nineteen. She nods
when her mother Rachele tells her the news:
"Ué Rosina vai a l'Ameriga figghe migghe."

Rosina says, *"Mo me n'i à scì!"* Now I will go!
Scene four: Rosina and Lucietta say goodbye to their mother
and father Nicola, and siblings and cousins and friends and aunts
and uncles and grandparents and goats and chickens
and land. Rosina says goodbye to Maria last.
Scene five: Their last sight of Italy from the boat.
The Neapolitan coast. A crowd in a blur. Rosina looks away.
She looks at the sky, then ahead, the endless water.
Scene six: Sick on the boat. Nausea. Tears.
Scene seven: Rosina and Lucietta meet a *paesana* on the boat
who shows a photo of her brothers in Massachusetts.
Rosina chooses Giuseppe to marry and taps his face on the photo.
Lucietta chooses Franco.
Scene eight: The two sisters marry the two brothers in America.

I asked Grandma Rose many questions when she was alive
but she always wanted to get back to the present moment.
She rather cook and sew and shop and chop and eat
rather than talk about the past. She rather twist
her shoemaker's knife into the earth and fill her paper
shopping bags with wild *cicoria*. She rather sew socks
crochet booties for us all. She rather fix, mend
make everything thing "nice'a nice."
I remember once a neighbor of ours lost her husband
and went into a depression, crying constantly.
After months of this, my grandmother grabbed her
by the shoulders and shook her hard and said:
"You have to be here now. For your children. For yourself."
That's how she shook trees to make crab apples fall.

Grandma Rose lived to a hundred and a half.
When she died, a peach tree sprouted where she spit pits
out my mother's window.
That's one of the many things I learned from her,
never throw a pit in the garbage.
Give it a chance to live a life.
Throw pits out the window into soil.
Where Grandma Rose spit pits at the earth, trees grew,
and from those trees other trees,
the birds now spread her pits.

Every fall I give away baby peach trees.
"La vita è dolcissima." That is her message.
Life is sweet truly, very very sweet, green, sweet,
and sap rises up out of earth
and down from sky
and up through trees
bulging into fruits we take
into our own skin.
Skin covers the sweetness
of peaches
and all souls.

Spaldeen Prada

Grandma Rose had her special way of making fun that I was a tomboy. She'd look me up and down with pursed eyebrows when I walked into a room and say: "Wha?! No pocka'book?!" Times I didn't have a watch on either was a double *vergonia*. "No pocka'book! A'no wristawatch! *Ayyy!* A'no nice!" The fact that I loved to sport holes in my dungarees made it all the more worse. I was supposed to be *organizzata* and on time, a woman who carried everything the world might need. "Nice'anice." Cut a *bella figura*.

Ninety years after she immigrated to the U.S.A., and eight years after she died, Grandma Rose's grand-nephew Oronzo came to New York with his wife and kids from *Acquaviva delle Fonti*. Oronzo was her sister Maria's grandson, Maria who was slated to come to *L'America* with their sister Lucia, but The Great War interrupted the plan. After the war, their mother, Rachele, Oronzo's and my great-grandmother, chose the youngest, Rosa, to go with Lucia instead. Rose was nineteen, Lucia twenty-one, Maria twenty-three. And so, Maria's family grew up in Acquaviva, and Rose and Lucia's family in the Bronx. Whenever I looked at Oronzo, I wondered how our lives would have turned out in the geographical reverse.

Oronzo was the first Italian Italian in our family to come meet us Bronx cousins. I'd ventured to *Acquaviva* right out of college; the first American to walk *Via Leandro Pecce* and reestablish ties. Maria was alive at the time, she looked so much like Grandma Rose I sat beside her and wept, held her hand, listened to her sing songs, wished we could all be together, knowing it would never happen in this life. I was deeply impressed with how profoundly well Maria was taken care of by her daughter Isabella, Oronzo's mother, and her example set a template in my mind for the course of my life: elders were to be cherished, kept home, cooked and cared for as children again. If they could accomplish this here, I thought, certainly we could in America.

The pain of the immigration split in the family hit me. I prayed I would get my mother over on a flight, to meet her cousins. Their lives would be so enriched by knowing one another. Thankfully, a decade later, I was able to make this happen. My Mom and her cousins didn't speak a word in common, but my mother had an ear for an archaic version of *Acquavivese*, which she heard growing up. So Isabella and my mother Rachele and all their cousins reverted to the old *Acquavivese* of

their parents, and talked and mimed and cried and hugged each other as tight as long lost sisters, as if to say: "I am so heartbroken that we didn't know each other all our lives and these few days will be it!" They held onto one another with hundred-year hugs and saw their parents in the expressions in each other's eyes.

One thing you have to understand is that after the great migration, when an American returns to Italy to meet the cousins, they treat you like the Queen is visiting, meet you at the train station with half the town in tow, all their friends celebrate in grand style, your arrival. The aunts have cooked for days, you must stay at every one of their houses, eat at all their tables, taste each of their homegrown *vino e olio,* visit the fields, the grapevines, the olive trees, hear stories of the world wars and how they survived, and begin to *capishe* a semblance of how this half of the family fared over the century. You meet all the neighbors and friends and get paraded around the piazza as a *cause célèbre;* neighbors wave to you from balconies and rooftops. So, when Oronzo wrote and said they were coming, I naturally wanted to embrace him with the same level of spiritual hospitality with which he'd received me. But how could I? What could I offer, given immigration's cumulative reckoning in our family here on this side of the Atlantic? Whereas from 1919 through the 1980s Grandma Rose sent money to *Acquaviva* when she could, now their quality of life and sense of community surpassed ours. What did all the pain and suffering of splitting the family in 1919 result in? What had us American *paesani* accomplished here in the United States? What did the myth of American prosperity truly hold? Tabulate consciousness. What kind of people had we become? How did my cousins picture our American lives? How far would they be let down? How could I explain any of it? My Italian wasn't *that* good.

I wrote Oronzo to prepare him that I didn't have a place to live, I'd recently been priced out of Brooklyn and was back sleeping on an air mattress on my Mom's floor. I didn't have a place where they could all stay —this was my embarrassment literally of the century. It was bigger than personal. It was for all of us descendants of Rose, especially my mother, Rose's last surviving child, who understood the significance of their visit and all visitors. My Mom had graciously cooked for and fed so many people, hundreds of friends of mine who came through New York, that if I tried to count, it would sound like an exaggeration. She always welcomed my friends to sleep over and share all we had. I described Mom's one bedroom apartment in the letter to Oronzo and worded my letter carefully.

No matter my wording, I felt I was committing a sin, a shame, a cosmic *vergonia*, to not be able to house my *cugini*. This was worse than not carrying a pocka'book. Oronzo would have to pay for a hotel. The immigration to the land of the free and the brave, and all our collective hard work over the century didn't add up to a room where the *cugini* could stay. My circumstances made little sense to me — let alone explain it to my Italian cousin. What series of events and history led to my impoverishment in America, the disintegration of so many of our familial bonds here — the fact that I couldn't rally anyone in New York to house them? I'm not sure which was more heart-wrenching, trying to explain my own sub-poverty level living conditions to the Italian cousins, or trying to explain the once-in-a-lifetime significance of their visit to the Americans.

On either side of the Atlantic, there were only a few family members who made the effort to re-build ties. Oronzo and I were the bridges. All other relationship building would come through our connection. I had an abundance of love for my *cugini* and would embrace them the best I could and show them all around town. I offered Oronzo all we had, one room where he and his wife and children could manage on blow-up mattresses. They opted for a midtown hotel.

Mom and I planned a "Welcome to America" party and we rallied the enthusiasm of some friends and relatives. It was a hot August. We had one air conditioner and would all be in Mom's living room, a sheet tacked in the doorway to keep in the cooled air. We borrowed chairs from neighbors. It was 2009, ninety years exactly after my grandmother, little teenage Rose, had left *Italia* — on a donkey to the train to the boat. I did lots of cooking: fried eggplant in chickpea flour, Mom's stuffed peppers, pasta, salad, a tableful of bounty. Grandma Rose's peach tree was having a 'wood' year — as they say: *one year wood, one year fruit;* this year — wood, nothing for the cousins to pick and eat.

I wanted to go get them at the airport and wondered how I would fit the four of them and all their luggage in a car. At the time Mom and I had a Dodge Spirit that our neighbor had given us as a gift. A blessed car, great for local runs, but white smoke blew out the tailpipe and I didn't dare risk driving it to Newark and breaking down with the *cugini* in tow. I rented the biggest American car I could find, a black Dodge Durango. This would be their introduction to *L'America,* the SUV. I waited at Newark Airport with all the limo drivers. Finally they got through U. S. Customs; only two small roller suitcases for the four of them. I was astounded. You could fit their family of four and a whole *Cinquecento* in

the Durango. They sat close together in the back seat. I told them to spread out. They didn't sit with their legs wide open like we did here.

From the airport, we drove to an old school diner—an iconic New York City experience, where the menu was as big as the Durango. My best friend, my niece and my brother enthusiastically came, and he generously picked up the tab. When the plates were served with leg of lamb, chicken, burgers, and sides, and one was put in front of Oronzo's wife Anna, she couldn't believe it. "All for me?" she repeated. One plate could have fed the four of them. As Americans we were living up to our rep. Everything was oversize, including our bodies. We were a good foot taller and double their girth. We ate triple their portions. They shook their heads in disbelief over the giant plates we were accustomed to; potatoes, string beans, salad, a Henry the Eighth size leg each. By the time the apple pie *à la mode* came, it looked ridiculous on the plate. Their eyes widened. They could never eat that giant a portion—the slice of pie looked almost as big as a New York slice of pizza. Cartoon comical. They took "to go" bags back to their hotel. They were lean, had no excess body fat, were well groomed, with designer eyewear and comfortable cotton clothes. I felt like a hulk; uncomfortable in my own bulk but at home in the city streets walking the avenues, talking to strangers, making the city come alive, cursing and cutting off cabs in traffic. Huge, bloated, American, just like the way one of my *contadino* uncles once described to me American fruit, double the size of what came off his trees, but no *sapore* he told me, fingers wringing the air.

One of their two compact suitcases was filled with presents for us from *Acquaviva*: rosary beads and holy relics from the church where Grandma Rose was baptized, *La concattedrale di Sant'Eustachio, group* photos of all the cousins, cotton flags from our province Bari, a cotton tablecloth from one of the Aunts—and a pocka'book! The most gorgeous pocka'book I ever saw—black and white checks from woven strips of leather, reminding me of a racecar "finishing line" flag motif. Prada. Soft. Fine craftsmanship. I figured I'd try it out. Why not? Test drive it. Grandma Rose always wanted me to carry a pocka'book! I put my Spaldeen inside it. I carried it around. I put lots of stuff in it. My fat wallet. Rescue inhalers. A bottle of water. A scarf for my neck. My steel carabiner clip keychain which could hold my body weight on a rope if I had to jump off a cliff for any reason. A notebook. Pens. All of a sudden I was the tomboy with the most gorgeous pocka'book around. People would stop me in restaurants and ask to pet it. I ain't kidding. You walk around in public with a Prada pocketbook and people approach you who never

would before. My friend Rosette took one look and corrected me: "You don't stuff all that in a Prada pocketbook! You don't carry Prada like it's a gym bag!" Whaddahmagonnado? I have a classy Italian pocka'book and the pink rubber soul of a Bronx street kid. I was sure Grandma Rose was shaking her head.

We gave the "Welcome to America" party everything we had. My Mom was so happy to see Oronzo and Anna again and their children who were babies when she was in *Acquaviva* and now were beautiful teenagers, approaching the age young Rosa and Lucia were when they immigrated. My Mom's cousins, the grandchildren of Lucia, drove all the way down from Boston and upstate New York to meet the *cugini,* and even chipped in, with others who couldn't make it to the party, to get Oronzo's family tickets for the Circle Line cruise around Manhattan island. A boat ride around the Statue of Liberty felt like an appropriate emblematic cap to their American journey. I read Grandma Rose's letters aloud that she had saved from her correspondence with Oronzo and Isabella over the decades. We all shared stories of the hardships and miracles of our lives. I translated when Oronzo recounted the history of *La Madonna di Constantinopile;* the *Madonna* was thrown into the sea during the sack of Constantinople, washed ashore at Bari, and carried to *Acquaviva* where they built her a church.

Oronzo looked around in surprise when he asked me: *"Dov'è il bagno? Sopra?"* Where's the bathroom? Upstairs?

"No. Qui." No, here, I answered: *"Non c'è un piano secondo."* There's no second floor.

These two rooms were "it"—the sum of our American lives, the sum of the century of immigration. I repeated my answer three times as Oronzo wanted to be sure he understood. I pointed to the bathroom door that didn't even close all the way, warped from years and layers of thick paint. Italians take great pride in making their beds and setting their tables and passing lacework onto future generations to build their families. Clearly looking around our apartment, the rupture of the generational building of comfort and care was visible. In America we had started from scratch, and I would have to start from scratch again. But if you listened carefully to us talk, and looked in our eyes, you would know that we didn't lose all our peasant wisdom here—in fact we peppered it with a *New Yorkese* intelligence, a skepticism of three generations of Bronx street smarts.

Oronzo astutely asked me how my elderly aunt had gotten to the party. How could I explain that her son had driven her, but not bothered to come inside to meet his cousins from Italy? Where's the logic? And why didn't the other relatives who lived nearby bother coming? This was the hard stuff, the mental states, the apathy. The family had undergone fission after fission; from the split between who stayed and who left Italy, to the further splits between who reached out toward one another and who didn't, to the furthest splits possible within minds and consciousness.

We drove the *cugini* all around the New York we knew and loved. My niece Nicole took us to Coney Island one night where under fireworks over the ocean, we experienced the best of our America, where within a few square feet of boardwalk slats, every kind of person imaginable stood and truly partook in the unalienable right to "the pursuit of happiness." Nicole took Oronzo's kids on the Cyclone and afterwards got us all a round of mangoes-on-a-stick. This was the America I was proud to be a part of.

I took that Circle Line cruise with them, we ate a *fritatta* my mother made for the boat ride, and biting into it in the open air on deck, we all knew, somehow that Rosa and Lucia also had a *fritatta* with them on their transatlantic boat, the *Duca degli Abruzzi*. There, under the torch and gaze of the Statue of Liberty where they entered the port at Ellis Island ninety years before, we talked of our grandmothers Maria and Rosa, whose places and destinies had been switched in 1919. As for that Italian pocka'book, I used it for ten years until it wore out, the Prada leather unraveled and peeled. I'm back to putting everything in my pants pockets again, and linking my carabiner keychain on my belt loop, about which my Aunt Lucy says: "You look like a jailer."

"Change always feels good at first," Tony says flipping his cigarette butt in the street, "but then you have to live with it."

See, See 12:

Bronx Speaks

Yo! Gimme five, man.
Madónn, I bunked into
Hoodycallit down at
the johnnypump on the
corner. Then this scooch
walks by actin' like
he's in cahootz about
the whaddyacall—
Ahh—fagetaboutit—one's
a chooch, the other's
a chibobi—bafanabla
I don't need any *imbroglio*
or *cazzamarole!*

How to Cross a Bronx Street, 1969

Step off the curb
Gauge the speed of oncoming cars
If there is two-way traffic
take it one lane at a time
stand between opposing lanes
Get as close to the car as you can
Life is a dare
As a street-crosser you are a *toreador*
Lean in as close to death as you can
Challenge the car
You live in the middle of the street
Swipe your index finger
along the side of the car as he whizzes by
Hold the pulp of your finger up to him
to show him he needs a wash

A Confession Unheard

What I can't describe is the heat inside my heart and hands.
I march down Courtlandt Avenue on a mission.
Church bells guide me to the spot, Immaculate Conception
on Ahun-fiftieth and Melrose in the South Bronx.
Times like these I'm glad my turf is organized:
blocks, straight walks, right angles.

Up the stairs, open the door, into the church:
Hup two, three, four. About face.
I stand behind the bullet proof glass,
slide a buck through the open slot like I'm in a bank
or seedy all night liquor store.
The church lady slides me a votive candle and a match.
    "Scuse me," I say, "I wanna talk to the priest."
I am here on business. Spiritual business.
The Priest steps out of a back door, takes his spot
four feet behind the glass.
I lower and tilt my head to get my voice through the opening.
    "Father!" I say, "I gotta axe you a question.
My father was an iceman in this neighborhood.
After he came home from fighting in Okinawa
in WWII with the Marines, he came here to say confession
and the priest threw him out."
    "What a you Italian?"
    "Yeah."
    "That's why."
    "He got thrown out because he was Italian?"
    "That's the way it was back then. He should have went
to the Italian church, Our Lady of Pity."
    "That's why the priest threw him out?"
    "This was a German church. It would have been the same
if a German boy went to the Italian church.
That's the way it was, and not just in this neighborhood."
    "My father was an iceman. Maybe you knew him.
He lived on Ahun-fifty-eighth."
    "There were a lot of icemen. I had a different one.

A few blocks away."
End of conversation. Except for my dead father
who smacked me in the back of the head
as I contemplated lighting the votive on the altar.
He told me in no uncertain terms:
    "Get the hell outta there."
Out the door, down the steps, to the curb, unlit match and candle.
All this time I'd imagined my father
might have did something
to get thrown out of the church.
Raged, yelled, threw a punch
or went wild in confession
about things they did at war.
I called my mother and her voice bounded in my head:
    "Those priests should be ashamed of themselves,
    not giving a serviceman confession.
    A church is a church.
    Anybody should be able to walk in. *Jackass!*
    Just think, our whole lives might'a been different
    had your father'd been able
    to make a full confession after the war.
    He didn't wanna do it in his home church
    where everybody knew everybody."

There's nobody left to talk to

now that Tony and Uncle Frank are gone
their hoarse Italian voices I miss
their wild brown eyes, vowels steeped in Bronx:
"Ayy!" "Eeeeee!" "O!" "Yo!"
"You! Yeah You!" "Hah?" "Eh?!" "Wha!"
their clasp and shake of my hand back shoulder
all the words they told me, the streets they knew
back doors, dumbwaiters, ice chutes, short cuts
every pothole from Flatbush to Bruckner
that hundred year old dip
in the right lane off the Manhattan Bridge
stories of old New York corners
thick with laughter car grease, rainbows in puddles,
the people they raised full *vino* glasses to
and swallowed hard. Tony who without a stomach ate
a Coney Island Nathan's hot dog and fries
to show his *cugini di Piacenza*
a once in a lifetime great Brooklyn time.
He knew he'd throw up later
but still he loved the moment of that hot dog.
Uncle Frank who without—geezus what organs did he have left?
Still he ate sausage and peppers 'til he sweat, hot cherry peppers
fork in one hand, white hanky in the other, organs gone
halves of organs gone—parts of him stitched up to other parts
how did he keep on eating, drinking, celebrating
every breath and meal every table sitting?

Rare men bridge worlds

There's nobody left to talk to who reminds me of my father
or my father's world or my father's mores
or my father's hands' knowledge
pipe cutters that they were
leaving the precise shine of fresh sliced copper on us all.
Maybe in other countries in other languages
where neighborhoods are still self-contained as ditches or ravines
but not here, not now, not for me—no more.

There's nobody left to talk to in New York

Now there's just apologists
people who say "I'm sorry" as soon as they meet you
with a veneer of politeness shellac
bunk into you in the grocery, "I'm sorry, I'm sorry."
My father, my father never apologized to nobody 'bout nuttin'
What would they say?
Tony or Uncle Frank or my father Joseph Rocco
to these "I'm sorry" people of the new New York today?

Bronx Rubicon

My inner Leopardi conflicts with my inner Whitman.
Optimism is an American trait and what of misery?
How *Mezzogiornese* is it, and what is Italian anyway?
Miseratz ki katz!
I wanna up and celebrate
sing praise songs about my cells
but I wish I could just fall and fallen tell you
how gravity skins misery
and keen for *Patria Mia* and lie there
the third time, three soldiers
to pick me up. Somebody carry this thing,
I can't lift no more. *Madonn'!*
Run your finger through the grooved lettering
on the marble
slab cool as skin

My Rubicon is the Cross Bronx Expressway
once you cross it, everything changes.
Alea iacta est—The die is cast.
I'll be buried in the Bronx
have to build a box to put myself in
at the end of the day
tuck this accent back into Bronx earth
oxygenate the soil catalyze tectonic plates
crashing up into mainland mountain folds
Where d'ya think a Bronx accent goes?
To the gneiss baby, into the bedrock.
Hey baby how ya doin? Yo! whatssupp man.
Put your ear to the gneiss,
you'll hear me whispering for *l'eternitá*

it's not so pretty it's not so serene
this is the Bronx it's not so clean
the graves are flat, the earth is round
they came to this country, they found this town
left *la paese* without a trace
came to the Bronx joined the fast pace race

of timeless time overhead subway cars
their steps got quicker, their kids got fed
baby girl fell outta sky down into alleyway
a doll fell out the window the neighbors say
they worked real hard, ate their daily bread
lived real long, now I'ma singa dis song

How can I tell you anything
Cugino mio uptown downtown crosstown
forget sleep—just hold onto my sleeve
the grid is my heart tempo, the grid is my lockstep
the grid and the diagonal,
you gotta be good on the zig and the zag
on the weave
pivot on toe
you gotta be sliding

How To Fast-Break

Do not honor time
Beat time
To the hoop, to the hoop, to the hoop
Stun the opponent
Rebound the ball
Spot your teammate running down the aisle of the court
Turn everyone else into a blur
Satellite the ball over everyone's heads like an arrow
With a fast arc, just ahead of the shooter
The fast-break is the ultimate assist
The fast-break is an act of faith
A communiqué between two
The downcourt runner has her hand flagged in the air
She does not call for the ball
She does not say, "I'm free"
She does not call any attention to herself
She is a silent panther,
    making herself visible to the rebounder only
Telepathic pass
The rebounder has fought hard to get the ball under the hoop
She hugs it tight to her body
protects it in her midsection, her belly
gives her back to the playing field, then glances
Sees her free runner down court
and without thinking, for hesitation costs time,
hesitation of heart, hesitation of weighing odds,
hesitation in calculating the kill of the runner
In hesitation all is lost
All reposition themselves, the runner is no longer alone
no longer is a fast-break thinkable
The rebounder acts with faith and in one movement
snatches the ball
pivots, sees, fires
the ball with one arm over all the heads
The ball is the highest then
in all the game

The newspaper lady tells me, "The good news is we are still here, but bad news sells better."

See, Saw 13:

Trach Kit

I just dropped a coupla' hundred bucks
on emergency trach kits
for my pocketbook and keychain.
The way things are going
dying of a closed-up throat feels increasingly likely.
So, I won't be caught without a trach kit
or knife and hollow Bic pen again.
My doctors don't like this train of thinking.
I'm not sure why.
Irradiated necks have more trouble breathing.
One paralyzed vocal chord from surgery
and radiation makes my airway smaller.
Any allergic reaction or infection reaction on top of that
leaves me clutching for air. And helpless.
When you're choking all people do is yell at you:
    "Are you alright? Are you alright?"
Makes me nuts. Makes me choke more.
My father was right when he said:
    "You're better off being around Marines"
when your life is threatened anyway.
A Marine will take action.
Marines don't just stand there.
A Marine will save your life.
As long as they're not battering you
a Marine will save you.

I bought the QuickTrach kit and the LifeStat keychain tool.
I'm on my own survivalist journey.
Wanting to breathe.
I watched videos from military folks,
woodland survivalists, EMS workers,
and heard a testimony of a cancer survivor
whose irradiated neck is rock hard as mine
from radiation fibrosis.
So this guy saved his own life
with a steak knife and Bic pen, twice.
That might be the easiest, two motions, slit and stick.

But I figured I'd buy the expensive toys nonetheless.
They're sharper than steak knives.
You just puncture, not slit.
Puncture is easier.
Joan River's death gave me pause.
If Joan had a trach kit, she coulda lived.
If Joan didn't go to the doctor that day, she woulda lived.
Ifs ain't worth nuttin's
but as a cancer survivor a couple of times over
stayin' alive is a job and I gotta try to do it good.

You can help.
1. If you hear me choking, don't question me
2. Bang me on the back
3. Get me water quick
4. Heimlich only if I've been eating
and no air at all is getting through
5. Help me puncture an airway

I won't be caught without a keychain
and pocketbook trach kit ever again.
And if you're the one to choke out in public
you'll be lucky
if I'm around to pop a hole in your
Cricothyroid membrane
and blow

For all the long-term survivors

of childhood cancers fueled by power ghosts
of cancer buddies lost along the way,
who played pool and made trivets out of tiles
and inpatient hours, porcelain dolphin 'fridge magnets,
stained glass crucifixes to hang by kitchen windows,
who flicked air bubbles
out of hospital roommate intravenous lines
during thousand hour nights,
who laid in each other's beds
and gave pre-thoracotomy rubdowns,
who hear voices, urge souls,
surge, purge, who make the most
of having a voicebox, hands,
heart, bone marrow, blood's ebb and flow,
who bear radiation fibrosed atrophied
necks, who shout to Madame Curie:

"Will you look at this? Your radium cured me Curie, yet killed
so much in me. I'm curied. Look at the atrophied rotator cuffs.
I can't pull my sword out of its scabbard.
Madame Curie, Madame Curie, listen to the deep dank cough
in the lower bases of my lungs, see the scarred lung tissue
pinched corners, name the secondary cancers caused by the radiation
to treat the first. Count all the –ectomies,
Madame Curie, Madame Curie, kiss the marrow
sucked from my bones, posterior ileac crest drilled to the core
like all earths. Visit my spleen and lymph nodes and tumors
in the tissue banks of the greatest cancer centers of the world.
Cancer cells outlive the world itself. I am racing to outlive the cells.
Madame Curie, Madame Curie, one day the world will learn
our cells' secrets; how to shut off senescence yes the magic
of saying "Nay!" to death. Live! Multiply!
Ah Madame Curie, Madame Curie, come solve these mysteries.
May I call you Marie?"

For the ones whose cells are keepers of everlasting life
holy holy holy grail, the sought after fountain of eternity,
for super cells whose codes one day the world will read
the forever cells sold to labs around the world.
For all the long-term survivors of childhood cancers
who still stand vertical, who know life's triage
who forgive quick, who brave radioactive beams
scalpels, pills, vials, injections, anesthesia, today's cures
who need to be cured of the cure
who stay alive to serve something in the world
who fly high above the tunnels of MRI machines
above the deafening jackhammer banter of
oversized magnetic resonance
that orients positive ions
through every finger stick, every red dot
on the tip of every one
of our middle fingers

Napkin Notes

forward fight, learn to breathe—breathe it in, get it out
power-woman, here is your shield, sword, torch, breath

Bladder tumors again after a lifetime of hair products,
cigarettes, dyes, sprays, colors—all Mom's habits
I suffer twice, each cigarette and manicure,
hairspray, nail polish and removers, the stink
of permanent wave solution as she soaked her sister's head.
As a kid I'd spank the air, pinch my nose, run from the apartment:
"I can't breathe!" Throw a wet towel over the pathetic louvre door
and bang it shut 'til it lost its place in the overhead groove.
Louvre doors ain't doors at all
can't keep a smell or sound out if they tried.
Now I bring Mom to get the bladder tumors cut out
every seven months they come back. Bladder chemo
every week we get up five a.m. to beat traffic.
She's tethered to oxygen, breathing less and less.

Charapay means 'shut up' the lady at the next table says
and this is what I did on my 31ˢᵗ Cure Day, 2013:
walked from Hudson and West 12th to *Rocco's* on Bleecker
coffee circles on white napkins and good absorbent ink
there's no feeding this hunger, gave money and collected money
for St. Ann's Orphanage in Kisumu, remembered the vat
of hot porridge each day if they're lucky,
nodded to a transvestite on Christopher and Bleecker
whose smile lingered from the northeast corner
where there used to be a pizzeria where you could rest.
Five o'clock shadow black stockings with runs
red pepper rim mason jar margarita
sliced meat sun-dried on a clothesline overhead.
This is my tribe, my dance around the fire
my body markings, the indigo dye in my hair
my shoebox diorama, my snowglobe
my rock sugar coated enchanted egg.

As a kid I peeled white birch bark with a pocketknife
to make an Iroquois longhouse. Meat hung to dry
on toothpick racks next to a sweat lodge of pine needles.
I created a world with clay, masking tape painted
with shoe polish. Now I have to do that with my own life.
Peel bark, start again.
Hang meat. People it anew.

Thirty-four years after Hodgkin's

I wake up with headaches that keep me in the chair all day.
The casual observer wouldn't say this is related
to cancer treatment three decades ago
but I know better the ravages of radiation over time
fibrosis of the neck—the inability to comfort the neck at night
the stress of not knowing how to survive the mundane world
shelter over my survivor's head, how to afford
the twenty percent Medicare doesn't cover
how to be a caregiver to my Mom when I can't button
my shirt, tie my shoes, zipper my coat or fasten my pants,
when I drop every plate and bowl post-Vincristine
peripheral neuropathy, when I can't afford aging,
eyeglasses, dental. How to breathe after Bleomycin
+ mantle field radiation—both lungs squeak and squeeze
God only knows what's goin' on in there.
How to have cash and energy
for the sidewalks of New York City
to see my nineteen doctors at Sloan-Kettering,
how to get from the breast building to the kidney building
to the skin building to the main campus all in one day:
how to make a 1:30 gynecological exam
then a 2:00 kidney ultrasound ten blocks away?
    "The computer factored in your travel time,"
the session assistant informs me.
This is a modern conversation
that never could have happened thirty years ago.
How to stop the questions asked of me
from spinning inside my head?
"Do you have diabetes?" the handsome debonair skin doc asks.
"Do you feel life is not worth living?" the sleepy old shrink asks.
"Her lungs are her Achilles' heel," the Long-Term Effects specialist
declares to his intern. With a paralyzed vocal chord
from surgery and radiation, how to speak to a classroom
of twelve year olds? I'm raspy and gasping for breath
and this spleenless girl body picks up Klebsiella bacteria
like a lint brush on a dusty stone floor.
And the meter
keeps ticking
relentless
time

Queensboro Bridge

Inside Sloan-Kettering was my first and last bed
in New York City. At eighteen I had a corner room
on the 15th floor overlooking East River sunrises
Rockefeller University geodesic dome, 59th Street Bridge
the Con Ed red striped smokestacks
I call The Three Wise Men. I watched the New York City
marathon stream over the bridge cross the river
duck behind buildings, disappear into clouds

My first month passed click by click
as the skyline changed from black to white to black again
long morning shadows of people walking down below
laid the paths out on sidewalks for their day. I watched
walkers in white coats on their way to work
my forehead pressed to the window glass that never opened.
An aqua '68 Mustang with a Brown University bumper sticker
parked down there every day on 68th between York and 1st.
Only doctors could park there back then.
Who did that car belong to? Where's that Mustang now?
In scattered parts well-placed, or still whole?

I walked out of Sloan-Kettering over fifteen hundred times.
It's been a lifetime occupation, growing and harvesting tumors.
I am the furrowed field that grows super cells
defiant of their surroundings, living renegade forever.

At forty-five I walked out with a list of homeless shelters.
The social worker had a stupid look on her face
looked everything up on the internet.
It used to be people knew stuff and phone numbers,
made a call, found things out, got things done,
helped one another. Now nobody knows nothin'
if it's not on the internet.
I stand outside the mammoth building housing cancer
pull my hospital bracelet stretch it 'til it rips
the respite from the handcuffs of great illness.
My tumors will have a home in this town forever.
I will not. My living body will not, just my aberrant cells.

I didn't know if I wanted to live in this town or leave it.
All I knew was I was vertical
and the wind on York Avenue was with me.

Thanks

For dying under different names
for never hating mondays
for wearing wigs despite it all
and drinking coffee anyway
show up time and time again on time
ignoring armpit lumps like plums
and joking about veins till they collapse
"i just lost my hair I can't do a thing with it"

For being human but better
believing all the way
in god, red meat, white light, christ's cross
good thoughts, what the doctor says, the bible
the qur'an and a thumbnail 'a dirt from chimayo

For scotch-taping saint christopher
medals on comatose arms
for the black beret on your sudden bald head
for giving away your license
for hypodermics and medical marijuana
for putting up with everyone who insisted
they had the answer to cancer

For flashing belly scars over your daughter's wedding cake
for dying a virgin
never hearing of a.i.d.s.
never capping your ears with a walkman
for choosing beatle tunes and jazz
to be played at your own funeral
for sketching your coffin and picking the pine
for finding ways to say the goodbye
and dying just when the leaves stopped
being green and fell
and letting me shovel dirt on top of you

Notes of a Long-Term Survivor

1. 1999 My body needs some kind of Magic Mountain
a place and enough time to rest my adrenal system
bolster my immune system,
understand my body in a new way.

2. 2006   Routine surveillance sonogram
and subsequent core biopsy found
a benign schwannoma in my right armpit.
The docs are discussing if it needs to be removed:
    "Soft tissue tumors can be a pain in the ass."
A psychic burlesque chic tells me:
    "Picture the schwannoma running away as a black kitten."

3. 2012 I'm alone all week.
My sister took Mom for a few days since she has a cough.
A MRSA colony is alive in my lungs.
Methicillin-resistant Staphylococcus aureus.

4. 2013   I came through surgery again at Sloan-Kettering.
The schwannoma is now gone from my armpit.
The surgeon stripped the nerve of sheath and tumor.
Bruises from the abdominal belts.
My neck felt like I was in a car wreck.
My throat ached from intubation.
Are we such delicate flowers post-treatment?
What do I have to tell all operative staff:
"Careful with the neck?"
I'd prefer to avoid positional pain in future surgeries.

5. 2015   Still wheezing here in quarantine
coughing up brackish gunk out of lungs,
broke through fevers and vomiting, stabbing headaches.
Metapneumovirus, related to childhood whooping cough.
I am coming out the other side, standing.
I still don't know the basics of protecting myself
spleenless out there in the city. Don't kiss me hello.

6. 2015   I plough through
I am the plow, pulled by the ox
I am the ox. I am the furrow
life is one hard ground
rocks must be unearthed
into sun

Gay Pride Before the Rainbow

Every October I get a flu shot
and in June a Gay Pride Booster Shot
vaccination of courage for the whole year through
recalibrates my bar of expression
I feel emboldened, relieved, accepted in the mass of bodies
of all types shapes, sizes, gender expressions
the strut and dance of our tribe in our Village
But this is all changed now
In my mind it will always be Gay Pride before the rainbow

On the avenue, 5th Avenue, New York City

We used to have to dance in dark corners
kiss at crumbling piers, meet in the woods
in shadows, clubs, back rooms,
underground dungeons where everything slowed
as you entered nets, nooks, brick corners
but on this day we all strut and shake and shimmy
in open daylight

On the avenue, 5th Avenue, New York City

By the end of Gay Pride 2015 I am bleeding from both legs
after the hours long march. It was a ballpoint pen
sticking out of my bag that stabbed me as I marched.
It was only when I sat finished marching that I saw
ink marks and drips of blood down my calves
The message is clear:
I bleed ink and blood. Go home and write.

A rumbling wheeze develops deep down in my lungs.
I take Ceftin and Prednisone,
Xopenex and Ipratroprium Bromide.
I give Mom her Lovenox. I sit and write.
My breathing worsens.
By July 3rd I'm back in Sloan-Kettering
stretchers line the hallway with bodies waiting.

It's ten p.m. The triage nurse leaves at midnight.
He's been here since noon without a break.
The patient escorts go home at eleven p.m.
then it takes a while to get wheeled up to X-ray
by the company with the graveyard contract.
A nurse brings me to a chair with a head and foot rest.
She wants my antecubital fossa vein
you know, my good vein that runs blue
up the centerline of my inner elbow.
The hell with that. I tell her matter-of-factly:
    "I save that for treatment. Put it in my hand."
I am reading "Italian Stories," by Joe Papaleo.
She puts a tourniquet around my arm
drops the butterfly needle on the floor,
goes to get a clean one, she pops the vein.
My hand golf balls up into a hard swelling.
    "The vein blew," she says blandly,
    "sometimes that happens."
She draws two vials of blood then applies pressure.
I continue the pressure and ask for an icepack.
A stretcher wants to pass.
They ask me to lower my feet.
    "I can't," I say, "I am holding my vein.
    You can put the foot rest down, but I can't."
I tell the nurse, "You had the tourniquet on too long
'cause you had to go get a sterile butterfly.
The pressure built up, that's why the vein blew."
    She smiles: "It happens."
My vein never blew before.

On the avenue, 5th Avenue, New York City

It was thirty-four years ago to the day
July 3rd 1981, The New York Times ran the headline
that changed the world as we knew it:
RARE CANCER SEEN IN 41 HOMOSEXUALS
My very first visit to Sloan-Kettering
was just four months later. I was eighteen.
A.I.D.S. hadn't yet been named.
H.I.V. wasn't a thought.

The New York City blood supply
that I received in transfusions was not yet screened.
Groups of gays were not yet a presence at Sloan-Kettering.
Infectious Disease doctors took on "orphan diseases"
and this—disease without a name.
Bone skinny, gaunt, pale, scared,
with lovers and friends, always in groups
group by group would come, with rumors of a gay cancer
Meanwhile we marched

On the avenue, 5th Avenue, New York City.

Tonight I sit here alone. I've been here my whole adult life.
Friends used to corral around me for every hospital stay.
Now it's *de riguer* that I am here on a Friday night.
I take my go-bag and get to 67th Street
a book to read, headphones,
a baseball hat to keep out the pervasive florescent light
ask for a sandwich and juice
put my feet up, don't fret about the vein
make myself at home.
Audrey texts me—she will come if I need her.
The doctor listens to my chest,
sees my elevated white count,
infiltrates on my chest X-ray
discusses antibiotics and asks
if I want to stay or go home.
I tell him I can go home. What's on my mind is
that I have to give Mom her morning Lovenox injection.
What a strange name, a blood thinner
that sounds like Noxious Love.
My mother needs her shot every day.

On the avenue, 5th Avenue, New York City

In 2015 thousands of rainbow flags are worn
as super hero capes. Someone's cashing in—
rainbow boas rainbow hats rainbow socks,
every one is out partying in the streets,
bands of straight folks wave rainbow flags.

It's become a kind of gay Halloween
spirit swallowed up in kitsch.
Company after company, so many businesses
are represented, even Sloan-Kettering
is in the Gay Pride Parade these days.
A casual observer might be impressed that so many queers
are so gainfully employed. Not the ones I know of course,
we remain on the sidelines, in the streets, creating art
with every good breath we have, honoring our dead peers.
I stood behind the barricades
with my oldest and dearest friends.

On the avenue, 5th Avenue, New York City

This year the Irish bring up the caboose of the Gay Parade.
The best for last. After the corporations
here come the artist activists.
Ireland has just become the first country
to legalize Gay Marriage by popular vote.
It's time to thank the Irish.
Activist/Director Brendan Francis Fay carries a banner
with author/playwright Honor Molloy:
    "Lavender and Green Alliance."
Activist/organizer Kathleen Walsh D'Arcy
and activist/poet Rosette Capotorto carry:
    "Thank you Ireland."
Brendan's husband Dr. Thomas Anthony Moulton,
a pediatric hematologist, carries the giant flag of Ireland.

I remember years ago Brendan being handcuffed
by NYPD in the rain at the Saint Patrick's Day Parade
when he put his body on the line for gays to be included
on 5th Avenue where we were forbidden to march.
Year after year he stepped out onto 5th Avenue
and got carted away hands behind his back.
But Brendan didn't stop there.
He created the all-inclusive parade "St. Pat's For All"
in Sunnyside and Woodside. Brendan and his comrades
ultimately won that tug of war. Gays are now allowed
on 5th Avenue in the St. Patrick's Day Parade.

I witnessed Brendan go from being arrested
to being honored in City Hall and in Dublin
where he and Kathleen Walsh D'Arcy
received the Irish Presidential Distinguished Service Award.
This is Gay History. This is Gay Pride.
From handcuffs to garlands.

On the avenue, 5th Avenue, New York City

I hop the barricade. It's time to march.
My friends and I join the Irish.
Artist/activist Brian Fleming with one frame drum
sets a beat that fills the block. One drum is all it takes
to set the feet in a beat in the street.
Our crowd grows. Others hop the barricade
when they see us coming. We grow and grow
and march and march and smile and shout and
hold onto one another arms linked, walking
down 5th Avenue and over on Christopher Street.
We have found each other in these multitudes.

On the avenue, 5th Avenue, New York City

Nurses

Nurses come in without knocking
throw on the lights
let you know they are there.

Their eyes are so big, hands so adept
at changing my I.V. bag without me knowing
like the way my Mom pulled my blanket
over my shoulders when I was a child.

Being sick is like being like a child
all over again.
People take care of you.
Nurses offer comfort with
soft hands, bright eyes, and wildly
vertical bodies.

Swiftly they come in, rearrange the medicine
ask me to open my mouth.

Where must I move?

Ninety percent humidity — days heavy
with New York questions

Another smoker sits
in the wind

I am dreaming
of Italy

Roman fountains whisper
"Come now, come now, come now!"

The wind off *Il Tevere*
swirls cigarette smoke

around the Bernini fountain
in the piazza

made into an ashtray
water falling into itself

pigeon stained sidewalk
A winged ram is my regal company

the artisanship of stonework
a pattern of arches in the sidewalk

Dr. Donat says she may want to take a quarter kidney
with the cysts, going in through the eleventh rib

the floating rib

When I think of Sloan-Kettering

I think of the long shine on the floors
men standing at the doors
that I want to go out of

I never had a surgeon sing me
a spiritual in an elevator
only the cleaning ladies

Bloods were drawn

Thyroid Stimulating Hormone is low
Spots on the thyroid bed
A great thyroid evaluation is the difference
between real life and half life
which I am living now
pulling myself up the stairs
trying to balance my head
on top of my thin fried neck
waiting as time divides
and divides again

Saint Nick Medley of 53rd Street

Sloan-Kettering got one thing right
hiring Nicki Medley as the concierge
for the Outpatient Building.
He boosts cure rates as much as any scientific advance.
The healing takes place in the entranceway, glass doors
open from the street and there stands Nick
behind the counter, a preacher at a glowing gold altar
in a bright tan suit where every day is Sunday.
I shout his name and he shouts mine
and opens his giant heart's arms.
The atrium fills with his spirit.
Nick works as hard as the sun, smiles to heal
all who walk by him, on their way to treatments,
scans, doctors and the most massive news of their lives.
I tell Nicki a doc just casually said I might be going blind.
He kisses my eye: "Everything will be okay."
The kiss bolts through the eye.
        "We're not gonna claim that.
        You'll be okay. You'll see."
I look into his eyes divine as sky.
He holds my head with two strong hands
clamps me to his chest, shakes sense into my soul:
        "Faith and focus. I got you. We got this."
I telephone my mother, and she says:
        "Just as you said that, I got a jolt
        through the phone, I felt his kiss
        through my whole body. A shock. Like lightning."
That is the power of Nick the living saint
a giant of a man in body and soul
barrel hugs and eyes Mom says are the color of the Madonna's robe
that light celestial blue.
A bear behind the counter embodying the spiritual power
of the ancient Keeper of the Gate:
To greet, to give courage to all who enter, to heal
in every living breathing moment
All Hail Nick! Sainted Keeper of the Gate
whose greetings are healings
and blesses the world with sacred power

Sister Elaine Appears in the Rooms

"Picture God as a little dog running at your heel.
He's always there. You can't get rid of Him,"
Sister Elaine Goodell has prayed over me
in Sloan-Kettering for decades.
Stands straight as a stalk, a curly white halo of hair,
round golden wire frame glasses, wide open eyes,
soft button down purple knit sweater, resonant voice,
luscious words, a conduit of The Holy Spirit, a woman in love
with God. All day room to room every day she talks
of God as a passionate lover, prays with scores of patients,
tells the day's miracle in signature prayers
about a bar of Lux soap on sale, ordinary things
that show God's constant activity and presence,

We arrived at the sign-in desk 5:30 a.m.:
"Can Sister Elaine come pray over Mom before surgery?"
6:20 she appears, an energized visitation, as if it's not early at all
as if it takes no exertion, in fact I've never seen her sit down.
       "This morning I couldn't find a comb. It was 5:30 a.m.
       I'm rifling through my drawer and I found this."
She cups her hands to hide her treasure, then unfurls them
to reveal one of my framed poems: "Command My Soul"
I'd given her three years before.
       "I said I'm gonna call Annie Lanzillotto today. I look
       up at the board to see the names on my list—
       I see Lanzillotto."
Every day holds a miracle to be part of. She holds our hands.
       "Think of this hospital admission as a new beginning.
       Think of today as a new beginning."
A doctor walks into pre-op and mistakenly tries to interrupt:
       "Excuse me. Hello I'm the Anesthesiologist."
Sister Elaine goes on praying. Anyone else would have halted
then resumed after the doctor's business.
Sister Elaine obeys a higher chain of command.
Nothing interrupts communiqué with God.
Sister Elaine prays on.
Her business is the opposite of Anesthesiology—

Awakeningiology!
The doctor just stood there. I opened my hand
to welcome the doctor into our circle. Sister Elaine prays on.
Afterwards the doctor said:
    "Thank you for including me in your prayer circle.
We are usually on the outside of these things."

days are long, years fast

See, Saw 14:

The Knave of Hearts

was the earliest character
in my nursery rhymes.
I don't know why
he stuck in my soul
for fifty years.
Fuzzy Wuzzy
Uncle Wiggly
Miss Pecksniff
are there too
the early ones
with the Five Chinese Brothers
holding hands in a circle.
They dance now
all together
the literary characters
of all the authors
I have ever loved and known.
All the characters
in all the books
written by friends of mine
are in the circle now too
the memoirists, their parents and lovers
and city mates
people they've known
and imagined
all there together
in an alternate
reality, dream space
literary landscape
in my brain
and will be
for all time
holding hands
one large circle
where we who write
end up, on the page
with everyone
we've meditated on
dancing
a great
swirl

Spiritual Imperatives

Sip the Nile
wearing a talisman from an old lover

Floor it so wind whips the top down
over the Brooklyn Bridge in rain

Roll naked
in snow

Shift into third into the *piazza* on a Vespa
like a teenager too good lookin' to be any one gender in particular

Run through the pine forest like a dog off her rope
straddle leap bear traps

Toll the gong, open hearts
and third eyes

Yank the rope of the church bell at midnight
to ring in the new millennium over East Harlem

Flex vaginal waves
to the galaxy in the universal tongue

Pose naked *Vitruviana* in the round glass window
of the straw bale house on the mountaintop of Left Hand Canyon

Lay naked on the face of the Flatirons, back against sun hot stones
defy their decree of return

Lay naked on top of the second pyramid at Giza
finger graffiti scratched by Napoleon's soldiers

Blow Mamma a kiss
goodbye

Leave Daddy unburied in the military cemetery
trust the backhoe to shovel plenty of good dirt on top of him

Take socks off in a prop plane
kick clouds

Hike above the thunderstorm
learn what the gods of Mount Olympus knew

Love and Joy

it's the things you don't anticipate that communicate care
the rendering of hours 'til long after candles melt away
it's the skills housepainters have
the knowing that the preparation and right tape
really are the most important parts of the task
as is the thorough cleaning of brushes
it's knowing that the planning of something is the thing itself
plowing and planting, reward enough
and yes it is right there in the furrow

To Do List for the Newly Married Couple

Linger kisses
so the pressure of lips lasts
after the boat sails away

Hug longer
than feels appropriate in public
for no matter how you count, it is all too brief

Memorize striations
of colors in each other's irises
at different times of day

Find places
on each other's bodies
only you know

Make up songs
to sing together
joyous anthems of your day

Hold on tight
when fears come
with the "hoops of steel" the Bard mentions

Learn something
together as often as possible
let the questions take you on their way

Protect each other
with reserves of strength
you don't yet know you have
Know the contours
of each other's breath
bask in the rhythm and sway

Take turns
listening to each other's heartbeats
for what they came to say

Streets of Souls

I want to write of roads
Earth roads, *terra viæ*
more for goat hoof than Goodyear
Roads for barefoot leather straps
wound round ankle bones
Roads that wind into the wind
carry thin-lipped pink horizons
train tracks cannot aspire to trace
just brace valleys, mountain passes, the cliff edge
of which I speak. Village roads of *il centro storico*
mud slum roads of Addis Ababa, constant scattering feet
Streets named for saints. Puddles,
chicken feet, well-worn stares
goat herd crossings. Streets etched along oceans
up ridges where donkeys tread. My streets of souls.
I can name each and tell what happened there.

Strada Provinciale 48
links two towns, the birthplaces
of Grandma Rose and Grandpa Giuseppe
a seven kilometer stretch through combed fields.
Take *Via Caduti di Tutte le Guerre*
        Street of the Fallen in All the Wars
out of *Acquaviva delle Fonti*
        Living Water of the Fountains
Vai sempre dritta, go always straight on
to *Cassano delle Murge*
        Murge are *Pugliese* elevations of sedimentary rock
carved into caves by my ancestors
along the heel of the boot.
Imagine them meeting,
two teenagers tending olive trees
grapevines almonds and figs
their eyes a respectable distance
from each other on this sturdy square of limestone

Zerega
a stretch of blacktop promised a contained life
from the deli to the church to the candy store
to the house to the school to the corner mailbox
to the churchyard to the pharmacy to the junk store
a white sleeve of bread I carried on the walk home
bit the hard end off up the stoop two steps at a time

Flatbush
on bricks in the shape of arcs I stood on
the triangle in the middle of the intersection
next to the bench under the tree not knowing
these coordinates would mark my home for years
a dog leash wound round each wrist tight
seventeen Brooklyn Septembers
fine as Dolores Street noons

Wickenden
Portuguese sweet bread offered mornings
a soft sweet landing atop the hill
passed dark windows, wood door
of *Babe's on the Sunny Side* where pool players
wrested eight balls out of corner pockets
Georgie M. Cohan kicked a can
scallop fisherman lifted their catch
by the Point Street Bridge over the Providence River
under the blue vaulted sky I'd sit to calm my cry
in Our Lady of the Rosary Church

What do I experience daily that is old, ancient and true?
Rock and sky. Rocks shaped like clouds.
Clouds shaped like rocks.
That's all that's left. To stare up or down.
In the city this century I do not see:
Grandma's cast iron pot over an open fire hearth
Barese green olives warmed in *meridionale* sun
the needle's glint piercing night's corners
two hand-rinsed cotton dresses on hangers over the tub
Grandpa's brown wingtip shoes by the door
shined every Friday, drinking water in earthen clay

amphorae by the roadside
hand-carved wood-handle knives of shoemakers
leather straps of the donkey chewing a stalk of sugarcane
tight rings of cloth around the crown of Grandma's head
to balance the basket of figs

I walk to feel my heart region's compass
ghost knocks at Saint Philip & Decatur
marble steps worn low by footfall on Elysian Fields
Qena Manfaloot lines the Nile as close
as a road can a river follow
shadows grab from behind on Delancey
money covered in soot on the Bowery
I grab pages of books to read
Broadway was once an Indian trail through the forest

There is no where to go on a street that leads no where

Winchester
a dead end named after a rifle
made good by Grandma Rose's peach tree
arching over the wooden bench in August
Sacred peach cave where I sit and sing *Ave Maria*
the world through a fragrant veil
of hundreds of baby peaches
branches rocking under fruit weight
graze the cement path and I believe again

Via Appia
Hot round stones curve underfoot and over Roman catacombs
One day I'll walk it all the way to Brindisi
where it ends at the Adriatic sea wall
then I'll sail the echoes of souls back to *Hellas*
and find out where the \-is\ ending came from
in my grandfather's surname

The curves of my arches, the souls of my feet.
Do you know that your two feet fit perfectly
over the contours of your lover's face?
Try it. The balls of your feet fit her eye sockets.

Her nose comes through the hollowed space
between your two arches. Your soles rest on her cheeks
your heels her chin, your toes, her brow.
Do you find this as spiritually comforting as I?
That we quite literally fit together?
Do you find this comforting as steady echoes
of footsteps and hooves,
the sense of not going anywhere
but of having been one place
that feels like the center of it all?

The finish line was the beginning only

See, Saw 15